Silent
Determination

One woman's battle to survive
and thrive with a rare brain
disease

PETER CAHILL

ISBN 979-8-89130-399-7 (paperback)
ISBN 979-8-89130-400-0 (digital)

Christian Faith Publishing
832 Park Avenue
Meadville, PA 16335
www.christianfaithpublishing.com

Printed in the United States of America

To my loving wife of forty-two years, Andrea Cahill. Without her in my life, not only would I not have written this book, but I wouldn't have also had the innumerable unique life experiences that I enjoyed every day we were together.

Also to my children, Natalie and Peter, whom I love dearly and who have been such a positive and supportive part of these life experiences.

To the multitude of doctors, NPs, clinicians, and hospital staff and administrators, in particular three Massachusetts General Hospital (MGH) doctors—the late Dr. Robert Ojemann, Dr. Scott Plotkin, and Dr. Fred Barker—who have supported, guided, and tended to us over the many years Andrea fought her war with neurofibromatosis (NF).

Additionally, to everyone afflicted with NF/schwannomatosis, I am with you in spirit as you fight your own battles and will continue to work tirelessly with MGH, its brain tumor center, and the NF clinic to support their efforts to find a cure.

Last, but far from least, to the grace of God, Who gave us the strength, direction, and hope to not only endure our struggles but also to thrive despite them.

Any and all proceeds from the sale of this book will be donated to the Andrea Cahill Foundation for NF2 research at the Massachusetts General Hospital. You can learn more about our foundation at https://because.massgeneral.org/acahill.

CONTENTS

Introduction...ix

Chapter 1: In the Beginning
(Of all the gin joints in all the towns in
all the world, she walks into mine!) 1
Chapter 2: How We Became Us..................................... 19
Chapter 3: Young and Innocent 37
Chapter 4: Can This Really Be Happening to Us?
(A Seismic Shift in Direction)........................ 52
Chapter 5: Not a Battle, but a Relentless War 67
Chapter 6: Well, It Can't Get Any Worse, Can It?
(Oh, Yes It Can—Much Worse than
We Could Ever Imagine) 79
Chapter 7: Figuring Out the "New Normal".................... 94
Chapter 8: Andrea's Brave New World 105
Chapter 9: And We Thought Deaf Was Deaf................. 116
Chapter 10: Deaf Ain't Dead (or Charting a Post
Apocalypse Road) 131
Chapter 11: God Deals the Cards; It's Up to You
How You Play Them 151
Chapter 12: Lucky Cards 174
Chapter 13: Smile When Your Heart Is Breaking............. 194

Chapter 14: Play Your ACES
(or When Times Get Tough, Get Back
to What You Do Best) 205

Chapter 15: Down but Not Out (Trust Me,
Miracles Really Do Happen) 217

Chapter 16: Stuck in a Lion's Den? Then Fight Like
a Gladiator 239

Chapter 17: The Biggest Collateral Damage
(or Handling the Kids with Kid Gloves) 262

Chapter 18: Can't Shed a Tear about Not Being
Able to Cry.. 283

Chapter 19: Brain Surgery Is…Well, Brain Surgery.......... 303

Chapter 20: This Is the Poison
that Will Make Things Better
(Maybe, Maybe Not; the Chemotherapy
Trials) 322

Chapter 21: What Doesn't Kill You Makes You
Stronger, Right?.. 341

Chapter 22: A Long, Strange Trip for the Grateful Living.... 356

Chapter 23: Some ABCs on QLAs (Quality-of-Life
Adjustments) 368

Chapter 24: Day Is Done, Fades the Light, God Is Nigh ... 385

Chapter 25: Stormy Headwinds, Spiritual Tailwinds,
and the "Rainbow Connection" 403

Chapter 26: Goodbye but Not Good Riddance................ 421

Epilogue 429

There is much wisdom in the words of Nietzsche
as regards to the meaning of life.
"He who has a Why to live for can bear almost any How."

— Friedrich Nietzsche; from Twilight of the Idols; 1889

INTRODUCTION

When my wife, Andrea, passed away on January 22, 2022, it was devastating to our family, as it usually is whenever wives, mothers, fathers, aunts, uncles, or friends move on. However, in my certainly slanted but maybe not completely delusional opinion, Andrea's situation was different. Her adult life consisted of constant conflict and never-ending challenges. She was born with the neurological disorder neurofibromatosis 2 (NF2) and battled it for thirty-five years of her adult life.

As I will chronicle in this book, NF2 is a chronic, progressive, and devastating disease that causes tumors to grow in the brain and spinal cord, creating innumerable physical problems. Andrea became profoundly deaf, lost her ability to walk, had significant cognitive and memory issues, and dealt with many other ancillary difficulties as a result of NF2 and her ensuing radiation and chemotherapy treatments. In addition to the physical and mental challenges, emotional trauma for Andrea, her family, and her friends was an inevitable, constant by-product.

Just for a moment, stop and think about what it might be like if, at the age of thirty-one, you suddenly become profoundly deaf, unable to do your job, are tasked with raising two young children, and have to wake up every morning knowing you have a chronic, progressive neurological disease that will slowly but surely dim the quality of your life, require multiple and ongoing brain surgeries, and eventually kill you.

The easier thing to do would have been to give into the disease and shrink in the face of its magnitude, but rather than succumb to the obstacles, Andrea picked herself up, faced her dilemma head-on, and tackled them with unwavering resolve, grace, and dignity.

This is Andrea's story, as told through my lens.

But fortunately, it's only the start of the story. The real plot is how she handled these trials from setback to setback, surgery to surgery, and year to year. She could have folded at any time, and no one would have thought any less of her. I often try to imagine what I would have done in her situation, and although I can't be sure, I doubt I would have risen to these challenges in the same manner that Andrea did.

Not only didn't she fold, but she didn't even give in an inch. In fact, she excelled, always putting herself second and finding ways to inspire others—and that's what made her so very special.

I only hope I can do her story justice in this book. I strived to capture not only the events, the dialogue, and the interesting/sometimes humorous situations, but also her personality, her struggles, her triumphs, her spirit, and, most importantly, her love.

For years, McDonald's touted their "secret sauce" on their Big Mac hamburger. It was advertised as something so secretive, so special, and so unique that was not only appealing by itself but also so fantastic that it made everything you put it on better. Well, Andrea's secret sauce was love. No matter what crazy situation popped up—oftentimes new to her, overwhelming to us, and almost always beyond her control—she handled it with grace, dignity, and love. Anyone involved in any interaction with her felt this love; they were impacted by her love, and they were better off because of her love.

I was the recipient of much of this love, and my fervent hope is that I can bring the depth of that love alive in the pages of this book.

In my mind, Andrea was put on this earth to show us all how to be better people—how to handle life's problems with honor, humor, and determination and how to fight for yourself, your family, and a cause.

This book is my perspective, as her husband and caregiver, on how she did all that and how, in doing it, she was able to reach so many people in so many ways that even I and those closest to her didn't fully understand the immensity of her impact until after she passed.

While life, specifically NF2, treated Andrea so very badly, as a result of her wisdom, faith, courage, and selflessness, all who knew her were far better off for the time she spent here on earth.

CHAPTER 1

In the Beginning
(Of all the gin joints in all the towns
in all the world, she walks into mine!)

I'm sitting in a dark, eerily quiet hospital room at 5:30 p.m. on a Tuesday evening. It's April 15, 1987. While the rest of the world is on the move—getting out of work, going out for a drink, worrying about filing their taxes on time, or heading home to their families—I'm waiting anxiously for my wife, Andrea, to open her eyes. Andrea was about to wake up after an all-day brain surgery to remove a large tumor on her auditory nerve. It was her third such operation in eighteen months to combat a disease that we had never heard of two years before, neurofibromatosis 2 (NF2). This operation would change the course of our lives forever.

As she opened her eyes with great difficulty and gave me a weak smile, I said, "Welcome back, hon." I got no response, so I said the words again, louder; and again, and again, and again, still louder—until my rantings drew the attention of one of the nurses. She peeked inside the doorway and said in a soft, kind voice, "Is everything OK?" I looked up at her blankly and replied, "No, it's not, and I'm not sure it ever will be." As she closed the door, I looked back at Andrea and realized that what the doctors had warned us about before the operation, had in fact happened. The delicate surgery had not spared the auditory nerve. Andrea had lost her hearing forever.

As she grabbed my hand and began to weep, I took a tiny bit of solace in the fact that the last words I said to her before she drifted off from the anesthesia, the last words she would ever hear, were, "I love you, Andy."

Amazingly, at least to us, profound deafness was just one of many challenges that Andrea would face over her remaining thirty-five years as a result of relentless body blows (literally and figuratively) that the disease NF2 would deliver. Only her silent determination would allow her to rise above her fate and become the special person she was meant to be.

Living in my wife's new world was a unique combination of F-bombs going off constantly like fireworks. The situation was F-ed up, to be sure, as well as frightening and frustrating. But it was also fascinating, fun-loving, faith-filled, and, especially for me, fortuitous. I was fortunate to spend most of my life with a woman who possessed and utilized an amazing range of gifts—gifts that could make you laugh and feel more fully alive, drive you to be a better person, or bring you to the brink of helplessness. She could inspire, illuminate, motivate, and also perplex. She could bring a smile to your face while insulting you, enlighten you while confusing you, bring you to the verge of tears with a casual slight, or show you how to chuckle at yourself by making fun of her own human foibles.

If the forty-five years I spent with Andrea demonstrated one thing to me, it was that she was extraordinary. In my mind, *extraordinary* would be a gross understatement. But for all her specialness, we were a pretty ordinary couple. We met while she was in college at Wheelock College in Boston, studying to become a teacher. I was a third-shift computer operator, working on the other side of town.

I was taken with her natural beauty, her boundless energy, and her amazing smile. She had an ease about her, a grace that made other people feel comfortable. She was stylish, classy, and funny. She had a zest for life, a loving family, and a wide circle of good friends. Her empathy was like a sixth sense. She also had a wide range of interests and so many endearing personality traits, but to me, everything seemed to come back to her amazing, bright-as-the-sun smile.

She was clearly out of my league.

That's because I was basically a street urchin. I came from a chaotic Irish American family of thirteen, the oldest of eleven siblings. All of us lived in a three-bedroom home, with one bathroom (one tub, no shower), one phone, a dog, and my usually cranky (for good reason, I came to realize) paternal grandmother living in the finished basement.

When I was a teenager, it got so crowded and strained for me in the house that I moved my bedroom out to the front porch. The upside was that I actually had my own space. The downside was that the room wasn't heated. To escape the zaniness going on inside the house, I happily spent three years, including three New England winters, pretty much living outside! It seemed like the *Wild Wild West*, and it pretty much was.

I was raised in the city of Quincy, Massachusetts, at the time a very blue-collar suburb of Boston. Quincy is known as the City of Presidents, being the birthplace of both John Adams and John Quincy Adams. It's steeped in history, tradition, and granite (it's also known as the Granite City for its famous quarries), and I loved growing up there. We were close to the ocean, I had a lot of friends, and we rode our bikes everywhere. We played all kinds of games, especially sports—anything with a ball. There was stickball before school, home run derby at recess, and pickup ball after school. In the summer, we were out virtually from sunup to sundown.

We were lower middle class on the socioeconomic scale. My father worked three jobs to put food on the table and keep us clothed. When the younger kids reached elementary school age, my mother went back to work. We had what we needed and not much else. But most of our neighborhood was in the same boat, and we never felt deprived.

I struggled, dodged, and BS'd my way through high school with very average grades. I was a little bit crazy, a social klutz (as one of my female classmates later put it, I was "a challenge"), a sports fanatic, and a kid who was all too familiar with trouble, most of it self-induced. If trouble didn't find me, I had a way of finding it—mostly as a result of my big mouth. I think the term we used back in the '70s was "a wise-ass."

I was also painfully skinny; my arms were so thin that I could wrap my hand around my biceps and touch my index finger to my thumb. I tried everything to gain weight—ice cream with breakfast, whole milk by the gallon, and every fat-filled, lard-encrusted meal I could get my hands on. The eat healthy, exercise more, live longer culture was just beginning to take hold, and when it came to food, I scoured magazines and TV for examples of healthy, low-fat diets and then did the exact opposite. It didn't matter what I did, including lifting weights like a demon (I had no fat to convert into muscle); I was stuck at what was probably the lowest fifth percentile in the weight class for my age/height.

It was at this point, as a young teenager, that I could have desperately used some parental guidance, a mentor, or a coach to point me in the right direction and help me with my physical issues and self-esteem. It just wasn't going to happen; my father was already way in over his head, and his military style of "do it my way or the highway," coupled with my "F—— you" attitude to everything he said, didn't make for a harmonious, team-oriented relationship. I wasn't quite good enough in any sport for any coach to take a real interest, and there was no boys' club around to suck me into a more constructive atmosphere. I was too much of an introvert to ask for guidance or support, so I resorted to guerilla warfare for kicks and, I guess, attention— quick shots at authority figures, enemies, and frenemies—and then faded back into the shadows of my basketball, my books, or my weights. Except there were too many times that I didn't get in and out fast enough, and I always seemed to pay for it.

It seemed like I somehow always managed to piss off the toughest guy around. Sometimes it was a classmate, sometimes the cops, and always it was my father. For example, in high school, a bunch of my friends and I worked after school and on weekends at a local deli. We constantly played pranks and hurled insults back and forth, mostly to pass the time. One of my buddy's older brothers started to work Saturdays with us. Recently back from Vietnam, and none too happy to be working alongside a bunch of wise-ass high school snots, he made it clear we should steer clear of him unless it was absolutely necessary. I, of course, needed to push the envelope and one day said something flip to him one too many times. He caught me in the big walk-in freezer and beat, kicked, and choked me within an inch of my life. I was a slow learner, but a pounding like that taught me to at least keep my mouth shut around guys like him who were far crazier than I'd ever be.

But maybe not. Another time, I somehow ended up in a brawl with a large portion of a biker gang in a bar. I'm not even sure I was at fault, but it didn't matter after I had a beer bottle smashed over my head, a chair thrown at me, and some bad dudes landed a couple of solid punches. I couldn't catch a break, and when the cops arrived to break it up, they put *me* in the back of the wagon, in cuffs, to "cool down."

After high school, I was determined to go to college. No one in my family had a college degree, and I wanted to set an example for my brothers and sisters. One thing I had going for me was that, although I was a very average student, I was a prolific reader. Fiction, nonfiction, magazines, newspapers, advertisements, sports box scores, and so forth—I would read anything. I was also a decent writer. When I was fourteen, I entered an essay contest for a free week at Ted Williams' Baseball Camp in southeastern Massachusetts. I won the contest and had a great week that included meeting and getting a casual hitting compliment from the Splendid Splinter himself! Talk about being on cloud nine!

While the baseball camp was a dream come true, the real benefit I got from winning the contest was getting bit by the writing bug. I started to write more seriously, essays, journals, and even poetry. I decided I wanted to be a journalist, and against all odds, I was accepted into the journalism program at Marquette University in Milwaukee, Wisconsin. I couldn't believe it. I was going to a big-name college and taking the first step in my dream of becoming a writer. When I told my parents, they looked at the costs for tuition, room, and board and broke out laughing. I think my father said something like, "You've got a better chance of going to the moon than that college in Wisconsin!" I was completely deflated, but I had to accept that it just wasn't going to happen.

I ended up spending two years at the local Bridgewater State College, where my goals were, in order, (1) to play basketball, (2) to drink beer, (3) to meet girls, and (4) to achieve the minimum GPA to stay in school to pursue objectives one, two, and three.

In my sophomore year, I tore up my ankle, couldn't play basketball, ran out of money, and lost interest in school. I dropped out (it would take me almost thirty years before I'd finally get my degree). I took a full-time job at the local supermarket at the deli, slicing meat.

I thought I'd hit rock bottom, and I pretty much had. At age twenty-one, I was heavily in debt, with a car that I seemed to push more than drive (I owed Sonny, the owner of the Gulf gas station at the end of my street, several times more than the car was worth. I finally had to work off my debts, pumping gas for him), not even a hint of a romantic relationship, walking to work, living at home in the garage, and working at a supermarket making minimum wage.

But fortunately, as the old saying goes, "The darkest hour is just before dawn."

I had two things going for me: I had a good work ethic (this was drilled into my head by my father, whom I'd worked alongside at one of his multiple side jobs, scrubbing floors and toilets, since I was thirteen years old), and I made a lot of friends. And when I say friends, I don't mean just drinking buddies (although we did like drinking together), I mean real friends. Despite my quiet, laid-back demeanor and social awkwardness, I somehow had a knack for making and keeping friends—a trait that would be critical to whatever success I had later in business and life.

One day, out of the blue, a high school buddy of mine called me and explained that an older guy from our neighborhood had returned from Vietnam and landed a job as a manager with a computer firm in Boston. He was hiring for lots of positions, including computer operators.

I had no idea what he was talking about, but I quickly gleaned a few things. I'd read somewhere that computers were the next big up-and-coming thing, and I would be working in the big city and making more money. The combination of these factors would likely increase my odds when it came to drinking beer and meeting girls. I jumped on it!

What an education I got. I worked the third shift from 11:00 p.m. to 7:00 a.m. with an ex-con with a gun, a judge's grandson, a guy who was in hiding because he messed around with a mob consigliore's girlfriend, and a gay boss who carried on intimate conversations with the large data processing machines and printers, which included rubdowns and hugs, in hopes of avoiding paper jams.

On my first night on the job, one of the guys pulled up a window and fired a revolver off the wall of the building, fifteen feet across the alley. He wanted to see if the bullet would ricochet back to our side of the building! On the next shift, one of my new "friends" told me that the new guy (me) makes the 2:00 a.m. doughnut run, and I could use his car. Later, I found out that he wanted me to start his car because he was worried it had been rigged with a bomb.

For me, the whole setup couldn't have been more exhilarating—learning new things, all kinds of crazy adventures going on every night, making new friends, and getting decent money. Now all I needed was a good woman!

And that's when Andrea appeared. The timing was perfect. But she hardly seemed like the perfect fit for me, and vice versa.

Andrea grew up in Winchester, a well-to-do town ten miles north of Boston. Though Quincy was the next town south of Boston, I'd never been to Winchester. There may as well have been a Berlin-like wall between what is known as the north and south shores of Boston.

Historically, Boston was a blue-blood white Anglo-Saxon Protestant bastion; according to the old saying, Boston was "the home of the bean and the cod, where the Lowells talk only to the Cabots, and the Cabots talk only to God." Indeed, there was a time when signs saying "Irish need not apply" and "Italians are not welcome here" were the norm rather than outliers.

Eventually, working-class Irish immigrants settled in South Boston, and Italians settled in the North End, and given this ethnic geographical flow (and probably Boston's legendary traffic issues), rarely did these populations interact.

Andrea's grandparents had emigrated from Italy, and her father, through hard work and street smarts, had risen to become the president of a large wine/liquor importing company. They had a well-maintained house in this pleasant suburb. She was the youngest of three children. Not only was she the only girl in her immediate family, but she was also the first girl born into her extended family after two brothers and eleven male cousins. I heard the term *princess* used a few times (never by me), but she never struck me as spoiled.

She was smart, highly focused on school, and very career oriented. She wanted to be a teacher since the age of five, and she wanted to go to Wheelock College, a small, private, all-women school in Boston that specialized in education. While the tuition there was a relative pittance by today's standards, it was not inexpensive in 1974 dollars. And while her parents had created a comfortable lifestyle, they were by no means wealthy.

They pushed hard for her to attend a state school. Her father was an imposing, strong-willed man, but he was dealing with a stubborn, idealistic teenager who early on identified what she wanted to do for her life's work. Yes, she really told her first-grade teacher that she was going to be a first-grade teacher when she grew up.

My money would have been on the big guy who, as I came to learn, was pretty much an immovable object. But Andrea was also an irrepressible force. She simultaneously argued, reasoned, charmed, pouted, and pushed her way across the finish line, and off to Wheelock she went.

Not surprisingly, she excelled in school (her grade point average was 3.9, and she was not happy about the fact it wasn't a 4.0), and she enjoyed every minute of her college experience. From the academic and social aspects of college life to the hands-on student teaching, every bit of her four years at Wheelock was pure joy.

So how did a laid-back, gritty city kid with enough street smarts to get by and more than enough balls and lip to get the crap beat out of him regularly end up with an ambitious, focused contessa from a leafy suburb? It's the stuff they write romance novels about, but in our case, it's all true.

The way we met in many ways reflected what was to come in our future relationship and lives together—unpredictable, humorous, frustrating, absurd, and, ultimately, with a happy ending.

On April 8, 1977, Good Friday for the Christian world (and what would turn out to be a very good Friday for me), I went with a group of my buddies to the Boston Garden to watch our beloved Boston Celtics play the New Orleans Jazz.

I was excited because one of my favorite non-Celtic, Pete Maravich, was playing for the Jazz. The legendary "Pistol Pete" had long shaggy hair, droopy socks, and a killer jump shot. It was also the nickname some of the guys down the park had given me.

I, too, had the long hair and disheveled dress, but that was where the resemblance ended. My Achilles' heel on the basketball court was my jump shot. Hustle, defense, getting to the hoop, fundamentals? Check, check, check, and check. The jumper, not so much.

The Celtics won that night 120–109 (Pistol Pete had thirty-nine points, but the more talented, well-balanced Celtics prevailed), and we decided to celebrate. We headed to an area in Kenmore Square near Fenway Park that was full of bars and also near a cluster of all-girls colleges, hoping to get lucky. There were a few places we liked to go, but that night, we picked a crowded bar named Copperfield's to top off an enjoyable night and kick off the weekend.

Copperfield's was a classic college bar. The heavily shellacked upstairs bar was wet and sticky from the spillage of cheap pitchers of beer. That same beer created a dank smell and a spongy grit on the dirty, slushy floors. A cloud of cigarette smoke clung to the ceiling. A bad band wailed in the corner, surrounded by oblivious, beer-guzzling college students. The bathrooms were downstairs, and you only ventured that way if you absolutely had to. In other words, our kind of place.

Copperfield's also had lots of coeds. There were four all-women colleges within a mile radius. In much the same way the seals off Cape Cod attract great white sharks, this environment drew in a lot of guys like us, interested in draft beer and pretty women.

It was getting late, and we were running short on both money and time when I made a last-ditch, desperate attempt to get one of the lingering coed's telephone number. She reluctantly agreed, and because we didn't have any paper to write it on, she took a dollar bill from her purse, wrote down her phone number, gave it to me, and hightailed it out of there with her friends.

I had consumed more than a few beers, but I knew two things with absolute certainty: (1) She was far too cute to be attracted to me, and as a result, there was no way in my mind those numbers on the dollar bill were her real phone number; and (2) I was out of money, and draft beers cost exactly one dollar. So I did what I think any reasonable, buzzed twenty-two-year-old man would do: I put the dollar bill on the bar and, just as they shouted last call, got myself one final ice-cold beer.

I didn't have much time to enjoy it, however. Out of the corner of my eye, I saw a pretty girl making a beeline in my direction. Based on the look on her face, I was pretty sure she wasn't coming over to hug me. Little did I know that the next few seconds would change my life forever, ultimately for the very better. But in the short term, I was about to meet and absorb the full wrath of one Ms. Andrea Marie Pirani.

I had no way of knowing it, but my future bride was having a very bad week. A straight-A student in both high school and college, she had been distracted earlier in the week, had forgotten she had an exam on Tuesday, and received a C– from her male professor.

Now in my admittedly warped world, depending on the subject, a C– was an occasion to celebrate. In my freshman year in college, my basketball coach had to inform me that my 1.6 GPA was not based on a 2.0 but rather a 4.0, and if I didn't raise it to a minimum of 1.9, I wouldn't be able to play basketball. I took that as a challenge and proudly showed him up by buckling down and bringing it up all the way to a sterling 2.1! Clearly, Andrea and I came from different worlds.

Her lousy grade wasn't even the worst of it. The prior weekend, she had finally broken off a longtime on-and-off relationship with her high school boyfriend. Her father, who had no love lost for this guy, was ecstatic. That made her even angrier. So as she approached me, she was thinking of just how pissed she was with three of the most important men in her life and decided she'd take all that hostility out on me.

The discussion started out like this:

ANDREA. Who do you think you are—leading that poor girl on and then buying a damn beer with that dollar bill after that nice girl gave you her phone number?

ME, *with my catchy comeback*. Who the hell are you?

ANDREA. I'll tell you who the hell I am. I'm someone who cares about people and especially other women!

Somehow, I'd managed to piss off an outspoken, altruistic, currently irritated-by-men feminist without saying a word to her. Probably not the best way to start a relationship.

At that moment, all I was interested in was finishing my beer and getting away from this maniac. But Andrea decided she would put on a full show for her girlfriends, lambasting me for a good five minutes. When one of my friends came over to try to bail me out, she turned on him. He took about thirty seconds of her tirade and informed me, "Good luck, pal. You're on your own."

I worked my way over to her circle of friends, hoping for any kind of relief, with Andrea tracking me like a predator hunting prey. I finally found a sympathetic (or at least empathetic) woman who revealed Andrea's mindset and explained how I had inadvertently stuck my head into a hornet's nest.

After a while, Andrea appeared to calm down. She even laughed when I asked if she would write *her* phone number on a dollar bill for me! We were actually having a reasonable conversation as a group when the bartender yelled out, "Lights out! Everyone out! Now!"

I said my goodbyes to the group, thanked Andrea for reaming me out in front of the entire bar, and walked out the door. (I never even had time to finish the damn beer!) And that would have been the end of it, except for one small but critical detail: There was no one outside waiting for me. My buddies had left and apparently gone home.

Evidently, in an extreme example of a complete lack of awareness, they thought I'd "gotten lucky." Lucky my ass! It was a cold April night. I was in Boston at 2:00 a.m. with no car, and the subways shut down. My friends had deserted me. I had no money, no way to contact anyone (cellphones were still twenty years in the future), and was in the company of a group of relatively hostile feminists, who had little empathy and no sympathy for my plight. That gave the word *lucky* a whole different meaning.

I did have a couple of things going for me. I was used to landing on my feet and being blessed with a silver tongue. Still, this was going to be an uphill battle, so I did the only logical thing I could think of: I begged.

Of course, the ladies had little pity for me. They figured I was lying about my friends leaving, that I was just trying to weasel my way into their dorm, and that I was a no-good SOB who deserved what I got. Some of that could have been true, but none of it was on this particular night. All I was asking for was a floor to sleep on and fifty cents to take the subway home the next day.

As they were mocking me, an unlikely voice rose to my support. It was Andrea. It wasn't the most rousing defense, and it went something like this: "I'm sure he's a dirtbag, but no one should have to sleep outside in the city in the cold."

I took that as a faint sign of hope. Slowly, the conversation turned from "We want nothing to do with this guy" to "How can we help him get through the night and then get rid of him?"

Once they agreed to help, they had to figure out how to sneak a man into their all-girls dorm. No problem. It seemed to me that this wasn't the first time they'd done it. Two of the women kissed up to the security guard—literally—while I walked in between the other three. First obstacle overcome.

Next, I needed somewhere to sleep. None of the women wanted me in their room—especially Andrea. Finally, they decided I could sleep in the closet, with the door closed and two beds pushed up against the outside of the door. They took shifts dozing in the farthest bed and keeping guard with a baseball bat. My friends thought I'd hit a home run, going back to an all-girls dorm with five pretty coeds; the truth was, I was locked in a closet with armed guards who, given the chance, would have liked nothing better than to whack me with a baseball bat!

I woke up the next morning, sweating, hung over, and nervous about what was awaiting me. Fortunately, my captors had determined that I was actually far from dangerous and, in fact, harmless. They brought me breakfast, let me use the shower, and seemed to generally tolerate me. That was good, but all I really wanted to do was get the hell out of there and get home.

As I was preparing to leave, Andrea asked me how I was getting home. I told her I'd try to call one of my so-called friends to come get me, or I'd jump the turnstile and sneak onto the subway.

"What the heck!" she said. "I'll give you a ride home."

You could have knocked me over with a feather. I asked her if I heard right, and she replied, "Get in the car before I change my mind, and I'm not going to say it again."

She did drive me home. We had a great conversation, and when we arrived at my house, she laughingly gave me her phone number (not on a dollar bill). She smiled that smile that defined her, waved goodbye, and headed home to help her mother cook Easter dinner.

I was intrigued. No, I was smitten.

It had turned out to be a very good, Good Friday, and an even better Holy Saturday!

CHAPTER 2

How We Became Us

I called her the next week, and we seemed to hit it off. I took her out on a couple of dates. She was interesting and funny. On our second date, we stopped at a jewelry store in downtown Boston and pretended to be engaged. She even picked out an engagement ring she liked!

It didn't take long before I was hooked on Andrea, and for the first and only time in my life, I was hooked on love. I still wasn't sure what this beautiful woman saw in me, but I figured it had to be fate. Rather than question it, I was going to ride this wave for as long as I could.

While we were dating, she introduced me to a new world of possibilities. While I was happy to lounge around with my friends and watch any sport on TV, drink beer, and read, Andrea had a far more expansive range of interests—from photography to dancing, grave rubbing, incredible crafts, and gardening. She was a whirlwind of curiosity and activity and seemed as passionate about one subject as the next.

And the questions! Andrea's curiosity was insatiable. She wanted to know all about my life—not the highlights but the details surrounding my family life, my school life, and my love life, right down to how many girlfriends I'd had, how serious was I with them, and how long I dated them.

She had lots of questions about my hopes and aspirations. I swear I gave out more of my personal information to this woman on our first couple of dates than I had cumulatively to anyone in my entire life.

And it wasn't just personal info. Andrea wanted to know how things worked, why they worked or didn't work, and what we should do to make them work. From people to politics, society, and arts and culture, Andrea wanted to understand it all. She wouldn't let up until it made sense to her. Since she had her own quirky perspective on a lot of things, making it make sense to her was sometimes a challenge.

She hadn't been particularly interested in my two passions: history and sports, but she was now. She didn't want just to know about John, John Quincy, and Abigail Adams; she wanted to visit their houses and the crypt where they were interned and to learn all about their families.

She desperately wanted to understand more about sports, especially football. In time, she became a huge New England Patriots (and Tom Brady) fan, but some aspects of the sport always perplexed and frustrated her, such as safeties, touchbacks, and fair catches. How was that "fair" to the kicking team? She'd ask. Already a Red Sox fan, she now also embraced the basketball Celtics. Over time, she became a more avid fan of all three teams than I was.

She opened up whole new worlds to me in many ways. I quickly realized that, in addition to the city-boy-meets-suburban girl, not-too-bright-guy-meets-straight-A-student, and sports-nut-meets-don't-really-care-about-anything-played-with-a-ball scenarios, there was one other difference—our ethnic backgrounds and family cultures. While both our families viewed our clans as very American and not primarily Irish (the Cahills) or Italian (the Piranis), there were more than a few vestiges left over from the Old World.

My Irish heritage at that time was one big cultural stereotype: lots of beer, Leprechauns and four-leaf clovers for luck, wearing green on Saint Patrick's Day, and so forth. My appreciation for my ancestry didn't come until many years later when I studied Irish history and visited Ireland and the villages and towns where my family emigrated from. I came to understand the plight of the Irish people, their struggle eternal with the United Kingdom, and the ongoing battle among themselves. A lot of things, in my family and in general, made a lot more sense after I gained a deeper feel for my people's history and struggles.

Before too long, Andrea brought me home to meet her parents and cook me fettuccine Alfredo (she'd already learned, from standing by her mother at the stove from the time she could walk, to be a marvelous Italian cook). Andrea's family was wonderful—down-to-earth, honest, caring, and loving. She was the youngest of three children, with two older brothers, John and Peter. Peter was around a lot; I didn't see much of John, who was six years older than Andrea and already married and off on his own. They lived beautifully intertwined between their Italian heritage (which they were proud of) and their American lives (of which they were even prouder).

Andrea's father was born and raised in the United States, by parents who emigrated from Italy and never learned to speak English. He spoke only Italian until he was five years old. Although he never went to college, he was one of the smartest men I've ever met.

He fought in World War II and was stationed in Italy, working for the office of strategic services (OSS, the predecessor to the modern-day CIA). He came home after the war, started a career as a salesman in the Italian food and spirits business, and rose to the position of president and CEO of the firm. His first name was Alvaro (our son's middle name), but he always went by Al. Even though I think he dreamed in Italian, he identified as a proud American.

The parents of Andrea's mother, Marian, also came from Italy. And although Marian also spoke Italian, it was deemed "lousy" by the fluent linguistic experts in the family. Marian was a wonderful cook, a doting mom to Andrea (today, she might be considered a "helicopter mom"), an avid gardener, and an amazing artist.

The house and yard were beautifully put together and maintained, everything was in perfect order, and meals were served promptly at the proper time. I came to realize that this sense of organization was primarily a by-product of Al and his personality. Marian, the artist at heart, was chaotic and spontaneous and said pretty much whatever was on her mind. We got along famously, and I came to love her for all these traits.

I learned so much from her family—elaborate Sunday dinners, how to properly pour a glass of wine, how to play bocce, and how to make ravioli and gnocchi. The only ravioli I'd ever had come out of a can, and I thought "New Gnocchi" was a large city where the Yankees played, two hundred miles south of Boston.

This cultural orientation required me to make some adjustments. The first time I came to Sunday dinner at their house at noon (sharp, every Sunday), I figured we'd be done eating in time for me to watch the basketball game at 1:00 p.m. In my house, because of the number of people in my family, we ate Sunday dinner in shifts, and if I could grab the early Sunday shift, I'd be finished by 12:30 p.m. and have plenty of time to catch the pregame show. Well, at the Pirani's, we were finished by 1:00 p.m.—with the first course! By the time I finished the six-course dinner and dessert, the game was long over, and I could barely get up from the table and walk back to the car!

It was all fascinating to me. The aroma of the food as I came up the walkway made me feel like I'd been transported into a Roman bistro. The never-ending courses of delicious food, much of it homemade, and the ongoing conversation that spanned a spectrum of tones ranging from complimentary to argumentative. Despite the sometimes acrimonious banter (and occasional ranting in Italian), all the people at the table appeared to be happy to be together for the entire day.

Her parents seemed to like me okay. I had the good fortune of being the next guy to meet them after Andrea jettisoned the guy they hated. Timing is everything!

While Andrea and I had hit off swimmingly, there was one fly in the ointment. My best friend growing up had been accepted into a master's degree program at UCal Berkeley, and since I didn't have much going for me at the time, I had agreed to join him and relocate to California. I told Andrea all along that this was the plan, but we pushed it to the background as our relationship evolved.

As we approached August, we talked about me staying in California for a short time—six to twelve months—while she finished college and got her teaching career started. We even discussed her coming out to visit and what an adventure that would be. I knew in my heart that I didn't want to leave Andrea. Who knew if we were going to work out, but the feeling was pretty special. At the same time, I just couldn't let my friend down. I'd made a commitment, and I felt I had to deliver. I was in a real conundrum, and although very conflicted, I continued with the plans for a cross-country journey and living arrangements in Berkeley. I even went so far as to quit my job.

Andrea had other plans. She wasn't conflicted at all, and I saw for the first time the determination that would become her hallmark in later years. She'd decided that we did have something special, and she wasn't willing to let it go. She began calling me several times a day—mind you, we had one phone in the kitchen and nowhere for a private conversation. My sisters, who could hear all of my side of the discussion, quickly sided with her and began to get in my ear as well. Her persistence was impressive, and over the course of a couple of weeks, she'd convinced me that going out west was a big mistake. While I'd come around to her way of thinking, I had two problems: I'd made a commitment to my buddy, and I now had no job.

I went to my friend first and explained the situation to him. I was prepared to honor my commitment if he held me to our agreement. Fortunately, he was both understanding and gracious. He easily let me off the hook and revamped his plans. He, too, was taken by Andrea and didn't want me to make a lifelong mistake. We remained good friends, and he was the best man at our wedding.

I then went back to my big boss with my tail between my legs and begged for my job back. He raked me over the coals just for sport and took me back. This guy became one of my best friends, my mentor, and my confidant over the next forty years.

Having dodged that bullet, we concluded that fall that we were meant to be, and we decided to get engaged and set a date to get married. On a beautiful starlit night, I proposed to Andrea on the rooftop of the same Wheelock dorm I had to be snuck into six months earlier. When she said, "Yes," I felt like I could have floated home off the top of the five-floor building.

The only thing brighter than the stars that night was her beautiful smile. A crazy fairy tale with a happy ending!

But when we told her mother, she was taken aback and tried to talk us out of it. She told me Andrea wasn't ready to be married, that she was too young, and that she was still in college, too immature, and couldn't cook well enough (that one had me laughing to myself).

I realized later on that her mom was really afraid of losing her best friend (which thankfully, she never did). When she realized it was a futile battle, she hugged us both, and by the end of the night, the wedding planning had started.

Her father, on the other hand, was very gracious when I asked him for his daughter's hand in marriage, but he struck a slightly different tone as I was leaving the house. As I walked toward the door, I heard him at the top of the stairs, his voice rising with each rant: "What the hell do you think you're doing? Are you crazy? Have you lost your mind?" I slipped out the door and didn't look back.

Welcome to the family!

But I guess he came around. About a week after we announced our engagement, Al decided that we should get together and toast to our future. There were four of us at the house, and he put out four short glasses—kind of like the old jelly jars that we used to reuse as juice glasses. I thought that was a little odd, but as he headed down to the basement, I perked up. I knew Al had a world-class wine cellar and figured he was going to bring up one of his best bottles to celebrate.

Andrea's and my jaws both dropped when we saw him emerge from the cellar with a single, dusty sixteen-ounce bottle of Rheingold beer from the spare refrigerator downstairs. Even Andrea, who was not a beer drinker, knew that was not a good beer.

Al cleaned off the bottle, which looked like he might have brought it back from the war thirty years earlier, and then proceeded to pour four ounces of beer into each of our glasses and raise his glass in a very nice toast to us. I had no idea what to do. I figured it must be some old, quirky family tradition, and so I threw it back like a shot of whiskey. My other three drinking buddies each took polite sips of their beer, like it was fine wine, and my future in-laws gave one another knowing looks that seemed to say, "Yep, he's the Irish guy." Despite the overt stereotyping, I think this was Al's way of making an effort to relate to me.

At my house, a slightly different scene played out. My father grabbed four sixteen-ounce cans of Schlitz (the beer that made Milwaukee famous), no glasses, and basically said to Andrea, "Good luck with him."

As we sat at the kitchen table, drinking our beers, Andrea's jaw dropped yet again. She looked over at the basement door where a cloud of marijuana smoke was drifting up from beneath the door and starting to fill the kitchen. A couple of my brothers and their girlfriends were in the basement, smoking pot, and my parents sat there, chatting with us, apparently completely oblivious to the Cheech-and-Chong skit that was playing out right in front of us!

Driving back to her house afterward, Andrea astutely observed that at her parents' house, it was virtually impossible to get a buzz and completely impossible *not* to do so at my family's place!

Boy, did we come together from two very different worlds!

Although Andrea had a small nuclear family, she had an enormous extended family of uncles, aunts, and cousins who came out of the woodwork, accepted me into their brood, and showed me a different type of family love. Those Sunday dinners were a wonderful tradition that went on for many years. I miss them to this day.

Andrea and her family also steered me into something that would later become essential in my life. The Irish Cahills and Italian Piranis were both Catholic, but when I met Andrea, I was at best a lukewarm Catholic.

I was brought up in the church and pretty much went through the motions. I guess the term that would apply best to me was a casual Catholic. But Andrea insisted we go to church every Sunday and later made sure we did as a family with our children. Baptisms, first communions, and confirmations were big deals in her house, and they later became important in our house too. As for myself, I certainly began putting more time into religion, and I got more out of it—but not a whole lot. However, as you'll see, this was the first step toward setting me up for great rewards later on.

But the real essence of the Pirani family seeped from the character of Andrea's parents. During this time, and over the next ten years until he passed away, Al and I became good friends, and he was a great sounding board and mentor to me. While he never quite figured me out, he accepted me. We had completely opposite personalities. Al was fastidious and precise, impeccably groomed, and a man of few words who chose those words carefully. I was a young goofball, who let almost everything slide off my shoulders—easygoing and fun loving. One day, when we were looking at something that was still broken on my car, which he had pointed out the week before, he threw up his hands in exasperation and said, "Doesn't anything matter to you?"

To which I quickly replied, "Only one thing, your daughter."

"Touché," he said and walked away with a wry smile on his face.

Al taught me how to use his tools, how to maintain a car, and ultimately how to take care of a house. Of course, we had our moments. I remember one particular puzzling interchange when he came to visit us at our first house. The toilet was flushing slowly, and he said to me, "Get me the snake." I stood there frozen. I knew he couldn't mean, "Get me a *snake*," but I had no idea that such a thing as a toilet auger (or snake) existed. My father's toolbox consisted of a hammer, a couple of screwdrivers, a pair of pliers, and several rolls of duct tape. We eyeballed each other for about thirty seconds, and he finally said to me, "You have no idea what I'm talking about, do you?" I didn't, but by the end of the evening, I not only knew what a toilet snake was but also how a toilet worked and how the municipal water system functioned! While I'm sure some of my blank spots made for good fodder at the office, his teaching style toward me was always patient and kind.

Marian was equally welcoming and influential. She was a mainstay at her parish, Saint Mary's, for over fifty years as a parishioner, a member of the choir, and a volunteer. She often touted her "special relationship with the Blessed Mother" as evidence of her great faith, which she certainly had. Indeed, the name Marian in Christianity means related to the Virgin Mary. In the Jewish faith it means "the precious one." By either measure, Marian certainly lived up to her name.

Marian was the youngest in a family of six. As was the case with many women from her generation, she was constantly fighting to be heard by her parents, her sisters, her husband, and even her children. It seemed to me they worked en masse to tamp her down, get her to adhere to the norms of that era, and insist she blend in with the conformity of her suburban landscape. In my eyes, she was a multitalented artist who could take a picture of an ocean scene in her mind and create a painting that would have you believe you were on the beach, a fabulous cook who could take anything laying around in the refrigerator and create a special meal, and someone with an inner warmth who would show me what unconditional love and loyalty was through her relationship with Andrea.

Of course, we had to adapt to one another. I remember at one point she told me she'd like to make me a painting—anything I wanted. Her face dropped when I brought her an album cover from my favorite rock group at the time (the Grateful Dead) and told her, "This is what I want." Somehow, the album disappeared, but I did end up with a beautiful painting of an ocean sunrise!

Many of her paintings continue to adorn and embellish my homes. As I reflect on the beauty of her art, I marvel at how she magnificently blended her artistic vision with poetic-like depth to create paintings that seemed to pull you in and embrace you.

My family ultimately came to adore Andrea. They basked in the love she resonated with. My sisters became the sisters she never had. My brothers accepted her as just another sister. No big deal to them. What's the difference between having six or seven sisters kicking around?

However, in the beginning, they were slow to warm up to her. Part of it was that they were protective of me. I was close to the older ones, and they felt like they were going to lose a brother—especially my sister Mary, who was particularly attached to me; she fought hard to dislike Andrea, but over time, they became extremely close. The other part was that Andrea brought a whole different perspective to fashion, college, arts and crafts, and cooking than they were used to. It all seemed a little intimidating at first. Of course, Andrea was anything but intimidating, and one by one, they each connected with her in their own way, and every one of them became a fast friend for life.

My parents also came to respect and admire Andrea, but with all the chaos that surrounded them, they initially came across as indifferent to her. My mother and father didn't have the natural warmth and closeness that Andrea was used to from her family. My father was reserved and cynical, and my mother, although outgoing and friendly, followed my father's lead at home. Andrea took this lack of affection to mean they didn't like her. Over the years, Andrea rubbed off on them, and even they became more connected and developed a strong bond. (Of course, it didn't hurt that we brought grandchildren into the fold!)

The next year and a half moved fast. I studied computer programming and became more established. Andrea graduated from Wheelock and landed her dream job a as first-grade teacher. Although I was pretty oblivious to it, the wedding preparations proceeded at a blistering pace.

During the time leading up to Andrea's graduation, I also became an accepted part of her Wheelock College family. I was enjoying the college experience that I never had, vicariously through Andrea and her friends. At this point, I was no longer "despicable" but "eccentric." I had clearly, in the minds of Andrea's friends, become more "enlightened." My rough-around-the-edges style was now considered "urban chic."

All this was exemplified by our story from the Blizzard of 1978. This snowstorm is legendary in New England. A storm that largely caught the weather forecasters by surprise, it dumped over three feet of snow in two days. Winds of over eighty miles per hour buffeted the region, creating massive snowdrifts that trapped people in their houses for days. The Massachusetts coastline looked like a war zone. Hundreds of houses were washed away, and large chunks of land were lost to the sea. Thousands of people were trapped in their cars on the roads surrounding Boston while trying to get home. Some ended up dying from carbon monoxide poisoning or freezing to death after they ran out of gas. In all, ninety-nine people perished as a result of the storm.

I was oblivious to what was going on around me that Monday. I was now working days, and the storm started slowly. The first fluffy white flakes began appearing around 11:00 a.m. My only concern was whether I would be able to get over to see Andrea that night. I wasn't worried. It was only about a twenty-minute subway ride, and the subway station was literally outside the front door of my office building.

About noon, someone caught on that this might be a big one. We were dismissed and told to get home while the getting was good. As my buddy and I walked out the door, we decided to go across the street, avoid the crowds rushing to the trains, and grab lunch. Well, we had lunch and a couple of beers, and we became enthralled by the weather reports on TV that were now touting this storm as the "blizzard of the century." As it turned out, they were finally right!

We bundled up and walked out the barroom door into a raging beast. In the four hours that we'd been eating and drinking our lunch, a foot of snow had accumulated on the ground, winds were blowing sixty miles an hour, the drifts were already four feet high, and we couldn't see beyond the end of our arms. We got to the subway station, only to learn that the trains had shut down an hour earlier. There were no cars on the streets, and the ones parked were already snowed in.

We went back to our office and settled in for what we thought would be a couple of hours of wait for the trains to start up again. That was Monday afternoon. It wasn't until Wednesday afternoon that we were able to even get out of the building and assess the situation. Boston was a ghost town. Streets weren't plowed, street signs and traffic signals had blown down, live electrical wires crackled in the wind, and the drifts were what you would imagine they'd be like in Antarctica.

With no public transportation available, there was still no way for me to get anywhere. Andrea was in a similar situation four miles across town, albeit with food, hot water, showers, and music. We, on the other hand, were low on food, though we had plenty of booze since we'd raided every executive suite and fridge in the building.

On Thursday, desperate to see Andrea, I told my buddy he was in charge, loaded up a backpack with as much food and liquor as I could carry, and set out on foot to find Wheelock College. Since we'd had no contact with the outside world since Monday, I had no idea how bad the storm was or the impact it created on people's lives, their property, and the region's infrastructure. All I knew was that I had to see Andrea.

It took me well over an hour to walk a mile. Although the snow had stopped, the wind continued to howl, and the temperatures dropped into the low twenties. By the time I completed the four-mile trek and arrived at the campus, darkness had set in, and I was frozen to the bone. But it was worth it. I got to spend the next few days with Andrea in a winter wonderland—completely separated from the reality of the horrors that the Blizzard of '78 had spewed on Boston and the neighboring communities.

My arrival at Wheelock also showed just how high my stock had risen there. A little less than a year earlier, I was a virtual pariah; now I was greeted like a returning hero, welcomed with open arms. Okay, the provisions might have had something to do with my popularity, but I'd still come a long way!

Andrea and I had a storybook wedding and honeymoon in June 1979. The ceremony was at the church that Andrea had attended all her life. The music was voiced by the choir that both she and her mother sang with. The reception for almost three hundred people was held at a beautiful country club with arched walkways and old stone, ivied buildings. Andrea was radiant and beaming from the start of the day to its end—basking in pomp and circumstance, the magnificence of the church and the reception, and most of all, enjoying the happiness of family and friends who celebrated with us.

There was an eclectic mix of guests that made for a lot of fun. As Andrea was the youngest in her family, there were many older cousins and in-laws. Her father had a large number of friends and business associates attending. My contingent was younger and rowdier; Andrea never forgave one of my "friends" who slithered across the dance floor doing the "worm." It was a nice blend of the old and the young, the traditional and the modern, and the reserved and the rambunctious.

The next day, we were off on our honeymoon to Acapulco and Mexico City. In Acapulco, we drove along the spectacular cliffs north of the city, swam and sailed in the ocean, and marveled at the high divers floating majestically from their craggy perch, slicing seamlessly in the turquoise Pacific 150 feet below. In Mexico City, we were horrified at the cruelty of the bullfights, amazed at the Aztec ruins, drank all the local tequila we could afford, chowed down on authentic Mexican food, and watched the pilgrims walk on their knees, some for miles, to enter the Shrine of Our Lady of Guadalupe. I looked on in amazement and fascination but without comprehension as to what would drive someone to do that. It would be many years before I developed the level of faith and belief needed to understand and become one of the true believers.

We flew home in the proverbial state of "fat, dumb, and happy," primed to resume living our dreamy life.

But life isn't always a fairy tale, and dreams don't always come true.

CHAPTER 3

Young and Innocent

Andrea graduated with high honors from Wheelock College in 1978 with degrees in elementary education and special needs services. And it only got better from there. She landed her dream job as a first-grade teacher in the idyllic Massachusetts coastal town of Rockport. Shortly after we returned from our honeymoon, we borrowed some money from Andrea's parents, mortgaged ourselves to the hilt, and bought a three-family house in the historic city of Salem, north of Boston and closer to the school where Andrea worked. We rented out the second and third floors and became landlords.

Salem is nicknamed "Witch City" after the famous Salem Witch Trials in 1692–1693, and as new, inexperienced home-owners and landlords, we were involved in more than our fair share of spooky events.

Here, a familiar pattern emerged. Andrea was interested in the big picture and building relationships, less so in most of the details, and wanted nothing to do with any problems or confrontations—with our tenants, guys working on the house, financial issues, or potential dustups with the city officials or neighbors. This made for a great team: She identified the opportunity or the problem, we collaborated on the solution, and I was the hammer that delivered the necessary messages. We were too young and stupid to know any better, so we followed our instincts and learned a lot more from our mistakes than from our successes.

And boy, did we make mistakes! Neither of us knew much about owning, maintaining, or running a house, much less dealing with tenants in a three-family dwelling. Andrea's father was a big help, but some stuff we just had to learn the hard way. I remember Andrea wanted to change the wall covering from wallpaper to paint in the second bedroom. What seemed like a weekend knockoff took me the better part of two months, every night after work. There were several layers of wallpaper separated by paint. After weeks of steaming, scrapping, and swearing, I finally got down to the bare walls, which unfortunately looked like Berlin after World War II.

While Andrea didn't really want to get involved (she had papers to grade), she was happy to function as quality control and make sure the work was done up to her standards. Of course, I managed to ruin the hardwood floor in the process, so I learned another new skill: floor sanding and finishing. When I was finally ready to paint, she changed her mind and decided to go with wallpaper. After another weekend of learning how to hang wallpaper, the room was finished. Andrea then refurbished it with money we didn't have and delighted in telling her family and friends what a great job "we" did and how much "fun we had doing it!"

We lived on the ground floor and went through an eclectic array of tenants above us: flight attendants, young parents with babies, students from the local college, and con men. We dealt with wild parties, bounced checks, deserted apartments, and scams. One tenant whose lease was ending threw a clam bake for thirty people in August and then left a week early without throwing out the shells. When we went to pick up the keys, they were long gone. When we opened the door, the smell created by shellfish remains marinating in ninety-degree heat for a week brought us to tears. The place had to be scrubbed down from top to bottom. The maggots on the decaying shells were the size of kittens.

With more confidence than skills or experience, we simply pushed on through the issues and focused on saving for our own one-family house.

We also had some additional help. Almost from the day I met Andrea, I became very close to her brother Peter and his wife, Rosemary. They were my age, we were interested in the same things, and they made me feel very welcome in my new extended family. Rosemary was the sister Andrea never had, and she stood by her through thick and thin. Peter was very handy and helped us with things around the house. Like his father, he guided me around new homeowner disasters more than once.

They had two small kids who we were delighted in babysitting. We spent a lot of time together and thoroughly enjoyed one another's company. Years later, whenever I really needed help, Peter, and especially Rosemary, would drop everything at a moment's notice and fly over to assist.

Mostly, Andrea and I just had fun. We enjoyed each other, our friends, our jobs, and especially traveling to new places and seeing different things, which our honeymoon in Mexico had kindled.

We both loved to travel and took full advantage of Andrea's summers off, venturing far and wide: to Montreal, the Great Lakes, Civil War battlefields, the California and Oregon coasts, Mount Saint Helens volcano in Washington State, Arizona, Las Vegas, and down the Eastern Seaboard. We took long road trips, camped at Kampgrounds of America campgrounds, and drank cheap wine.

We had incredible adventures and met all kinds of characters.

During our visit to Washington, Mount Saint Helen's had just erupted. There were piles of ash that were reminiscent of the snowdrifts from the Blizzard of '78. We thought it would be a grand idea to drive up the mountain to see how close we could get to the crater. No mind that the national park was closed and that we were engaging with a still-active volcano.

We got about halfway up the mountain when we became stuck in the ash—it was more than a foot deep. We were almost literally up to our ashes (sorry for the bad pun). We were also, as my father would say, "up shit's creek without a paddle." With no one on the road (why would there be?) and darkness approaching, we were resigned to sleeping in our car on the mountain when, out of nowhere, we saw a pickup truck coming *down* the mountain. The driver, who bore an amazing resemblance to Grizzly Adams, turned his truck around without a word, hooked the bumper of our rental car with a chain, and pulled us off the mountain. At the gate, he unhooked the chain, threw it in the back of his truck, and drove away without saying a word. It was one of the many times on our travels when Andrea and I looked at each other with a "Did that really just happen?" look.

At a San Francisco Giants baseball game, Andrea insisted on letting what appeared to me to be a homeless guy sit with us. She had a great conversation with him while I watched the game. She even bought him a hot dog, a beer, and peanuts. After he left and we got up to leave at the end of the game, we realized he'd stolen Andrea's pocketbook. She was despondent. Andrea, through her innocent naivete, always saw the good in people and couldn't believe that someone she'd treated so nicely would do such a thing. We shrugged it off and finished our trip. Two weeks later, we received a package in the mail; a couple in San Jose had found Andrea's pocketbook—intact, though minus the fifty dollars she had in her wallet—and mailed it back to us. Faith in humanity restored!

We came to a much fuller appreciation for the vastness and beauty of America. We swam in Lake Tahoe; kayaked in San Francisco Bay with the seals; rode horses in Sedona (in the same valley where John Wayne filmed some of his movies); snuck into Tijuana, Mexico (where I tried to talk her into a tattoo, to no avail); picked tulips in Holland, Michigan; and felt the ghosts of Civil War battles in Gettysburg and Vicksburg. This love of travel would lead us to visit all fifty states and twenty countries—by car, train, tram, plane, boat, ship, Vespa, bicycle, and on foot.

In 1980, we sold our multifamily house in Salem and moved into an apartment on the water in Rockport, where Andrea worked. Rockport is famous for its beauty, its seafaring people, and the universally acclaimed painting by Jeri Borst Haagens, known as *Motif 2*, of a red fishing shack that has become iconic of the artist colony that emerged in Rockport.

Andrea took to Rockport, and Rockport took to Andrea. She and another first-year teacher fresh out of Radcliffe, Maureen, became rock stars in this quiet town. They were young, bright, energetic, creative, and innovative.

They were also very accessible, and it was not at all unusual for Andrea's students' parents to stop by our apartment on Front Beach to check on something or just ask a question. Sometimes they brought cookies and stayed for coffee. Other times, we opened a bottle of wine, and they stayed for dinner. Watching Andrea in this environment was like watching what I envision an angel in heaven must be like—totally in her element, very much at peace, and completely at ease.

Of course, there were challenging moments. With youth comes idealism and naiveté. Andrea was overflowing with educational concepts and ideas. Some of them fit within the frame-work of the school's curriculum, and some of them clearly did not. Andrea and Maureen's boss, Selma, a wonderful woman and longtime teacher-administrator with deep, strong ties to the community, became a mentor to both women. She alternatively coddled them, admonished them, and pushed them beyond their experience levels into the real world. While she was always open to new ideas, she was a traditionalist who needed to sometimes rein in young Andrea when she wanted to teach first graders a foreign language or use her husband as a guest lecturer on basketball as a career option.

Andrea walked to work, arrived early, and left late; built out a classroom that was vibrant, funny, and educational (a reflection of her personality); and was totally in her element. She would bring me in to see her class, and I would watch her teach, much like I would with my daughter many years later, with great pride.

Andrea was a marvelous teacher. I realize it's impossible for me to be objective, but watching how she interacted with her first-grade class was magical. The kids were learning every minute, but they'd also, at times, be squealing with joy at a game she'd created or an exercise they were doing. They'd follow her around on the playground like she was the Pied Piper. It was another one of Andrea's magic tricks. I saw it so many times, but I was amazed and delighted every time!

Occasionally, I would stop by and shoot baskets with her kids at recess. I'd pick them up near the rim so they could make a hoop, and when they did, they'd immediately look for Andrea and scream, "Ms. Pirani, Ms. Pirani, I made a basket. Watch me!" She would beam with pride at the joy "her kids" were having and the glow on their cherubic faces.

I watched her teach babies to read. It was beyond my comprehension how she did it, but every one of those kids could read and comprehend a book by the end of the year. Not only could they read, but they also all seemed to love reading.

Andrea decided to learn how to play the guitar, and she got to be pretty damn good. The kids loved singing along with her to tunes like "one, two, three, four, five, I caught a fish alive," and "Puff the Magic Dragon." The "Rainbow Connection" from *The Muppet Movie* was the class favorite, and I can still hear and see Andrea strumming her guitar with her voice filling the classroom, tiny kids shouting out the chorus ("someday we'll find it, the rainbow connection, the lovers, the poets, and me") as loud as they could with huge toothy grins on their faces.

We socialized with Selma and her husband; it was a very tight community, and they treated us to real small-town New England hospitality, as well as providing us with access to the inner sanctums of the town. Selma was a smart and savvy woman who could seamlessly separate her roles as boss, mentor, and friend, depending on the venue. In doing so, she looked to round Andrea out, not only as a teacher but also as a more complete educator.

For example, for reasons that didn't make a lot of sense to me at the time, but were in retrospect a part of a plan to expose Andrea to the many aspects of education beyond class-room teaching, her boss put her on the teacher's union negotiating team. There were many nights when the anguished young teacher would come back to our apartment after a brutal negotiating session and scream at me, "All I want to do is TEACH MY KIDS; I don't want to deal with any more bullshit politics!"

That was a trait that she never lost. Her intentions, whether it was with her first graders, her friends, her adult students, or me, were forever pure. She always let you know where she stood, but she never wanted to complicate relationships with icky things like money, gossip, or politics. I think this was one of the elements of her personality that drew people to her. They not only felt welcomed, but they also felt safe.

We also became fast friends with Maureen and her husband, James. We went to happy hours after work, had dinner together when we could afford it, and spent a lot of time playing board games and drinking cheap wine. Between Andrea and me, we were making about twelve thousand a year (skinny even by 1979 standards), but we literally didn't have a care in the world.

Andrea took a job in a craft store in a quaint tourist area (I guess that's a real oxymoron) in a place called Bearskin Neck. She loved interacting with customers and tourists, and she quickly became an ambassador for Rockport and all it had to offer. We walked, frolicked on the beach, and loved the setting we lived in, especially during the nor'easters that would slam mighty waves from the north Atlantic off the rocks and up against our picture glass window. We'd sit on the couch and taunt the waves. We were poor financially but happy and rich in spirit, laughing at the world from our own delightful little bubble. Every morning, we'd awaken to the rhythmic sound of the waves breaking on the beach just yards off the back of our apartment.

Andrea taught in Rockport for five short years, but it was by far one of the happiest and most meaningful periods in our lives.

However, our larger plan was to buy a piece of land on the south shore of Boston, build a house that was near the ocean and my office, and have children of our own. The plan eventually came to fruition, but living in Rockport made it tough. We loved the town and the people, and Andrea loved her job. We lived on the beach next to a bookstore and within walking distance of all kinds of shops and restaurants. We made a lot of good friends. But practically speaking, living on an isolated peninsula forty-five miles north of Boston wasn't going to work for my job or the need to be close to our families.

Crazily enough, one of the factors that contributed to our decision to move was the temperature of the ocean water. We loved to swim, but the area where we lived was beyond the reach of the warmer Gulf Stream currents. While we lived on the beach with a spectacular view of the North Atlantic, I found out the hard way that we weren't in Florida, or even the relatively temperate waters of Cape Cod.

We moved into our apartment on a steamy July day. The temperatures were in the nineties, and we were overheated from moving boxes, refrigerators, and furniture. As we finished, just before we fired up the grill to cook for the people who helped us move, I thought it would be a good idea to go for a quick swim. I bounded across the hard sand and ran toward it, then dove into the beautiful, clear water. After about three seconds, I thought I was going to have a heart attack. I grew up by the ocean, but this water was ten degrees colder than anything I'd ever been exposed to. It was like a polar plunge on New Year's Day—in July!

For the next two years that we lived there, I never went back in that water. As I looked out our bay window, it tempted me, seduced me, and constantly tortured me—I could look but not touch! No way were we going to live on the ocean and not be able to go swimming.

Rockport was a wonderful interlude for both of us, especially Andrea who excelled at her job and adored her school kids. But she had those other aspirations, namely having kids of her own.

First, we needed a house. Our friends Sue and Mike helped us find a two-acre lot of land in the town of Hingham, just south of Boston, and Mike built our new home. I learned to use a chainsaw and cleared the land for the English Tudor house we built. Andrea and I did all of the painting and the landscaping. It was an exciting, overwhelming, learning experience. In a little over three years, we went from barely understanding how to maintain a house to building our dream house.

Life was good—and then it got even better! After four years of marriage, we had our first child, a beautiful girl with enormous blue eyes, whom we named Natalie. If I thought Andrea was on cloud nine when we got married or even when she fulfilled her life's ambition and became a teacher, motherhood took her to another level. From that moment on, nothing in her life was more important to her than her children and their well-being. Just in time for Natalie's homecoming, we completed building and moved into our own brand-new house.

Andrea decided that she would take a break from teaching and become a full-time mom. Selma was not happy when Andrea told her we were moving out of town. I think she hoped and expected that Andrea would be a fixture in the Rockport Public Schools for many years to come.

As for my career, a couple of years earlier, I joined three of my colleagues and started what was to become a very successful software consulting business called Atlantic Data Services (ADS). We helped banks develop software and financial products, assisted with the many bank mergers that were taking place in the '80s and '90s, and provided project management for large, transformational projects. There were great growth opportunities, and the first big one tested our newly expanded family unit.

Andrea displayed her mettle when our company signed our first remote client, a large bank processing center in the remote outpost of Swedesboro, in southern New Jersey. As ADS's operations manager, it was up to me to make sure we not only got the work done but that we also used it as a model for future expansion.

This was going to be a lot of work and require me to have a big on-site presence. I started out flying down on Sunday nights and flying back home on Thursday or Friday nights, repeating that script week after week. Although Andrea's mom was around to help with the baby, it was clear that this situation was not sustainable.

Our CEO, Bob Howe, asked me if I'd be willing to move down to New Jersey for some time and solidify the client model and expand the business. After many conversations, Andrea agreed, with the stipulation that we would go there for six months and not a day longer. I concurred and gained the same hard commitment from my company. With these parameters in place, off we went to our new home away from home and another big adventure.

Though Andrea agreed to go, that didn't mean she had to like or accept the relocation. She was leaving her new dream house, with a new baby, far away from family and friends. The house we had built south of Boston was only about twenty miles from her parents' home north of the city. To her family, but especially her mother, it may as well have been two hundred miles. Although Mom was never happy with the location of our home, to her credit, she was always there to support Andrea.

Even though the move to New Jersey was only temporary, now we were talking about actually moving hundreds of miles away, and her mom was beside herself. I tried to emphasize the word *temporary*, but the words she chose to hear were "hundreds of miles away." Andrea, although conflicted, finally told her mom, "We're a family now, and where one of us goes, we all go." And that was the end of that.

But it soon became clear that Andrea was right to be dubious about our new situation. The good news was that we had a townhouse with plenty of space, within easy walking distance for me to the client site. The bad news was that it was the middle of January, Andrea had a six-month-old to take care of and no friends or neighbors, and the nearest decent supermarket was over fifteen miles away across the Delaware Memorial Bridge in a different state.

As we always attempted to do, we tried to make the best of the situation and persevere. The weather got better, we started meeting people, and we had some visitors (though her mother, in an act of stubbornness, never came down). We explored Philadelphia, Baltimore, Amish country, the Jersey Shore, and Washington, DC.

While it was far from ideal, it was okay, and it was a big stepping stone for the company, which Andrea never let Bob forget. For the next more than three decades, every time Andrea came in contact with Bob, she'd admonish him for exiling us to New Jersey.

ANDREA. You owe us big time. Peter saved the company for you guys, and you better not forget it!

CEO Bob. Well, I don't know if he actually *saved* the company, but we're very appreciative of the sacrifices you both made.

Andrea. You're darn right we made sacrifices, and he did save the company, and I don't want you to ever forget it!

CEO Bob, *throwing up his hands*. Okay, okay. He saved the company!

So fresh off from saving the company (I hadn't, and regardless, I was far more interested in the new postion and raise I received), we successfully navigated that bump in the road and moved back to our newly minted house with one-year-old Natalie.

It was hard to believe that life could get any better. And all of sudden, it didn't.

CHAPTER 4

Can This Really Be Happening to Us?
(A Seismic Shift in Direction)

In early 1985, Andrea was feeling fine overall, but she began to experience some strange symptoms, highlighted by sharp pains that would migrate to different parts of her body, but mostly affecting her neck and head.

She saw a variety of doctors—her general practitioner, an otolaryngologist (ear, nose, and throat doctor), a headache specialist, and even a dentist. She tried yoga and acupuncture. They poked, probed, and needled her (including a cortisone shot in the tongue that Andrea would forever tell me was more painful than brain surgery).

Since these pains were sporadic and she otherwise remained healthy, we didn't dwell on them. We had a new house, a new baby, a new community, and a new company to distract us. We were also in the naive medical phase where we believed that, no matter what was wrong, eventually the doctors would find the problem and fix it. Boy, did we have a lot to learn.

Finally, someone came up with the bright idea to do a CAT scan of her brain. I was in New Jersey when I got a call from Andrea that the scan revealed a tumor on her left auditory nerve. We were in shock. All kinds of thoughts raced through my mind as I grabbed the first flight back to Boston. My immediate feeling was one of disbelief—disbelief that God would allow this to happen and disbelief that our seemingly charmed life could be so suddenly and dramatically turned upside down. In my mind, tumors were associated with cancer, and I knew that brain cancer was a particularly bad form. As we caucused that night and readied ourselves for the meeting at the hospital later in the week, we—for the first time, but not by any stretch the last—prayed for the best-case scenario.

This was the moment in time when our fairy-tale existence morphed into what would become our forever personal nightmare. It was also the first time that we instinctively reached out to God as our lifeline, begging for a positive outcome. God answered us, but not quite in the way we prayed. It was a lesson we would eventually appreciate—God does things as he sees fit, for his own reasons, in ways that we can't understand.

We met with the doctors and learned that the tumor in Andrea's head was not malignant. But before we could even wrap our heads around what appeared to be good news, we learned a new word that would change our lives forevermore: *neurofibromatosis* (NF), or more precisely, as we came to understand it, the subtype neurofibromatosis 2, or NF2. While we heard the diagnosis and learned to pronounce the name of the disease, we had no clue as to the magnitude that moment was going to have on us for the rest of our lives together.

Not too many people are familiar with this illness, so allow me to give you my short primer on neurofibromatosis, with apologies to much more capable neurologists and neuro-surgeons. NF is a nasty disease that causes benign tumors to grow slowly in or on your body, often on nerves, for some still unknown reason.

NF is a genetic disease, and you're born with it. There are two types of NF. With NF1, tumors grow on the outside of your body. This type of NF disease is possibly what affected the protagonist of the movie *The Elephant Man*. With NF2, tumors grow inside the body, mainly in the brain and spinal cord. NF2 can cause a multitude of issues—the tumors can create deaf-ness, balance problems, cognitive issues, eye problems, facial paralysis, neuropathy, and more. The only way to exorcise the tumors is through surgery.

NF can present itself in two different fashions. NF can be genetically transmitted, that is, passed down from generation to generation in the form of a mutated gene. A parent who has NF has a fifty-fifty chance of passing it on to their child. On the receiving end, a child either does or doesn't get the mutated gene and the disease. Unlike some diseases with gene markers, like cystic fibrosis, NF does not skip generations. Once the indi-vidual in the NF genetic chain does not receive the NF-altered gene, they are free from the disease and cannot pass it on.

The second way you can "get" NF is spontaneous. In this case, there is no genetic component in the receiving process; it just happens—a stroke of very bad luck. 50% of NF cases are genetic, and 50% are spontaneous.

Basically, if one of your parents has NF, you're living on a roulette wheel, with a 50% chance of winning and an equal chance of losing. An even more grotesque analogy is that you're playing Russian roulette with one pull, and one bullet in the gun's chamber—it's all or nothing.

We don't know for sure how Andrea acquired her NF2. Her maternal grandmother had benign tumors and ultimately died from the effects of these tumors in the 1960s. But the awareness of NF and the tools required to diagnose and treat it were in their infancy then, so there is no way to confirm what caused her grandmother's tumors or whether she had, or passed on, NF2.

Fast-forward to the early 2000s, researchers were able to identify the specific gene and mutations that cause NF2. With a simple blood test, doctors could determine if a person's NF2 gene was mutated (NF-positive and causing NF2 disease) or not (no NF2).

This became especially important to us and our children (more on that later). Our doctors wanted Andrea's family, especially her mother, to take the test. The hope was to provide them with some interesting data on the possible link back to Andrea's grandmother, to assess whether Andrea's mom had NF2, and to help advance their general research on this little-understood disease.

But Andrea's mother would have nothing to do with it and steadfastly refused. She was in her seventies and very old school when it came to medicine and doctors. She was in perfect health, hadn't seen a doctor since Andrea had been born, and was of the mindset that if it ain't broke, don't touch it. The doctors pleaded, bribed, and harassed her, but there was no way she was going to get tested, and she never did.

At the time, I thought it was odd and maybe even a little bit selfish. Andrea and I had already thrown ourselves into finding out as much as we could about NF2. We had even started a foundation to raise funds to advance knowledge about the disease. In fact, we were told that some of the money we raised had been used to fund a researcher who was a part of the team that helped discover the breakthrough NF2 testing methodology. Why wouldn't her mother take a simple blood test if it would help the research, potentially be beneficial to future generations of NF2 sufferers, and maybe in some way even have an impact on Andrea?

It was a while before I fully understood this lesson. NF2 and most serious chronic diseases have obvious physical impacts on its victims, including tests, scans, treatments, drugs, operations, pain, and rehab. But there's also a difficult and heartbreaking emotional aspect of the disease that takes its toll on not only the patient but also many others in the supporting cast. Like a stone tossed into a pool of water, the greatest impact may be the point where the stone hits the water, but the ripples from this action resonate in all directions. The bigger the stone, the bigger the ripples. And NF2 proved to be a doozy of a boulder.

It was only after Andrea and I had been in the exact same boat that her mother was in with our own children that I was able to see her mom's perspective. She felt that she wouldn't have been able to deal with the guilt she'd have if she knew that she had passed NF2 on to her daughter. Added to that, the whole situation no doubt dredged up unpleasant memories of what she went through with her own mother. Andrea herself agonized over the fact that she could pass NF onto her children—a thought so devastating that she told me it would have been far worse for her than having the disease herself. Of all the emotional traumas Andrea dealt with, having to deal with one of her children diagnosed with NF2 might have been the thing to push her over the edge.

Intellectually and rationally, it makes no sense. Of course, no one in the chain from Andrea's grandmother to her mother to Andrea would have had any control over getting or passing on NF. No one was lax, negligent, or malicious. It was always the cunning NF2 that was the villain, not the people caught in its ugly web. Damn you, NF2!

But try to tell that to a father who passed the disease on to his baby and knows that the baby will suffer greatly and has a high probability of early death. Tell that to a mother who has to watch her beautiful adult child endure what feels like an endless series of brain and spinal surgeries to try to control a disease for which there is no cure. Tell that to a child who is forced into a scary, strange life with their newly deafened mom, who can't easily communicate with you anymore and is now forever different from all the other moms. Damn you, NF2!

Despite the relative lack of research and definitive understanding of NF2 at the time Andrea was diagnosed, the doctors assured us that it could be managed. The first piece of good news was that the tumors created by NF2 are almost always benign. The other comforting news was that the tumor resting on Andrea's left auditory nerve could be completely removed with surgery and would not grow back. It turns out that when a tumor created by NF2 is completely removed, there is a very small likelihood it will regenerate. Conversely, when any part of the tumor is not fully removed, there is a near certainty that it will grow back.

The auditory nerve is the conduit that transmits sound from the ear to the brain. If it's not functioning properly, some level of hearing will be degraded, ranging from difficulty hearing to profound deafness. We all have two matching auditory nerves, one each on our left and right sides. A tumor that NF2 creates on the auditory nerve is called an acoustic neuroma.

Our surgeon explained to us that he was confident he would be able to remove the entire tumor, and we could rest assured that it would not grow back. The simplest analogy is a weed in your garden. Pull it out roots and all, and it's gone. But if you can pull away only part of the weed and leave any of the roots intact, the weed will likely return.

In Andrea's case, removing the entire tumor to preclude future damage would definitely compromise her left auditory nerve, and she would lose hearing in that ear. However, we were told that NF2 tumors on both acoustic nerves (bilateral acoustic neuromas) were uncommon, so the chance of Andrea developing a tumor on her right acoustic nerve was slim. While the surgery would cause Andrea to lose her hearing in one ear, she would be able to adapt with one working ear, and full deafness was an unlikely prognosis.

So while it was indeed brain surgery and certainly nothing to be taken lightly, we looked at it as kind of a one-and-done operation—no doubt serious, but one with a strong probability of success. In addition, we had an eminently qualified surgeon with a significant degree of confidence at a highly reputable hospital. Andrea demonstrated amazing grace under tremendous pressure—she was scared, a young mother, starting a new life—but as we drove to the hospital to prep for the surgery, she flashed that Andreaeque smile and said to me, "I can do this!"

With that attitude and a solid hospital and surgeon in our corner, what could go wrong?

Well, in this instance, nothing. While the surgery was stressful for all of us, Andrea came through it with flying colors. After Andrea woke up after surgery, she went through a short hospital stay, a relatively brief stint in rehab, and a quick convalescence at her parents' house. They were unbelievable during the whole ordeal, including taking full care and control of now-toddler Natalie. Except for the partially shaved head and a grotesque row of staple marks, Andrea was back on her feet in what seemed to be no time at all.

We all celebrated with her parents over a Rheingold split four ways (apparently, there was plenty of leftover from our engagement toast!), and we soon headed back home to pick up our life where we left off. We were told that there would be periodic follow-up scans, but for the most part, Andrea could expect that life would return to normal. We accepted this prognosis without question and blissfully slipped back comfortably into our former lives.

Unfortunately, we were still ignorant regarding NF2. Our surgeon was highly focused on the tumor in front of him, and he did a perfect job. The problem was that no one at the hospital was looking at, or talking to us about, the bigger picture. No one was telling us about the potential for more tumors on Andrea's other acoustic nerve and in other parts of her brain and spinal cord. No one was telling us about the impact NF2 could have on our lives, Andrea's health, and our children beyond the "unlikely" potential for another acoustic neuroma and the even more remote chance of deafness. No one was clearly explaining the hereditary realities. No one was giving us a full picture of the wanton level of destruction and heartbreak NF2 could (and would) impose on our future.

Later, I heard the adage, "Doctor's doctor, and surgeons cut." While the hospital we used was good and the neurosurgeon was clearly competent, we didn't have a neurologist who was looking out for Andrea's overall well-being beyond the surgery itself—someone to guide us through choppy waters that could lie ahead of her. We didn't have a psychologist who would help Andrea or me try to make sense of what was happening. We didn't have a support team that would help her deal with the quality of life issues.

Of course, we didn't know what we didn't know, but we also lacked not only the experience in this area but also the guidance necessary to develop a support system to help us fill this void. This was the first faint warning signal that we needed to be more in charge, to advocate, and to operate in our own best interests. It would be a long time, and we would have to fight through a lot of medical haze before we got to that point, but eventually, we would become cynical, savvy medical consumers in a high-stakes game of NF2 "chicken."

For the most part, for a while, life did return to normal. Andrea extended her hiatus from teaching and was now a stay-at-home mom. She made friends easily and soon helped organize a play group with other moms. Ever the teacher, she created activities that not only were enjoyable but also developed the children's skills while making learning and socialization fun. It was kind of like she was back in the classroom again.

She used her personality and background to help solidify this group of women, who went on to become tight-knit friends. Although they didn't know what they were getting into at the time, many of them stood fast by her and had her back for the rest of her life.

We were busy with our new home, I was working hard helping to get the new company off the ground, and we moved forward with our new normal.

It wasn't so bad. Until it was.

The next body blow came when we found out Andrea was pregnant with our second child. Either we hadn't understood, or we were never told, but the genetic aspect of NF2 that I explained earlier hit us right between the eyes for the first (but unfortunately, not the last) time.

Since genetic mapping wasn't available in 1985, the only way to know if the baby of an NF2 parent would have the disease was to wait and see if symptoms developed later in life. Receiving and fully digesting this information—with one small child already at home and another one on the way—was a real gut punch. Amazingly, this aspect of the disease had not been made clear to us. We'd been so focused on Andrea's operation, recovery, and well-being that we collectively had skirted over the genetic attributes of the disease.

When you're in these types of high-stress medical situations, it's frightening how much important information can be missed, misunderstood, or omitted. Questions and answers that seem so obvious after the fact somehow get skewed or lost in the process of shock and information overload.

Because no definitive connection could be established between the tumors of Andrea's grandmother and Andrea's NF2 and because her mother showed no signs of the disease, perhaps we concluded that the mutated disease started with Andrea and would stop with her. Perhaps we didn't want to know the hard reality and never pursued that line of questioning. Perhaps we were simply misinformed. Maybe we were so excited to have children and a family that we glossed over it. At this point, all the *perhaps*es and *maybe*s became meaningless, and we were left with the cold certainty that Andrea carried the NF2 gene, and was potentially a genetic conduit to our children.

This realization was almost worse for us than Andrea herself contacting the disease. We were adults who could reason, evaluate, and make educated decisions, but now we were talking about bringing a baby into this evolving nightmare through no choice of his or hers. To make matters more difficult, we also had to now deal with the same issues with toddler Natalie, who had been unknowingly put in the same position before we even knew what the term NF2 meant!

There was a school of thought that suggested to us that Andrea consider having an abortion. Their logic, from a very clinical perspective, was that we already had one child at risk of developing NF2, why increase the odds by introducing a second baby into the equation? To muddy the waters even further, doctors were also assessing an emerging theory that pregnancy in mothers with NF2, stimulated hormones that, in turn, could trigger the development of more tumors in the mothers. This added yet another level to our angst.

The doctors focused on the science—statistical probabilities, most likely outcomes, and theories—but we were consumed by the baby growing in Andrea's belly. We were very uncomfortable taking a life—even one that we had created and ultimately had control over. It was neither a political nor feminist issue to us, but it was something we'd come to believe through our faith and something personally important to both of us. We firmly believed that only God had the right to create or terminate a life—period. But it's easy to profess faith in a vacuum—another whole deal when reality stares you down and you come to understand the gravity of the pain, heartache, and consequences attached to your decisions.

We agonized over this conundrum, which seemed to have no good answer. A Solomon-like dilemma: protect Andrea and harm the baby, or protect the baby and potentially put Andrea at greater risk. Did we really have the confidence in our beliefs to allow a scenario to be set in motion that could forever complicate and likely denigrate our lives and the lives of our children? Did our faith only exist in the abstract for us, or were we willing to roll the dice with God at our craps table and accept his will?

With the clock ticking, we decided to retreat to a bed-and-breakfast for a weekend and figure things out as best we could. We were truly, to quote Bob Seger, "working on mysteries, without any clues." This was a huge decision with potentially terrifying, lifelong consequences. We were two scared, young parents, trying to sort out something mind-boggling to us—intellectually, physically, emotionally, and spiritually.

It was also complex. As much as we thought we knew and understood about NF2, it seemed we were getting new and usually more frightening information every week. We were also getting a lot of opinions and, in some cases, pressure from family, friends, and doctors. Worst of all, we still didn't know what we didn't know.

The B and B's peaceful setting in the New Hampshire Mountains belied the turmoil we were struggling with. For two days, we contemplated and talked through the alternatives and consequences, cried and screamed at each other, bargained with God, and prayed, finally arriving at our decision: Andrea would have the baby, and we would live with the outcome and consequences. While we hadn't found a perfect solution, we found a path. Most importantly, at least for the moment, we found a modicum of peace.

Although Andrea would always pooh-pooh anyone who called her brave, this was a blatant act of bravery on her part. She stared down NF right into its soulless eyes and didn't blink. We decided to follow our instincts and faith, willing to accept whatever the future would hold. We made a decision, choosing to trust our faith in God as opposed to what was being presented as the more rational and scientific route. In this instance, as we would do again and again in the future, we fully embraced the words, "Please, God, watch over us and help us!"

It turned out to be a nerve-racking but routine pregnancy. In what we hoped wasn't an omen, a hurricane hit New England that October and dropped two large oak trees on our house. On December 12, 1985, we were rewarded and blessed with a healthy, happy baby boy, Peter Alvaro (or "re-Pete," as I liked to call him). While mother and son did great, we would have to wait twenty long years to find out if this innocent, cuddly newborn was harboring NF2.

So once again, we returned home to yet another phase of our young life, hoping and praying that we could move on with a mundane—dare I say, boring—existence.

Unfortunately for us, God had other plans!

CHAPTER 5

Not a Battle, but a Relentless War

Dark storm clouds were gathering on the horizon of our life. The kind of menacing clouds that move fast and mean business. Their inky black color and deep contours made it clear that their goal was to wreak havoc and cause disruption. Psalm 18:9 (NIV) appeared to be embracing our life: "He opened up the heavens, and came down; dark storm clouds were beneath his feet." This terrifying account of God's furious judgment seems like an all-too-real representation of what we were experiencing.

While pregnant with Peter, Andrea had begun to experience some of the old, pre-NF2 diagnosis symptoms. We did our best to ignore them, but by now, we were starting to learn that this monster called NF2 never retreats. In fact, NF2 was already spoiling for a second round.

Each day, Andrea would remain in bed, wide awake, for as long as she could. It allowed her a last snatch of peace and contemplation before she had to get up, go out, and face down her increasingly surreal world. She would lie in bed and plan her day like all of us do, but then she would try to sort out where she was with her new lifetime companion, NF2.

Did she have any new symptoms? Were the current symptoms any worse? Did she have any doctor's appointments coming up? Was her support system intact in case she had to move quickly on an issue? How were the kids affected? What was going to happen in the long term with our children?

We were starting to understand that the NF2 was in control of Andrea's body and mind. We had a voice in every medical matter that arose, but NF2 always had the final say. It was a suffocating reality. While NF2 hadn't ground us down yet, the constant presence of the elephant in the room was oppressive. The weight of what was and what was to come felt almost biblical in nature.

Like the classic video game Pac-Man, with its insatiable appetite for the next series of dots, NF2 moved slowly and relentlessly forward—at first ringing the faintest of alarms that grow louder and louder, demanding that you pay attention to it. Like a perpetually colicky baby, it offered little relief, only intermittent breaks, with us always on edge, waiting for the next signs of progression.

Sure enough, an MRI showed another tumor growing on the right auditory nerve. Something we had been told was "unlikely" had, in fact, happened. The only thing that could potentially stop it was another surgery. This had staggering implications. We had dealt with brain surgery and come to grips with the hereditary aspects of NF2, but now we were faced with the stark realization that this was a match that not only had no end but also followed its own rules and progressed without mercy.

We needed to take a step backward, try to compose ourselves, and attempt to map out a plan. Unlike most young families, who were busy making vacation plans, evaluating schools for their kids, and thinking about moving into a bigger house, we were consumed with a tornado-like swirl of confusion, uncertainty, and despair.

This was our "Aha!" moment with NF2. We arrived at the realization that we alone had to make the life-altering decisions facing us, and they were going to be hard ones, almost always without any assurances of success. At this point, we had to lock in on the battle against NF2, or we were going to succumb and allow it free rein to control almost every aspect of our lives.

At the same time, we also came to understand that while we had a lot of support from family, friends, and the medical community, they could do only so much. In a life-and-death situation, it's a different, unnerving feeling when you reach the point where you realize that ultimately you alone are responsible for your own decisions—no one else can make them for you. Blind trust in your older family members, wise friends, or even doctors is not going to magically make things right or diminish the downstream consequences.

We decided we were all in. I was determined not to get blindsided again because of a lack of knowledge, misinformation, or misunderstanding. We started by learning as much as we could about NF2. A lot of this fell on my shoulders. There was not much good news to be found, and the dire information I started to come across was simply too much for Andrea to handle at this point. I did my homework. I did as much research as I could into NF2, treatments, and best hospitals—a daunting task at the time before the Internet. I spent a lot of time in the library, on the phone, and writing letters asking for information.

We'd been happy with the hospital where Andrea had her first surgery. Though not a nationally recognized medical facility, it was a regional hospital with an excellent reputation. However, we realized the primary reason we'd gone there was that it was close to the house of Andrea's parents and was where she had her initial MRI that showed us her first tumor.

We had a similar level of trust in her surgeon. While we vetted him before Andrea's surgery, we didn't check out any alternatives or other facilities. We only confirmed that he was competent. Fortunately, he *was* competent. He was also highly respected, if not renowned, and he had successfully removed the initial tumor without any complications.

However, the more research we did on NF, the more we understood the complexity of the disease and the need for not only a very good facility and surgeon but also the best alternative available. We were determined to find the optimum landing spot for Andrea and follow the research wherever it took us.

Our research did lead us to a world-class facility, as fate would have it, right up the street from us: Massachusetts General Hospital (MGH). After doing as much due diligence as I knew how, using all my contacts and relationships for validation, and much soul-searching, we decided this was the best place for Andrea, both in the short and long term.

I contacted Andrea's original surgeon and thanked him for all he had done but let him know we had decided to change doctors and hospitals. It was tough because we'd become close with him through the follow-up to Andrea's surgery. He was very professional and empathetic, but I know it hurt him. He was one of the top-tier guys in his field. However, we'd concluded that we needed *the* top guy in this field. Unfortunately, he became a small piece of collateral damage in what had become our full-fledged war against NF2. There would be many more pieces of collateral damage ahead.

This was the point when we really began to view NF2 in terms of warfare. A war of desperation, for sure, because no one had ever beaten NF2, but it was a war we were willing to fight. We didn't ask for this war, but if we were going to be dragged into it, we were going full bore. As they might have said in my father's submarine days, "Damn the torpedoes."

Before we fully understood the war analogy, we looked at the diagnosis and first operation as a single battle—a one-time serious event that was over and done, and that we'd won. What we came to appreciate was that our struggle was not that clean or linear; like a war, it would involve many battles, a lot of pain, and much ancillary damage.

Real wars usually end with negotiated settlements—even if the settlement terms are jammed down the loser's throat. The biggest frustration we had fighting this medical war for Andrea's well-being was accepting the fact that NF doesn't negotiate; it doesn't offer terms; it never falls back; and while it can be slowed down, it has never been stopped.

In our minds, it was time to throw rational thinking out the window. We couldn't play by established rules because NF didn't follow any rules. We vowed to pursue every avenue, every new technology, and every possible clinical trial in an attempt to slow down and eventually harness this beast.

The first steps in this process over the next several months were a complete whirlwind. We kicked off what would be a lifelong partnership with MGH and worked to forge emerging relationships with our new neurosurgeon, Dr. Robert Ojemann, and various other doctors and support staff at the hospital while coping with the reality and the impacts of another brain surgery on Andrea, our family, and our lives.

Our previous hospital had been a well-run, technologically proficient medical campus, but we quickly learned that MGH functioned at a different level. This is where everything was cutting-edge and the very best doctors came to practice. This is where the first public demonstration of the use of ether as anesthesia for surgery took place in 1846. The first North American book on tumors was written by cofounder Dr. John Collins in

1837. The electrocardiogram was first used in North America here in 1914.

It's the hospital of choice for Arab sheiks, Russian oligarchs, the rich and famous, and world leaders. It's also the place where ordinary people like us came from all over the country to be treated. The beauty of it to me was that we seemed to get the same level of access and attention from the best of the best as the elite class did. It was pretty amazing.

The first indication that we were in a whole new world was the requirement to redo all of Andrea's tests. MGH wouldn't accept any results, prognoses, or conclusions from any other hospital. They needed to do their own evaluation to ensure the data was clean and the strategy was sound. Andrea had to go through the entire testing process again, from consultation and blood work to neurological testing and MRIs. We were assigned a neurologist whose primary job was to watch over, assess, and improve Andrea's quality of life. While in the long term this proved to be an integral part of Andrea's care, for the first part of Andrea's MGH experience, it would prove to be a challenge.

The result of the reevaluation confirmed the initial prognosis: The second tumor, on the opposite auditory nerve, was growing and would need to be surgically removed. We went in to meet the now most important man in our lives, Andrea's new neurosurgeon. As we emerged from the elevator and made our way to his office for our initial visit, it was freaky, and we were very unnerved. Within this ultramodern facility, we were in an area of the original hospital, called the White building—

built in 1939 and named after George Robert White, a prominent Boston philanthropist and owner of the Potter Drug & Chemical Corporation, maker of antibacterial soaps. It was as if nothing had changed for decades. The walls were off-white, the lighting was muted, and the linoleum floors were so highly polished we could see our reflections as we walked. It reminded me of the hospital in the movie *One Flew over the Cuckoo's Nest*.

Most noticeably, it was eerily quiet. The echoing of our shoes on the hard floor was the only noise—that is, until we heard a soft sobbing sound in the distance. Coming around the corner, we saw a middle-aged couple embracing on a wooden bench, clinging to each other, with tears streaming down their faces. Andrea turned away, but I tried to give them an empathetic acknowledgment. There was no reaction in their hollow eyes, only immense sorrow. As we would learn, this was a place where people came not to be cured but rather to face their demons.

We sat down with Dr. Ojemann and developed a strategy. Dr. OJ, as Andrea quickly dubbed him and he seemed to enjoy, was a large, quiet man who reeked of competence. He had a small, unpretentious office in the front of the building, from which you could see all the comings and goings at the main entrance. It was like being in a bubble—watching the rhythm of everyday normal life outside while contemplating the relative insanity of your own situation in this tiny room.

Dr. OJ was so quiet and unassuming that you could almost question if he was the right guy for the job. He delivered information and answered questions in a measured tone, picking his words carefully. Initially, it seemed like he was struggling for the right answers. I later realized that he was getting a feel for our current mindset and how much we understood.

Two things struck me during our visit that helped me put to rest our initial notion that he might not be the right doctor. First, behind his desk, there were numerous wall hangings, similar to what you might see in any doctor's office. He graduated from the University of Iowa, went to medical school at the University of Iowa Medical School, and did his residency at MGH. There were pictures of him with his wife and his family. Pretty standard stuff.

Farther in the far corner, almost out of view, were a few more photos and proclamations—photos of him with Ronald Reagan; one of him giving a speech to what appeared to be a large conference; a scroll extolling him as the president of the American Academy of Neurological Surgeons, the Congress of Neurological Surgeons, and the Society of Neurological Surgeons; and more pictures of him with other dignitaries from around the world. It didn't come across as bragging; in fact, it was more like he was trying to hide them. They seemed to be there more to remind him of where he'd come from and what he'd been able to accomplish than to impress his patients.

Of course, Andrea hounded him with questions about who was in *that* picture, where was *that* meeting, and when did you do *that*. Although he was an incredibly busy man, on every occasion, he impressed me with how he patiently took the time to answer her questions and often chuckle at her comments.

Andrea had the amazing ability to carry on routine, easygoing banter in tense, pressure-filled situations. It was like she was able to shift into a different gear to diffuse the gravity of the moment. Even as we conversed about the most serious issues imaginable, Andrea would carry on in this fashion:

ANDREA. Did you meet Nancy Reagan when you met the president?

DR. OJ. I did.

ANDREA. Don't you just love her? I think she carries herself so nicely.

DR. OJ. She's a very nice woman.

ANDREA. Did you have dinner at the White House?

DR. OJ. I did.

ANDREA. What did they serve?

DR. OJ, *realizing that if he didn't cap this conversation, it could skew the remainder of his schedule.* I don't remember, but let's get back to talking about you.

The second thing that raised our level of confidence, as we became more familiar, was his knowledge and style. He delivered serious, complicated, and yes, emotional information with clarity, certainty, confidence, and a type of blunt compassion.

He certainly wasn't about to sugarcoat any topic, but he also appreciated the enormity and emotional impact that some of the news he delivered would have on his patients. I suspect this delivery style was one that he honed over the years as a result of having to give his patients both good and devastating news, helping them appreciate the impact of this information and getting them to focus on the next steps.

Unfortunately, in his line of business, bad news was often very bad indeed. We collectively agreed to have Dr. OJ try to remove a large portion of the new tumor on the right auditory nerve while attempting to preserve the integrity of the nerve and thus maintain all—or at worst, some—of Andrea's hearing on that side.

While confident about the surgery, I don't think Dr. OJ was particularly optimistic about the results. We all knew that even if he successfully removed a part of the tumor and saved some of Andrea's hearing, the tumor was going to regenerate and present the same issues at a later date. We hoped that, because these tumors often grew very slowly, the surgery might provide Andrea with a window—months or maybe even years—of hearing and a period to come to grips with the reality that someday she would become deaf.

There were also discussions about other and emerging options, such as radiation, laser, or gamma knife surgeries that might help Andrea in the future, if he could save a portion of her hearing now. In that sense, we were trying to buy time.

While this was marginally hopeful news to us, Dr. OJ was primarily focused on the task at hand: the surgery. Like a world-class athlete preparing for the big game, we could see him moving into the zone as the surgery drew closer. As the big day approached, Andrea and I thought a lot about her new doctor, who would shortly hold her life in his hands. Was he getting enough sleep? Was he eating well? Did he limit himself to a glass of wine at dinner? What if he oversleeps on the day of the surgery?

What was happening all seemed so far beyond our comprehension that our heads were spinning. We prayed for Dr. OJ, for Andrea, for our kids, and for our future, but the apprehension and anxiety overwhelmed us, and even prayer brought us little solace. Unlike the first surgery, where we were new to NF and thought of it as an event rather than a process, and where it was over almost before we knew it started, this one was more complicated, more real, and more sinister. For the first time, we were coming to grips with the expansiveness and depth of the NF experience.

CHAPTER 6

Well, It Can't Get Any Worse, Can It? (Oh, Yes It Can—Much Worse than We Could Ever Imagine)

The surgery was long, difficult, intricate, and tedious. Unlike the first tumor, which could be removed with complete disregard for the left auditory nerve's future function, this second operation on the right auditory nerve was an intense effort to preserve her remaining hearing.

The surgery was a success, but this time, the results would prove to be a stunning failure. Dr. OJ was able to remove a significant portion of the tumor—that was the good news. He also did it without any unintended consequences like facial paralysis, stroke, or the diminishment of any of her other functions. But for whatever reason, the second surgery was much harder on Andrea than the first; the recovery process was slower, the pain sharper, and the prognoses for the future much murkier. Here, the rehab hospital stay was longer and more challenging.

As she recovered physically from the surgery, the day-to-day impact on her life and the emotional trauma were beginning to take their toll. Andrea had lost a good portion of her hearing in her "good" ear, and although she was fitted for a hearing aid, it was a cumbersome and relatively ineffective solution (we never again could stand to see a hearing-aid commercial on TV!). She would later tell me that being deaf in one ear and significantly hard of hearing in the other ear was worse for her than being profoundly deaf.

While we were hoping against hope, over time, the writing on the wall became clearer and impossible to ignore; we fought through our sadness and frustration and prepared for the future. We hoped for the best while making preparations for what we thought was the worst: profound deafness. No sound at all—incomprehensible to a person born hearing—was now a quickly emerging likelihood.

Against the background of potentially becoming deaf, the strain of dealing with an infant and a toddler was increasingly strenuous. Some of our family and friends were in denial; some rose to the occasion; still, others distanced themselves from us, unable to deal with the enormity of the situation. Andrea began to feel isolated as her situation became more and more all-encompassing. While many of Andrea's friends stuck by her side, some completely bailed on her, something that would continue at various points in her life as the disease progressed. More collateral damage.

Additional MRIs showed that remnants of the tumor on the right auditory nerve were already beginning to grow back—and in an unusually aggressive fashion. It became evident to Dr. OJ, and eventually to us, that a third surgery was inevitable to completely remove the tumor before it became even more of a problem.

I don't remember a lot of discussion or pushback on this strategy. We were out of options as it related to this battle. We were worn down and beat up. Andrea's quality of life was bad and headed toward worse. She was depressed and at her lowest point so far in the evolution of the disease. Having a sword of Damocles hanging over her head was becoming more problematic than having her hearing cut off.

With our backs against the wall, we rallied. We began to consider solutions to our problems rather than just dwelling on the troubles. We charted a course of getting to what we thought and feared was the endgame—total deafness—and then rebuilding our life around a bad, but hopefully manageable, situation. Some of that turned out to be true; some not so much.

We accepted that a third surgery was now inevitable, and we began to prepare in earnest for our post-surgery, deaf-world life. This was a strange period. We were trying to get ready for a traumatic, life-altering event, but we were at the same time working to stay positive and keep up Andrea's spirits. I tried to keep Andrea busy with anything to distract her from reality. But when the conversation invariably came back to her situation and she'd ask me, "Petes, what's going to happen to me, to us, to the kids?" I had no answers. I had only a blurry inkling of what our future held, but I clung to one certainty: I was going to do everything I could to hold us together, whatever that entailed. But like the biblical passage in which Peter denies Christ three times before the cock crows, this certainty, and my faith, would be put to the test in ways I couldn't imagine.

In the midst of everything going on, we still had to pay attention to our toddler Natalie and our big, healthy, now one-year-old Peter, aka Bam Bam. Once again, Andrea amazed me with her ability to prioritize, compartmentalize, and love. It is difficult to explain just how extraordinary Andrea was during this time. She not only knew she was going to become deaf, but to get there, she also had to go through a third major brain surgery that could also leave her unable to speak or walk, become fully paralyzed, or worse. She was having trouble sleeping and eating. This woman had the weight of the world on her shoulders.

Within that context, she found the strength to take the kids to playgroups, visit with their cousins, read to them, and sing them lullabies as they drifted off to sleep. Her children remained the most important thing in her life—NF2 be damned! The mundane aspects of life became a blessing, a welcome distraction from the impending surgery. Andrea took the kids to their doctor's appointments and playdates; she did the shopping and the cleaning; she had coffee with her friends and went to the gym—anything to keep her mind off the ticking clock.

Finally, after what seemed to be an interminable amount of waiting, Andrea entered MGH for yet another serious brain surgery. This time, the surgery was a medical success, and the second tumor was completely removed. The result was exactly what we expected: Andrea was plunged into her scary new reality of total deafness—hearing only the sounds of silence.

When she awoke, she looked me in the eye and, in a flat voice tinged with resignation, said simply, "Petes, I can't hear… anything." I felt helpless, with no words I could say, or that would be understood, that I felt would offer any comfort. I tried to give her a reassuring hug, mindful of the tubes, monitors, and, most significantly, the many staples protruding from her shaved scalp. As I sat next to her hospital bed and watched as she drifted back asleep, I realized I would never again whisper a secret in her ear, call her on the phone, or say, "Good night. I love you," after the lights were out. A frightening and sad new reality, for sure.

As I watched her drift back off to sleep, I had a flashback to the quote in her college yearbook. From David Crosby; it said, "If you smile at me I will understand, 'cause this is something everybody, everywhere does in the same language." How prophetic that she would find a way to use that magnificent smile of hers to transcend the chasm between her newfound deafness and her now lost hearing world.

As she recovered, I think that, for the first time in this more than two-year saga, it started to finally dawn on me: Life was never going to be the same, and the foundation under us was always going to be shifting and eroding, whether or not we choose to accept it. I was used to controlling things, and this situation was beyond my control. I focused on just keeping my head above water, but like a capsized sailor alone in the ocean, the energy and stress to do this were enormous. I could feel myself slipping away.

I also felt very alone. Loneliness was just one of the tidal waves of emotion that seemed to, like the tides, wash over me daily. Frustration, hope, hopelessness, anger, love, and disinterest intermingled to form a constant cyclone of confusion and disorientation. Andrea needed to focus on herself and eventually the kids, so in that sense, I'd lost a part of my partner—at least for the moment. I had plenty of people around me—at work, at home, in the hospital, and from my family and friends, but I was feeling invisible in the crowd. I was sick of reexplaining the NF2 saga again and again; I was sick of the well-meaning advice from people who had no way of knowing my reality; I was sick of being told to "hang in there" and "be strong" or that "God never gives us more that we can handle." What I really wanted was peace, control back over my life, to have things back they used to be, to not be bound by the terms brain surgery or NF2, schwannoma, bilateral acoustic neuroma, or a gamma knife. I wanted everything I couldn't have—but somehow, some way, I had to find a way to accept everything that was thrust on me, on us. Damn you, NF2!

Being well-versed in learning things the hard way, I chose not to accept those realities easily. Hence, some key lessons had to be delivered, comprehended, and driven home. Like almost everything else in my life, I was going to learn them by getting a master's degree from the school of hard knocks.

With a one-year-old and a three-year-old at home, a demanding business career, and an incapacitated wife, I did what I thought anyone in my position would do: I tried to play Superman. Exactly the wrong approach, but at the time, I simply didn't know any better. I was stubborn, and I was going to show myself and the world how tough I was. I had studied and learned a lot about NF2, but I was still a novice when it came to being an effective caregiver and taking care of myself.

I refused to adapt, change my lifestyle, or acknowledge a higher power, and I kept pushing the envelope. Even with great family support and friends, my life was unraveling, and I had no idea what was happening or how to stop it.

Now I wasn't sleeping or eating well. My stress levels were off the charts. Continuing every day to go to work, take care of the kids, and now tend to my newly deafened wife, who was moved from MGH to a rehab hospital for six weeks, was taking a toll on me, and in short order, hit me like a ton of bricks, almost literally.

Each day, in the late afternoon, after work and visiting Andrea in rehab, I headed home for the second-shift part of my day. Back at the house, I fed the kids, put them to bed, gave instructions to whoever was staying with them, and then swung by the office to work on some time-sensitive business proposals. Most nights, I was sleeping in a chair at the rehab hospital next to Andrea. Between Andrea, the kids, and work, I was routinely working sixteen- to eighteen-hour days, but since I was invincible, what difference did it make? I wasn't sleeping anyway, so why not work?

As had become my habit, after visiting Andrea in rehab in the late afternoon, I'd grab a six-pack to bring home and finish off the first beer before I left the hospital parking lot. Shortly thereafter, I'd polish off the second one. I knew at some level that self-medicating was a bad idea, but I easily rationalized it by telling myself that I was under a lot of pressure and deserved a little relaxation. After all, I wasn't hurting anyone. I was, however, like Icarus, getting too close to the sun and tempting fate.

One afternoon, as I weaved in and out of traffic, I was also proofreading the proposal on my lap I needed to finish that night. I looked up to see my car barreling straight toward the rear end of a car stopped in front of me. My only option to avoid ramming the car was to swerve left, but that was into a lane with oncoming traffic. A car was coming at me from the opposite way, but miraculously, its driver was adept enough to turn up onto the sidewalk to avoid hitting me head-on.

I thank God to this day that there were no pedestrians on that sidewalk when that car jumped the curb. There I sat, at a dead stop in the middle of the wrong lane, inches from a car on either side of me, and caught between the justifiable wraths of both drivers whom I'd almost killed.

I apologized profusely. Amazingly, no one was hurt, and no cars were damaged. I maneuvered my car to the side of the road, where I sat for several minutes, trying to regain my composure and calm myself down.

There I had my first, and perhaps my most important, epiphany. I realized that I could continue down the path of this self-destructive behavior and put everything I loved and valued at great risk, or I could accept that God had given us a new life—and play this crappy hand the best way possible.

Thanks be to God, I chose the latter. In doing so, a lesson that Andrea had passed on to me as she steered me back toward the church early in our relationship flashed into my head: I remembered the involvement, faith, and dedication Andrea and her mother had in Jesus and in her mom's patron saint, Mary. I recalled the serenity, confidence, and spiritual happiness it gave them. At that moment, it made me long for something more than just being casually faithful. I had to more fully accept and embrace the presence of a higher being; to me, that was Jesus Christ.

I was also taught another lesson: It's impossible to take care of anyone else until you take care of yourself first. As the flight attendant announces before every plane takes off, "In the unlikely event oxygen masks should be needed, be sure to place the mask over your own face first before attempting to help others."

Accepting the presence of a higher power came to me in very real terms that fateful day. While it would be years before I was fully able to unpack my relationship with God, this was my awakening moment and the first step on that road.

Unfortunately, I would have to relearn the lesson of taking care of myself first multiple times throughout our journey.

Before I restarted the car to drive home, I poured the remaining beers out on the sidewalk and put the empty six-pack in the trash. That was as close as I had come to the edge—actually hanging over it and staring down into the abyss—and I vowed never to allow myself to return.

There are points in your life where you can question or lose your identity. The bad news is that you're lost without a compass. The good news is that we all have choices: to continue on, to change, to give up, or to work to be better. We can choose to ignore or pay attention. We can choose action over indifference. What we do makes us who we are or will become. I was fortunate to have the opportunity to make a choice that changed my life for the better. Was it luck, divine involvement, my upbringing, or the good fortune to have Andrea by my side? I have no idea. I do know that for whatever reason, from that point forward, I moved ahead with a different perspective and mindset, one that continued to evolve in a positive, healthier direction and gave me the courage to cope with the ups and downs of our life with NF2. It didn't happen overnight, and there were certainly some potholes in the road, but at least I felt like I had roadmap, and one hell of a copilot to keep me moving in the right direction.

Andrea finally got back home from the rehab hospital, and she continued to punch back and pick up the pieces of her life. Although it took her a long time to regain her strength and stamina and do the things she was used to doing, she took on the task of rebuilding her body (and life) with vigor. Almost every day, she would work out in a small gym we built at home. She saw a personal trainer who drove her hard. She even joined a gym so she could have access to some of the equipment we didn't have at the house. She pushed herself to the limit, and eventually, she was in better physical condition than she'd ever been.

Emotionally, we bonded under the mantra that "happiness is a choice, and we choose to be happy." We chanted it when we were happy and even louder when we were down and out. I think the term used now is gas lighting—we said it so much that we not only believed it, it became a part of who we were. It served us very well over the years.

We also developed our basic playbook or strategy for moving ahead. I was the eternal optimist, always staying positive for Andrea and the kids. I internalized the quote by the American author Seth Godin, who said, "Optimism is the most important human trait because it allows us to evolve our ideas, to improve our situation, and to *hope for a better tomorrow*." Andrea was a dreamer, who, although often seeing the glass half empty, was willing to draft off my optimism and used her resiliency to push through the ups and downs. Finally, we honed our support system to fill in the gaps. We were extremely fortunate to have family and friends who never let us down.

Along with rehabbing herself physically, Andrea also had to adapt to her newly minted deafness. As she did, she began to demonstrate the determination and energy that would become her legacy. In short, she proved to be one tough woman.

Where and how she found the inner strength and courage not only to deal with but also to tackle this unimaginable situation head-on, I never fully understood. I guess it was a combination of her personal makeup, her determination, her joy for life, her faith, and her sense of humor that pulled her through. Within her own gentle, outgoing, and giving personality, she demonstrated a streak of tenacity that would propel her through this nightmare and many future horrors.

For me, watching her was like trying to figure out how an enormous cargo plane stays up in the air. I've seen it a hundred times, and it's been explained to me, but it still makes no sense in my brain. I saw Andrea's persona on display every day, marveled at it often, and came to appreciate it more fully, but I never really completely figured it out.

Andrea's ways were mysterious. I don't think even she entirely understood them, but they allowed her to deal with the unknown, create good from bad, and not only forge a new pathway but also bring a whole swath of people along with her down that path.

Andrea with her mother Marian and
father Al at her college graduation.

Andrea, ever the teacher, with her first
grade class in Rockport, Massachusetts.

Just married! 1979...

A beaming Andrea on our
honeymoon in Acapulco,
Mexico—oh, that smile!

For years, the Fitzwilliam Inn,
in Fitzwilliam, New Hampshire,
was our respite, where we could
re-orient, refocus, and re-energize.

Us as a young couple starting
out; little did we know what
unforeseen challenges lie ahead.

While there were the usual fun
and games, Andrea emphasized
reading, social skills and, of course,
sign language at a very young age.

Always a marvelous mother,
even NF couldn't change that.

Normalcy, before Andrea's world
was turned upside down.

CHAPTER 7

Figuring Out the "New Normal"

One of the annoying pieces of nouveau phraseology that emerged during the COVID-19 pandemic was the quickly overused term *new normal*. Like much in the COVID-19 era, it was politicized by many of the talking heads. But it really bothered me because Andrea and I had already coined the term more than thirty years earlier.

I distinctly remembered talking to Andrea after her third brain surgery about "getting back to normal." Either I was still in denial or I didn't see the freight train named NF that was hurtling toward us in a deliberate but unstoppable fashion.

Andrea did, and from her hospital bed, she replied, "There is no 'back to normal.' That's gone. We have to figure out what our new normal is." While she may have struggled to come to grips with her battle with NF2, she was very aware of the impact it was going to have on our lives.

As much as her wisdom and foresight blew me away, it also scared the shit out of me as I came to fully and painfully understand what the "new normal" became for us. I just wish I had trademarked the damn slogan in 1986!

Andrea was down, but she was far from out – she battled back with a vengeance.

She amazed us all by quickly becoming a highly proficient lip reader. I don't mean she could just read the football coaches' lips on TV when they said a bad word. She could read lips so well that, at times, people thought she was lying about being deaf! People would be utterly amazed when she would casually mention that the person speaking to her had an accent, and she was always right. Sometimes at a party, Andrea would be looking across the noisy room and would turn to me with a devilish smile and say, "Do you want to know what she really thinks about the hostess?"

In addition, over the thirty-five years that she was deaf, she never lost her ability to speak clearly and enunciate words perfectly. Speech pathologists will tell you this is almost unheard of. We monitor the clarity and tone of our voice by hearing ourselves speak and by constantly recalibrating our brains to process words and deliver them clearly. That's why you will often hear deaf and hard-of-hearing people talking in a monotone.

Some of this capability came from Andrea's background in special needs education and her understanding of how words are formed on the lips, and some of it came from her trademark hard work ethic. Andrea would stand in front of a mirror, watching how words were formed on her lips, and repeat certain phrases in an almost Zen-like fashion. She would regularly ask me if she was pronouncing a word correctly, always saying it back to me several times—followed by, "I want to make sure I say it right."

Andrea's voice was of particular concern to her, and like many parts of her life, it was complicated by NF2. One of the surgeries had left her with a frozen, unusable vocal cord. With only one functioning vocal cord, she was one tweak or virus away from not being able to speak at all. This was an example of another of the many hidden impacts of NF we had to deal with, and Andrea had to worry about.

As a result of the frozen vocal cord, once or twice a year, she had to go to the Massachusetts Eye and Ear Infirmary for a laryngoscopy. This procedure was relatively simple—uncomfortable, but not painful.

But a week of anticipation and nerve-racking anxiety leading up to the procedure culminated in the tension of sitting with the doctor waiting to hear if Andrea's "bad" vocal cord was further damaged or if her "good" vocal cord was compromised. Either case could create the need for surgery and lead to a loss of voice or the need for a tracheotomy. Many were the nights when Andrea didn't sleep, constantly replaying her fears in her mind, imagining herself mute, and giving herself headaches from the stress.

Between Andrea's second and third surgeries (the one that left her totally deaf), we started to see what was coming. Her hearing was not good, the hearing aids weren't helping, and she continued to hear less and less.

As frightening as the prospect of her becoming deaf was, we decided that it was in our best interests to try to get ahead of what was now starting to feel inevitable. We realized that if we wanted to communicate with each other, we'd need to learn sign language. When we said learn sign language, we don't mean being able to fingerspell the ABCs and a few common words or phrases. We meant learning to become proficient to the same level of communication that we had when Andrea could hear.

I was blown away at how many spouses and families didn't learn sign language after a family member became deaf. Our neurologist told us, that in his experience, less than 5% of the families faced with a family member losing their hearing learned to sign proficiently. We were going to do everything we could to buck that trend.

Beyond statistics, it just felt cruel to me to ever leave Andrea alone on an island in this new, strange, terrifying land-scape without her best friend supporting her. I was determined to make this new situation work. We were always partners, but this is the point where we created a partnership, determined to create the best possible outcome for us and our children. Sign language turned out to be the keystone for rebuilding our lives.

In the beginning, it was admittedly old school, especially pre-Internet. We started with sign language books. *Joy of Signing* was the first, and I still have my tattered, original version. These introduced us to the signs, the concepts, and some of the nuances of American Sign Language, or ASL.

After work, I'd go up to our bedroom with a couple of books, and I'd practice signing, often for two or three hours a night. Andrea would practice during the day, and we'd work together, honing our skills at mealtimes or sitting around, watching TV. We also took several increasingly more advanced sign language courses.

When we felt competent enough, Andrea decided it was time to teach our family. It was a difficult exercise. Once a week, Andrea and I would go up to the Pirani house to teach a small group of family and friends rudimentary sign language. While Andrea viewed this as a positive exercise, there were a lot of different smoldering emotions in the room. Some members of the family never showed up, leading to feelings that ranged from "they're too busy" to "they can't handle it." Others tried but were so bad they never conquered the manual alphabet. Her father, devastated by this monster NF2 that was chewing up his beautiful daughter, was stoic, and unwilling to look even a little silly (a prerequisite for learning sign language), left the house unable to continue with the group. The tension was palpable.

Clearly, at this point in time, there was a lot more going on than just learning sign language. While people were grieving for Andrea, we were playing games, joking around, and cheerfully showing them hand gestures. Some of the group got it, particularly Andrea's sister-in-law Rosemary, my sister Cheri, a couple of friends, and to some extent, her mother. They became part of an important subset of our support system—those who could communicate with Andrea on her terms.

Andrea picked up sign language quickly and began teaching our children. Natalie easily grasped the vocabulary and moved quickly onto sentences. Peter's first signs all revolved around getting food into that Baby Huey body: "cracker," "juice," "milk," and "more." Even within the context of teaching the kids to sign, there was always a heavy cloud of forbearance hanging over our heads. While showing Peter some new signs, Andrea had tears running down her face when unexpectedly her baby boy started babbling just before her third surgery, and she was able to hear him speak words for the first and last time. The image of the two of them hugging and sitting cross-legged on the kitchen floor, Andrea's face soaked in tears and Peter with a huge grin on his face, is forever seared into my mind.

We eventually utilized the emerging technology to check out signs and phrases with new apps on our smart phones. We watched deaf movies without subtitles, we visited deaf schools, and we attended deaf socials. We continued to take courses. Recognizing its importance, learning sign language became our top priority—we did everything we could to immerse ourselves in all faucets of this fascinating language.

Learning ASL was certainly to our mutual benefit and the betterment of our relationship, but being able to sign fluently also allowed me to be a much stronger advocate for Andrea—to ensure that she understood what was taking place at all times and that she had all the information that I had. In the medical world, where we spent a great deal of time, this was paramount.

As our skills and her comprehension of ASL improved, it allowed her to more fully process what she "heard," ask questions, and have discussions with me and the doctors about the next steps and options. The time and energy we put into learning sign language and understanding deafness made me a better advocate for her and made both of us better advocates for the deaf and the NF communities.

At some point early on in her deafness, she found out about and began to research hearing service dogs. These dogs had been around for years for the blind, but we'd never heard of a hearing dog for the deaf. Today, these dogs would be categorized as rescue dogs with specialized skills.

We identified a place in New England that acquired, raised, and trained hearing dogs: Red Acre Farm (RAF). Andrea decided that she wanted—no, needed—a hearing dog. It seemed like a perfect fit. RAF's purpose was to make deaf people more independent, and Andrea seemed to check all the boxes— except one big one. Red Acre Farm had an internal policy that prohibited supplying hearing dogs to individuals with families. Their rational was that if children were present in the owner/ dog relationship, it was more likely the dog would devolve into a pet, and the value of the service to the deaf person could vastly diminish. Because of the scarcity of these dogs and the cost to train them, RAF was very careful about placing them in the best spots, with what they believed had the greatest impact and highest potential for success.

Andrea quickly went from being a model candidate for getting a dog to being rejected when her family situation came to light. Andrea realized the value a hearing dog could have on her life, and she recognized that if she was going to get one, she would have to fight for it. The battle royal was on.

An official at Red Acre Farm, who had once been our pleasant advocate, dug in her heels and was unwilling or unable to consider bending the rules. There was a waiting list of people looking to get a dog, and if someone didn't qualify, she just moved to the next person on the list. Nothing personal, just business.

Unfortunately for her, it was personal for Andrea, and the rejection only caused *her* to dig in *her* heels deeper. Andrea was unwilling to take no for an answer. Once more, we prayed for guidance and resolution, and one more time, we rested our hopes on the combination of prayer and dogged determination that was becoming Andrea's modus operandi.

For every argument the RAF program administrator made, Andrea made three counterpoints. Andrea communicated with the administrator through a typing device, connected to a phone line, called a teletypewriter (TTY). I could tell when it was RAF on the line by watching Andrea's furious fingers flashing across the keyboard. Figurative sparks flew from the TTY. Like a tennis match with endless volleys between two titans, this back and forth went on for weeks before an ominous-looking official letter from RAF arrived in the mail. Much to our surprise and delight, it bore good news. RAF had decided to make an exception to its own bylaws, and they had a hearing dog, Amber, waiting for Andrea!

Unrelenting perseverance and determination had carried the day. For Andrea, it became the blueprint for future battles and victories.

Andrea was grateful and gracious. She promised farm officials that they wouldn't be sorry about their decision and that Amber would never become a pet—and she kept that vow for a long as she had the dog. While Amber certainly became part of our family for the next fourteen years, she never did become a family pet. For evermore, we thanked Red Acre Farm for listening to us, working with us, and allowing Amber to make such a positive influence on our lives.

Amber was a game changer. She was a good-natured dog who was fiercely loyal to Andrea. Picked up as a stray on the side of the road in North Carolina, this mixed-breed Australian cattle dog had the disposition of an angel, the tenacity of a warrior, and the intelligence of a Mensan.

She connected Andrea to her own home, her kids, and the outside world. Amber could answer the doorbell, usher Andrea out of the house if the smoke detector went off, or lead her to the cries of her baby boy. As I traveled more extensively for my job, Amber assured us that Andrea could even stay alone if I arrived home late or eventually stay overnight.

Despite the love the kids had for Amber, the times they secretly fed her food under the table and the way my son would occasionally pull her around by her tail, Amber never wavered from her loyalty to Andrea (and amazingly, the dog never even growled at the kids!). She was by her side as her constant companion, at her feet when she sat down, and next to the bed at night. They were inseparable, and as a result, both of them thrived.

What's more, Andrea and Amber became highly visible advocates for deaf service animals. Andrea often went into stores and restaurants wearing her RAF T-shirt and handing out literature about the farm. When managers told her that dogs weren't allowed or welcome, Andrea would quietly explain, sometimes to an increasingly hostile, frustrated gatekeeper in front of a crowd of gawkers, that Amber wasn't a dog; she was a *service dog*.

She would not only produce the paperwork that by law allowed Amber to accompany her, but she would also include a little lecture on the role and value of a hearing dog. She always ended her spiel with the line, "As you will soon come to appreciate, my dog is much better behaved than my kids."

It didn't take too long to prove that point. One evening when I was working late, she took the kids and Amber to a local Chinese restaurant. It was late for the kids to be out, and they were not on their best behavior. Occasionally, they would take advantage of Andrea's deafness to raise some inappropriate level of hell when I wasn't there. I guess several guests complained, and the manager eventually asked them to leave, letting Andrea know as they exited, "And I don't want to see these kids in here ever again, but the dog is welcome."

Another time, a local bagel store owner gave Andrea a more vocal lambasting about "pets" in the store. Andrea—after her normal, rational explanation got her nowhere—gave it right back to her and stormed out of the store. She wrote a letter to the local newspaper, which prompted an apology from the bagel shop owner. Andrea accepted the apology but was otherwise unmoved; we never again patronized this establishment!

Amber was a great example of Andrea not wallowing, or worse, getting further weighted down by her dilemma. Instead of accepting or lamenting her situation, Andrea constantly sought out solutions and opportunities to make things better for her and her family.

Woman and dog developed a remarkable relationship. Andrea and RAF had given Amber a second lease on life. Amber, in turn, gave Andrea a purpose as an advocate for service animals; even more importantly, the dog allowed her to reclaim a piece of her independence as well as her zest for life. The newfound gleam in her eye was, as the credit card commercial extolls, priceless!

CHAPTER 8

Andrea's Brave New World

Once she recovered from operations two and three, Amber helped Andrea get back to being what she believed was most important to her: being a full-time mother. Andrea immediately looked for ways to do that as independently as possible. She reconnected with the "band of mothers" who she had helped to organize.

This mothers' group was not just a bunch of youngish, suburban mothers sitting around drinking lattes and eating croissants while their kids ran wild around the playground. Not even close. It was a group of about a dozen of highly educated women who had left or paused their professional careers to become full-time moms. They were committed to this pursuit. They wanted to not only raise their children to have fun but also help them learn how to establish relationships, socialize, and grow up to be solid citizens.

These women included teachers, artists, graphic designers, medical workers, and businesswomen. They discussed not only child-rearing strategies and philosophies but also their own interests, as well as local, national, and international news. If something was happening in town, at the White House, or around the world, they were discussing it, and everyone had an opinion.

I'd get home from work, and Andrea would pepper me with questions about social issues, the economy, and politics. I had to pay closer attention to current events just so I could keep up with her and her group.

Andrea's mom also played a key role in helping her on the road back to independence. Mother Marian was willing to do anything for her "miracle girl," and she was a critical part of rebuilding Andrea's confidence. As Andrea reclaimed many aspects of life that we take for granted, Marian always gave her space to grow while acting as a backstop if something didn't quite work the first few times. Marian was also there to make sure the kids were cared for and safe. She was the most consistent presence in Andrea's life, encouraging her to move forward but at the same time watching over her like a hawk.

As a result of the tumors, Andrea not only lost her hearing but was also left with fine and gross motor deficiencies and some processing issues. Andrea's initial inability to do these things independently—such as putting away the contents from the dishwasher, cooking a meal, taking a shower, or writing out a shopping list—was frustrating, but her mom knew how much leeway to give her when there was potential danger and when she was trying to do too much.

In fact, there was danger lurking around almost every corner of Andrea's new world—at least until her mind and body adapted to the shock it had been through. It was easy to drop a glass, let the sauce boil over in the pan, or slip in the shower. It was maddening to get to the supermarket and not be able to read your own writing or remember what you needed.

Andrea also tired easily and needed to nap one or two times a day. She knew she could rest for as long as she needed because Marian was on top of every aspect of the house. What a benefit for Andrea, and what a relief for me.

Around the house, Andrea had to adapt to many things in the context of being deaf. First, she had to learn to work with Amber so she could be more independent. Next, she had to figure out how to interact with the kids. Sign language was the key to communication. Our daughter, Natalie, ever the student, took to sign language like a duck to water. Our son, Peter, on the other hand, quickly learned that his mother was an expert lip reader and became a laissez-faire signer, doing enough to get by. We made it work.

There were many hidden aspects of late-onset deafness that Andrea had to cope with that weren't immediately apparent. For example, Andrea could inadvertently push a bowl of pasta off the countertop and not realize she did it—a messy and potentially dangerous situation with a couple of toddlers running around. She could leave the water in the bathtub running and flood the bathroom without knowing it until, on one occasion, the water came dripping through the kitchen ceiling.

There were times when you could hear her coming up the street in the car a half mile away because she had inadvertently cranked the radio to full volume. She was a terror in Walmart, using their electric carts to weave up and down the aisles, knocking things off the shelves, and in one instance clipping an entire display and reducing it to a pile of cans while continuing on, oblivious to the sounds of the merchandise carnage left in her path. Her electric toothbrush was always dead from forgetting to turn it off; many meals in the oven became charred blocks from not hearing the timer ring; visitors came and left without getting in, even though sometimes they'd climb up on railing and rap furiously on the windows to try to get an unsuspecting Andrea to spot them.

She overcame many obstacles presented by her new deafness by increasing her sense of awareness and sharpening her visual skills. Eventually, her visual skills became much more pronounced, allowing her to use her enhanced sense of sight to compensate for her loss of hearing. As she became more experienced, it seemed as though she could anticipate a situation or potential disaster and adjust to it before it created an issue.

Since Andrea now had no clue as to the loudness of music or noise in a room, she had to learn to modulate her voice. Sometimes she would speak too softly to be understood (not a big deal, but tiring for her to have to constantly repeat herself). On other occasions, she would speak very loudly in quieter environments (she could tell she did it when people turned their heads to look at her after she spoke).

Of course, in keeping with Murphy's law, it seemed that she would often speak loudly just as the room or the conversation went quiet—leading to some hilarious situations. One time at one of the kid's second-grade plays when there was a lull in the action, she said to me, very loudly, "These kids are AWFUL." As most of the auditorium turned to look at us, she leaned over, and said to me in a much quieter voice, "I said that too loud, didn't I?" She learned the hard way a couple of times that when you don't know how loud you're talking, nothing is private.

Between her near-perfect speech and her lip-reading ability, some people met her and refused to believe she was deaf. She would laugh at me and say, "How bad is that—I'm profoundly deaf, and sometimes I can't even get any credit for it!"

One of the most important traits Andrea exhibited, even in her darkest hours, was that kind of humor. She could laugh at almost anything and anyone. She, of course, loved picking on me, but most important for her well-being was her ability to laugh at herself. She went out of her way to knock herself down a peg to lighten the moment or put you at ease.

As well as she adjusted, as much as we believed in divine providence, as hard as Andrea worked and utilized her sense of humor, there were often issues. Once our children realized that she really was profoundly deaf, they could and would take advantage of the situation. If Andrea told them to turn off the TV or the computer, they would yes her to death, knowing that they could buy themselves another fifteen minutes before she realized they were still at it, and had to come in again. It was the same thing when they were listening to the radio in bed, had other kids over, or were fighting with each other. This constant back-and-forth game was frustrating and time-consuming—driving Andrea crazy.

There were setbacks and mini tragedies immersed in her progress. One day, young Peter went down to the basement to play without telling his mom. Andrea locked him down there—for how long we don't know—but by the time she figured it out, he was sitting on the top step, banging on the door, screaming, and crying.

When Peter was two years old, we took the kids to Disney World. Peter wandered onto the tram alone, and later, when we found him, the woman who brought him to the "lost and found" told me he was looking at Andrea and calling out, "Mama, mama, mama." Tragedy avoided, but a scary deaf-related drama that shook all of us.

Despite the inherent risks, I encouraged Andrea to spread her wings and take more chances on her way back from her initial dark days. I had seen firsthand how Andrea's spirit, drive, and capability often allowed her to flip difficult situations to create opportunities. I worked with her on the practical aspects of life, such as shopping, going out to restaurants, reconnecting with our friends, and driving. I knew these were things that were going to facilitate her self-esteem and socialization as well as her independence.

And for the most part, things went according to plan—well, with the possible exception of the driving. Andrea was never a very good driver, and deafness and brain surgery didn't help. She initially became extremely cautious behind the wheel, spending minutes rather than seconds at a stop sign and getting into traffic going twenty-five miles per hour in a forty-five-mile-per-hour zone, with a trail of a dozen cars behind her with horns blaring. Not hearing a thing, Andrea blissfully proceeded along her merry way like Mr. Magoo (now I'm really dating myself!). Especially in the car, it took a while for her to retrain and fine-tune her visual capabilities to compensate for her hearing loss and the resulting apprehension.

Before she got back on the road, we'd practice in the town cemetery. Can't hurt anyone there, right? Well, while she didn't hit any headstones, she might have done a little landscaping and widened a couple of the narrow roads. In typical Andrea fashion, she would demand I talk to the cemetery caretaker and tell him that if the roads were too narrow for her to drive through, they'd never be able to get a hearse in there!

Many times, she tried to widen the entrance to our garage. She drove a silver Mustang, and the garage was painted brown. More than we would have liked, I'd come home from work and see that the trim on the garage was freshly damaged. The height of that damage exactly matched the level of a new brown streak on the Mustang. Without exception, even when she was the only one with access to the car, Andrea would deny it. Of course, she deserved some slack because she didn't hear it, but to her, if she didn't see it, it simply never happened—evidence be damned.

The closest she came to admitting an indiscretion with the car was the day she took out the free-standing basketball hoop in the driveway. She rolled over the base, and the stanchion collapsed, barely missing the car as it fell. Since it was too heavy for her to move, she had to come clean when I got home—almost. "It's possible I might have hit the basketball hoop," she said, followed by, "I'm not saying I did. I'm just saying it's possible!" Not a problem. I went out and bought a new backboard and rim—and mounted it to the front of the garage, where even Andrea, in her most adventuresome moments, wouldn't be able to get to it.

As usual, there were moments that, if this were a movie, would appear to be scripted, but Andrea had a way of creating situations that seemed right out of a TV sitcom.

One day I was working in the garage. Andrea had gone food shopping. I heard a police siren in the distance, but since we were off a major thruway, I didn't give it a second thought. However, as I looked up to see Andrea pulling up the driveway, I realized that the siren was much louder and, in fact, belonged to the police cruiser that pulled in behind her.

As I got down off the ladder I was standing on, I saw the police officer (PO) approach Andrea and initiate the following discussion:

PO. Why didn't you pull over when I put the siren on and used the loudspeaker in my cruiser?

ANDREA. I didn't see you behind me.

PO. What do you mean, "See me behind you," didn't you hear me?

ANDREA. Of course not, I'm deaf.

PO. How are you conversing with me right now?

Andrea. I'm reading your lips.

PO, *turning now to me.* Is she really deaf?

ME. Profoundly. Can't hear a thing.

PO. No SH——T!

ANDREA. Is there a problem? I have to get the groceries in the refrigerator.

PO. You were doing twenty-five miles per hour in a forty-five-mile-per-hour zone.

ANDREA. So I wasn't speeding?

PO, *resigned that this is going nowhere.* Try to be more aware of your surroundings when you're driving.

ANDREA. I will. I promise I'll never go faster than the speed limit.

Andrea did finally master driving again and drove for another three decades. During that period, I had exactly two minor fender benders. Andrea—you guessed it—never got a ticket or had an insurance-related accident. Whenever our insurance was renewed and we checked our safe-driver rating, Andrea's was always better than mine.

Don't think she didn't take great delight in reminding me about that anytime I even mentioned her driving capabilities. It was all good. I was happy when she one-upped me. She was losing too many of the wrong kinds of battles, so wherever she could grab a win was good for her mind and spirit.

Through all the trials, tribulations, and triumphs, we continued to try to reconcile a God Who gave us strength with a God Who gave us NF2.

I truly believe God brought Andrea through that third surgery and back to a meaningful life. I'm equally certain that God gave Andrea NF2 and all the challenges and heartache that came along with the disease. How can I reconcile these two realities—the God Who gives and the God Who takes? For me, the only thing that made sense is that God has a much bigger plan for each one of us. One that is far beyond our comprehension. I don't know how else to balance what Andrea achieved and endured to achieve it.

If God is all knowing and all-powerful, and we give Him credit for answering our prayers, shouldn't He also get "credit" for the bad things that happen in the world? To me, the answer is yes, and the reason is His plan. Faith is the belief in His plan when we haven't seen it, don't understand it, and watch bad things happen to good people. This philosophy not only gave me great hope for the future after this life, but also gave me a sense of comfort about what happened to Andrea and me while she was here on Earth.

Looking back, it was really incredible that a woman could weather three brain surgeries, months in rehab hospitals, completely lose her hearing, acquire and train a service dog, and come back into large segments of her former life so seamlessly in a relatively short time. It was a real tribute to Andrea's bulldog spirit and her loving relationships.

We took a lot of what happened for granted, when in reality, it, and she, were nothing short of astonishing.

CHAPTER 9

And We Thought Deaf Was Deaf

Andrea and I thought we were beginning to get a handle on this deafness thing. But we quickly found out that it had complex dichotomies that we never suspected.

People who were born deaf, as opposed to those who became deaf later in life, had their own way of looking at the world. Andrea and I began to learn the fascinating saga of Deaf culture—the challenges faced by born-Deaf individuals and their families, their perspectives on the hearing world, and their desire to protect their culture and live their lives on their terms. It is an us-against-the-world mentality, with the born-Deaf individuals seemingly always fighting for their culture and their jobs, fighting to be heard, and, at times, fighting for their dignity.

In the born-Deaf world, I detected a ranking system for different groups. This system, from bottom to top, looked something like this to me:

4. Hearing people
3. Hard-of-hearing people
2. deaf
1. Deaf

The difference between levels two and one isn't a typo. As we learned, sometimes cruelly and painfully, the difference between a lowercase *d* and an uppercase *D* makes all the difference in the Deaf world.

It took a while for us to catch on. The uppercase *D* is a description of a way of life and culture, not a condition. A cultural identity. Unlike Andrea, for the born-Deaf (or "Deafies," the term coined by the writer Ken Glickman in his book, *Deafinitions for Signlets*, published in 1986; Glickman also referred to hearing people as "Hearies") deafness was not a disability, but a badge of honor—something to be cherished and protected. They most certainly didn't want any sympathy. In my experience, they just wanted to live their lives and not be badgered by the "noise" from the hearing world.

Their Deafness became a tremendous sense of pride and cultural reaffirmation. Perhaps you remember the Deaf Pride rallies at Gallaudet University in the 1980s when students at the only college for the deaf in the United States rallied against the hiring of a hearing president. They believed, and in my opinion rightfully so, that a hearing person could not possibly understand their situation, the discrimination and challenges they encountered, and the culture they sought to preserve—this hearing-centric perspective is known as audism. All of us who had any appreciation for Deaf culture cheered when the university backed down and named a Deaf president.

The two movies that captured, at least in my mind, deafness and Deaf culture are *Children of a Lesser God* (1986) and *CODA* (2021). CODA stands for *Child of Deaf Adult.*

In *Children of a Lesser God,* the film's star, Marlee Matlin, who won an Oscar for best actress, plays a born-Deaf woman named Sarah. Sarah was in constant conflict between the hearing world and the born-Deaf world. When asked why she slept with so many of her hearing sister's friends when she was a teenager, she replied, "Because sex is something I could do as well as the hearing girls. Better!" It made her feel "normal." At that point in the movie, she was trying to fit in with the hearing world on *their* terms. But as she grew older and became more attuned to Deaf culture, she encountered the hearing world on *her* terms—as a born-Deaf woman.

CODA highlights the challenges of raising a hearing child in a Deaf family. It captures some of the issues our own children had to deal with—albeit with only one deaf parent and without the added complexity of living in a born-Deaf culture that doesn't fully understand the hearing world any more than the hearing world understands them.

In *CODA*, the parents' instincts to battle to protect their language, traditions, and way of life, while having to exist as a tiny minority in an insensitive hearing world, creates inevitable and painful conflicts. Their daughter Ruby is forced to become an interpreter and as a result, although the youngest, becomes the de facto adult when connecting with the hearing world. This dynamic drives a wedge between her and her parents, and her older brother. The movie portrays the comical (when Ruby interprets for her parents at a doctor's appointment and has to explain her parents jock itch), and heartbreaking (the one-time Rudy didn't show up for work on the boat, the coast guard pulled the boat over and because her father and brother couldn't hear the commands, and they were hit with a hefty fine that almost cost them their fishing license), aspects of the disconnects between the Deaf and hearing worlds.

As I had learned, when Deaf parents had hearing children, they were often disappointed. To them, it was dwindling their numbers, fragmenting their family, and diluting their culture. Ruby's mother loved her as much as any mother, but admitted that she was disappointed when the doctors tested Ruby's hearing and exclaimed, "she can hear." This mindset and cultural orientation were well depicted in *Children of a Lesser God* when Sarah, asked by her hearing boyfriend what she wants, replied, "Children. *Deaf* children." His reply demonstrates the telling cultural gap between hearing and born-Deaf people: "You want me to say I want deaf children? I don't, but I would accept them." While he exhibited somewhat of a progressive stance on the issue, he still viewed deafness as a disability, while Sarah saw it as something to honor.

In 1984, the Food and Drug Administration formally approved the use of a medical procedure called a cochlear implant. Doctors could restore a portion of a deaf person's hearing with an electronic device that bypasses damaged portions of the ear to deliver sound signals to the auditory nerve (because Andrea's auditory nerve was compromised, this was never an option for her.) Many in the Deaf community, especially the elders, refused to consider the operation. Hearing doctors were perplexed that their Deaf patients didn't want to be "fixed" and become more integrated into the hearing world. The doctors didn't understand that many Deaf people never saw themselves as "broken" and therefore didn't need to be "fixed." Getting some kind of entry pass into the hearing world was perceived as a step backward to them.

Among younger Deaf people, cochlear implants created a Civil War–like divisiveness not seen in the Deaf world since the 1880's when Alexander Grahm Bell successfully lobbied for Deaf schools in the United States to move from ASL as the preferred method of communication for teaching Deaf students, to the oral method, delivering a blow to Deaf education and Deaf culture that would take a century to reverse. In the battle over cochlear implants, those who did and didn't choose to get the surgery struggled over friendships, hearing-world influences, and Deaf culture. From my observations, being Deaf was a complicated lot in life.

Even their language was proprietary and something that needed to be protected. Hearing people assume that Deaf people communicate in sign language in a way that mimics how English is spoken. Hearing people say, for example, "Welcome, come on into my house and meet my children." Hearing people presume that sign language would literally translate the vocabulary into a series of hand gestures that would reflect individual words: "Welcome-come-into-my-house-and-meet-my-children." But that's an adaptive-sign language called Signed English. It was created by hearing people in the United States from a sense of misplaced arrogance that spoken English is the be-all-and-end-all for languages.

If I signed in that fashion to a Deaf person, most might stare back at me and probably not even offer me a response. They would likely see that type of signing as a reflection of the superior attitude that hearing people often display toward the Deaf community. They might even consider it offensive.

Their language is American Sign Language (ASL). Other than a shared vocabulary, ASL has very little to do with Signed English. It is a beautiful, spatial, multidimensional language in which the sentence structure is completely different, and the meaning of what you are "saying" is conveyed via fluid moments, defined by hand positioning, facial expressions, the severity or gentleness of the movements, body language, and last and least, the vocabulary itself. Hearing people may be insulting Deaf folks when they tout Signed English as an effective representation of ASL.

By the way, in ASL, "Welcome, come on into my house and meet my children" could be signed in many different ways, one of which might be, "House-welcome-children-meet." The meaning, however, has much more to do with the sizing of the signs, the facial expressions (for example, very happy; matter-of-fact; wish you weren't here), and body language. Not that those aren't also used by hearing people, but they take a back seat to the words themselves and the tone used in communicating spoken messages.

As a recent *New York Times* article ("The Evolution of American Sign Language"; July 27, 2022) pointed out that ASL is a relatively young language, and like all languages, it is itself continually evolving to reflect changes in concepts and phrases in society. "Meme," as a concept or word, didn't exist just a few years ago, for anyone, whether hearing or Deaf. But it now exists in both English and ASL. The sign for the word *phone* has evolved as the phone has itself—from a clunky object on a wall to a more streamlined version that sits on a table to a mobile phone that fits in your pocket.

This progressive nature of language, along with the emerging technology, can create conflict in the Deaf community. Once you had to be face-to-face to sign; now you can use smartphones, tablets, and even smart TVs to communicate via ASL. But as the *Times* article points out, "the pace of innovation, while exciting, can drive a wedge between generations of Deaf Culture." Older generations of Deaf people often see this electronic transmission of signing as too impersonal and too small to read, and they may see evolving signs as an affront to past generations.

It's not fair to generalize, so I can only speak from my own experience, but there also seems to be a hard edge to Deaf culture. Deaf people can be leery of hearing people, and that can come across with a standoffish attitude, especially when they are in their own environment. The Deaf can also be dismissive to hearing people and downright mean to late-deafened people like Andrea. Some of our interactions were hilarious (even when I was the butt of their jokes and laughter), and some were just plain cruel.

For example, when Andrea was losing her hearing, we went several times a week to an accelerated class to learn ASL at a school for the deaf. As you might imagine, it was a traumatic time for us, and we were certainly on edge and completely out of our element. Only the teachers spoke, and when on campus, they spoke sparsely, always signing and using ASL as the primary means of communication.

I noticed one day that when I made the sign for "make," our instructor would smile, and the Deaf kids on the other side of the room would laugh out loud. I mentioned it to Andrea, and she said I was probably being overly sensitive and using the wrong sign. Well, this went on for the next three sessions, and finally, I asked our instructor what was so funny. This time, with a wide grin, she informed me that I hadn't been signing the word "make" at all but rather the sign for "masturbate"!

I felt a little silly, and we all had a good laugh and moved on. But I was annoyed with our instructor for not correcting me the first time I made the wrong sign and sparing me some ridicule from the Deaf students. That said, I learned a valuable lesson: Slight variations in hand formation or motion can have a dramatic difference in the meaning of the sign. I was keenly aware of this in the future!

Years later, when I gained a better appreciation for Deaf culture, I also understood that situation in a much clearer context. The Deaf kids in the back were having a little fun dumping on the hearing guy. The instructor let it go because she had to maintain her connection with the Deaf crowd. By aligning with them, at my expense, it helped her keep her standing in their culture even though she was a hearing person.

I warned you it was complicated!

Occasionally, however, the interactions became more ominous in nature. At some point, we began to attend all-Deaf socials. It was a great way for Andrea to try to connect with the local Deaf community, maybe make some friends within this group, and for both of us to improve our sign language.

Sometimes it worked out okay. Other times, some of the Deaf crowd would turn their backs to us or sign in a dialect they knew we didn't understand. It was their way of shunning us and reminding us that, when we were on their turf, they were in charge. Other times, it was even more hurtful. Andrea and a hearing friend (who went on to become a sign language interpreter) decided to get their master's degrees in deaf studies at a well-known university in Boston. Many nights, Andrea came home distraught after class. The two born-Deaf women who ran the program made it so difficult and embarrassing for Andrea that she ended up dropping out of the program. Our friend fought her way through and did get her degree, but in this case, I think they were harder on Andrea than her hearing friend because she was late-deafened. She was deaf, but not Deaf.

We persevered, determined to figure this "D" versus "d" thing out and understand where Andrea fit on the spectrum. We continued going to the Deaf socials, and we became more educated regarding Deaf culture. We visited the Horace Mann School for the Deaf and Hard of Hearing in Boston, the American School for the Deaf in Hartford in Connecticut (the oldest school for the deaf in the country), and the holy grail of schools for the deaf, Gallaudet University. While we were there, we stayed on campus, ate and studied with the students, and immersed ourselves in their world. It was fascinating, frightening, and enlightening.

At one point, I volunteered as a teacher's aide in a deaf school in Boston, but I was the one who got the education on adolescent Deaf culture, real street-level sign language, and the educational realities and challenges of getting these kids (some of whom were not only deaf but also didn't speak English!) ready for the "real" world. I gained a whole new level of respect for both the educators and the students.

The teachers, both hearing and deaf, were off-the-charts outstanding, and while I observed a lot of frustration and pain, I also saw joy and improbable success stories. I watched things that opened my eyes and made me smile. Deaf classrooms are loud, very loud, with kids talking, making noises, and clowning around. Almost all of the noise was good-natured or a way to get the teachers' or other students' attention. It was not at all unusual for a student to throw a shoe or other object across the room at someone to catch their eye—just another form of communication!

This experience led me to consider a career change and become an ASL interpreter. I began to study in earnest and was accepted into a college program. While my signing skills and knowledge of Deaf culture were advanced, I struggled with my receptive capabilities (reading signs). As I got deeper into the program, the speed, the slang, and the nuances of the language proved to be too much for me, and I dropped the idea. Being in the program demonstrated to me how difficult professional interpreting really was. On the upside, it allowed Andrea and me to further improve our skills and communicate with one each other more effectively.

It was always amazing to me how many difficult choices hard-of-hearing and deaf people had to make. Gut-wrenching choices, such as whether to go to a school for the deaf or the hearing, whether to use the oral method of communication or learn ASL, or whether to explore a cochlear implant. Small choices, such as whether to go to a party where you're the only deaf person—with the likelihood of having as much fun as a piece of furniture while everyone around you "parties like it's 1999." When you don't understand what a hearing person is saying, do you ask them to repeat what they said (sometimes more than once), or do you just fake it and nod in passive agreement?

I learned that many of these important life choices were deeply personal and that there usually wasn't a clear right-or-wrong, good-or-bad aspect to these situations. Decisions were made depending on people's backgrounds and influences, how they felt at a particular time, the guidance they were getting, or what best suited their personalities and current goals.

One apparent milestone in our deaf journey was when our daughter, Natalie, took a job as a teacher at a prestigious school for the deaf. We were so proud of her, as an educator, a hearing person who was sensitive to Deaf culture, an expert signer, and her mother's daughter.

But while she met some nice people and even made some friends, it was pretty obvious to me from the beginning that she was not accepted at the school—not by the students but by some of the teachers and administrators. In what appeared to me to be a case of reverse discrimination, they marginalized her, excluded her, and set her up for failure. Finally, it became so bad she had to leave to maintain her own mental health. Another piece of collateral damage added to the growing pile!

I don't want to imply that all Deaf people were unfriendly or mean to us. As with any group in our society, we interacted with all types of different people. Some of the Deaf we encountered made us feel at home; some shunned us. Some welcomed us; some ignored us. Some helped us with our signing; some mocked us.

I do think that some of the institutional discrimination that has existed for many years is part of what may have created a hard edge and some bitterness in the hearing world. My earliest, and maybe only, interaction with deaf people—until Andrea—was at airports and train stations where they sold pencils because they couldn't get work. There are different statistics, but one I see most often shows that about 43% of the Deaf community are not in the labor pool, as opposed to 21% of the hearing population (National Deaf Center; Deaf People and Employment in the United States: 2019.) The study showed that while deaf unemployment is only slightly higher than it is with hearing people, that figure belies that many deaf people are working at lower paying jobs.

Because they often didn't understand the spoken word or speak clearly, they were labeled as stupid. Since they couldn't listen to the radio or watch TV, the primary outlets for information before the advent of the internet, they were less informed and deemed ignorant. Prior to the advent of technology (TTYs, closed-captioning, cellphones for texting, cochlear implants, etc.), communication was limited, often to their family and a small group of Deaf friends, making socialization difficult and setting the stage for "higher levels of depression and perceived risk than hearing control groups" (Turner, O., Windfuhr, K. &

Kapur, N. Suicide in deaf populations: a literature review. *Ann Gen Psychiatry* **6**, 26 (2007). https://doi.org/10.1186/1744-859X-6-26.) A born-Deaf person in the hearing world is constantly swimming upstream, fighting an uphill battle.

What made it more arduous for Andrea was that she was in the breach. She was never going to be one of them, but she was like them in a lot of ways. She faced many of the same challenges, discrimination, and frustrations and dealt with similar types of intolerance and ignorance. That made it difficult for Andrea to reconcile what she was experiencing in the hearing world with how she was sometimes being treated in the Deaf world.

From my observations, the Deaf world seemed somewhat analogous to what I had experienced in Amish country while doing work in Lititz, Pennsylvania. The Amish worked hard to protect their culture and values in a world that had moved away from their way of life. Like the Deaf, a faction of the Amish was more militant. They wanted to become more insular, conservative, and staunch about maintaining a way of life. The outside world was a threat to them. The more moderate, usually younger faction, also wanted to protect some of the old ways, but at the same time wanted to become more integrated into the modern world.

These divergent outlooks led to internal conflicts, as well as bad blood at times with the outside world. The movie *Witness* is a great representation of the struggles and turmoil that arise when the two worlds inevitably conflict.

The Deaf culture encounters many obstacles and challenges in their everyday lives. While I obviously can't fully relate to many of these tribulations, I can stand back and appreciate the culture that's been created, the pride of the people in that culture, and their desire to protect their way of life.

All of these experiences with the Deaf Community represented real growing pains for Andrea. She was, by her nature, a caring, happy, and inclusive woman. Now that she'd lost her hearing, she was thrown into this maze of deafness, conflict, sign language, and Deaf culture that she would never easily navigate, forever straddling the hearing and deaf/Deaf worlds. All she knew was that she couldn't hear, and as a result, she was no longer part of the hearing world, but because she once heard, she would never be accepted into the Deaf world.

There were cultural obstacles that existed regardless of which side of the fence she found herself on, but she'd figure it out because, in the end, it would be her deftness, not her deafness, that defined her!

CHAPTER 10

Deaf Ain't Dead (or Charting a Post Apocalypse Road)

Deaf might not have been deaf, but Andrea was Andrea, and damn it, she was determined to find a way to make this thing work.

The president of my firm had a brother who was married to a deaf woman. After Andrea became deaf, Bob introduced us to his sister-in-law, a human whirlwind named Marylyn Howe. Like Andrea, Marylyn lost her hearing as an adult (she was nineteen years old), and also like Andrea, that only seemed to ignite an additional level of inner energy.

Marylyn was a force to be reckoned with. She was intelligent and strong-willed, a product of a military family. Her father was one of the pilots who flew the atomic missions in Hiroshima and Nagasaki. Marylyn made a mark for herself in many ways. She graduated from Boston University, got her master's degree in disability studies at Suffolk University, became director of public policy at the Massachusetts Development Disabilities Council, and became a member of the National Council on Disability for five years.

When she and Andrea met, they talked about how difficult it was to be late-deafened adults—essentially how they no longer fit into either the hearing world or the Deaf world. Marylyn had some residual hearing, and like Andrea, she was highly proficient at reading lips. Unlike Andrea, she had a difficult time learning sign language, as no one in her family or circle of friends signed. Unlike the Cahill family, Marylyn had no one to sign with.

It was against this backdrop of Andrea's evolving knowledge and understanding of Deaf culture that Marylyn became aware of a group based in Chicago, the Association of Late Deafened Adults (ALDA), an organization created for people who were not born deaf but for a variety of reasons became deaf after a period of normal hearing and language acquisition. ALDA recognized that adults with acquired hearing loss had no cultural identity and sought to create one. Marylyn and Andrea were not only excited to join, but also decided to start a Boston area chapter.

ALDA's purpose was to provide late-deafened adults with a social, emotional, and pragmatic support system. ALDA's website reflects these tenets:

> The ALDA mission is to support the empowerment of deafened people. Late-deafened Adults are people who have lost the ability to understand speech with or without hearing aids after acquiring spoken language.

ALDA is committed to providing a support network and a sense of belonging by sharing our unique experiences, challenges, and coping strategies, helping one another find practical solutions, and emotional support, and working together with other organizations for our common good.

It sounded great!

ALDA was started as a social club by a man named Bill Graham. Through the force of his personality and organizational skills, ALDA thrived and grew to become not only a social vehicle but also a networking system, a resource center, and a job-opportunity clearinghouse. It successfully filled a tremendous void in this segment of the deaf community in Chicago, and Andrea and Marylyn wanted to expand that network and offer it to late-deafened adults in greater Boston. ALDA Boston became the first official chapter outside of Chicago, a model for the dozens more that eventually sprung up around the country. ALDA remains active today, and from what I can tell, it continues to fill that need. Bill remains revered within ALDA as the founder, the visionary, and the mover and shaker who makes things happen.

ALDA Chicago provided the model for the Boston Chapter: Members networked, met for drinks and events, shared research, worked on coping strategies, and helped one another with employment issues. Employment is a particularly difficult hurdle for most late-deafened adults, many of whom can no longer do the jobs they'd been trained for and often either drop out of the workforce or have to accept lower-paying jobs that don't require hearing.

My sense from the stories I've heard, and what I observed, was that Bill Graham offered a couple of additional elements to the late-deafened adults in the Chicago area—one of which we had realized was critical to moving forward early on in our own scary journey—*hope*. Hope that if they all pulled together, they could improve their lot, have a career, socialize, and have fun. And as Marylyn reminded me when I spoke with her regarding this book, Bill brought one other key element to this frightening new arena—*humor*. As Marylyn pointed out, "He taught us all that it was okay to poke fun at ourselves and see the humor as we navigated this brave new world of deafness." He knew, intuitively, that while this was serious business, it would never jell and be able to thrive without laughter, frivolity, and fun.

Becoming deaf later in life is a desperate situation to be thrown into. It affects virtually every aspect of your life—negatively. If you find yourself in this boat, you'll be far more likely to become confused, depressed, addicted, angry, hurt, and lonely. Late-deafened adults have to deal with communication challenges, financial problems, and self-esteem issues. In some cases, educated, highly trained, and well-paid professionals are forced to settle for menial, low-end jobs. In other cases, they end up in the unemployment line. This is a heartbreaking situation, one that ALDA strove to mitigate.

Hearing people just didn't get it, and for many, never will. To most hearing people, deafness is a concept. When they think of "peace and quiet," it conjures up an image of serenity and restfulness. Being deaf, from what Andrea would tell me, was anything but serene. The need to constantly use your eyes to pick up cues, read lips, and watch facial expressions was tiring. The requirement to hold your focus while someone drones on, half understanding what they're saying, can be boring. The constant anticipation of being caught off guard or not keeping up with the conversation is nerve-racking. The feeling of loneliness, even when you're surrounded by a crowd, is sad. The constant clichés and platitudes about how well you speak/communicate/interact/understand feel condescending. For late-deafened adults who know what casual conversation in a crowded restaurant is like or recall the sound of big band music wafting over a dance floor, these triggers can be painful.

There were times when this theater of the absurd made me laugh out loud. I had a client who I was very close to—a very funny guy who was both a brilliant businessman and a certifiably insane human being. While very empathetic about Andrea being sick (he was my client in New Jersey when Andrea was diagnosed with NF2), he was a little bit strangely jubilant when I told him she'd lost her hearing. The conversation went like this:

ME. Andrea had another brain operation. She's going to recover, but she is now profoundly deaf.
SAM. Profoundly deaf? That means she can't hear anything at all?

ME. Correct! A 21-gun salute could be fired off in our living room, and she wouldn't even look up.

SAM, *quiet for a moment.* I'm jealous.

ME. Jealous, what do you mean?

SAM. If my wife became profoundly deaf, that means I could come home loaded at any hour and never wake her up— how good would that be!

ME, *thinking to myself.* That's simultaneously hilarious and sad.

In our long journey through late deafness, we encountered many emotions and clichés, but the one that exemplified Andrea's challenges and grated on her as much as anything was, "You need to talk louder so she can hear you." Andrea literally could not hear a single sound—if a bomb went off in the backyard, she wouldn't twitch unless the vibrations shook the foundation of the house. She would tell people that, and they would yell at her. She would remind them again, and sometimes they'd yell louder. Yelling and overaccentuating only made it harder for Andrea to read lips and understand. Of course, Andrea, being Andrea, would let them know, but always in a patient manner, regardless of how many times they raised their voice. Even though they didn't mean it, it still made her crazy.

This cliché illustrates the frustration that all Deaf, deaf, late-deafened, and hard-of-hearing people face. When my daughter was very young, she thought her mom could hear if she only "tried harder." Many adults have similar childish attitudes toward deaf people. After struggling to talk to Andrea at a party, they'd simply slide away to the next hearing conversation. Andrea would be held captive to her deafness the entire evening, interaction after interaction. Because she was almost always a minority of one, the requirement to make it work was all on her—she had to read lips, she had to ask people to repeat what they said, and she had to feign understanding of the conversation. Most hearing people just didn't care enough to put any real effort into the interchange.

By the end of the night, she'd be so tired that she could barely change out of her clothes to get into bed. Much of the joy she might have experienced that evening was vastly diminished. Peace and quiet my foot.

Andrea also took a lot of unintentional abuse because she happened to be late-deafened. Even some people who knew her well when she was hearing redefined who she was after she became deaf. You can make the case that she was, in fact, a different person because of her deafness. Or as I would argue, she was the same person who happened to have no hearing. I know Andrea didn't want to be treated any differently, but she was.

Andrea didn't become any less smart because of her deafness. She wasn't any less caring or less personable. She remained a remarkable wife and mother. However, a fair number of people, perhaps because of those old stereotypes and memories of deaf people selling pencils and stickers in the airport, did see her and, worse, treated her differently.

They continued to yell at her even when she told them she was profoundly deaf. They talked behind her back (sometimes about her!). They grew frustrated with having to repeat themselves and, in some cases, resorted to rude and condescending behavior. Even friends carried on conversations in front of her without including her. Merchants refused to allow her into their stores with her hearing dog, even though it was the law and she had the legal papers to prove it. Her students said inappropriate things to her and one another when she would turn her back to write on the whiteboard or look down at her papers. Sometimes she knew; sometimes she didn't.

Andrea accepted these slights much better than I did. She saw life through a different prism. She urged me to try to look at things through the other guys' eyes, to understand that they might be fighting a battle we know nothing about, to accept human failings and faults, and, most importantly, to forgive and move on. I tried, but the insensitivity and ignorance of hearing people to the deaf were now so much more evident to me, and so very disheartening. Andrea always had an indomitable spirit, one that seemed to draw strength from adversity, and it burned even brighter in the face of deafness and NF. It often occurred to me that Andrea, without hearing, was able to take heart and listen, while so many people she came in contact with who could hear never took the time or made the effort to tune in and be present.

Against this backdrop of struggling to fit in, many late-deafened people in the Chicago area found ALDA to be a godsend, a lifeline to others in their same situation. In this case, there really was strength in numbers as they navigated through this new, daunting terrain.

So Andrea and Marylyn, these two well-educated, highly intelligent, strong-willed, determined women, joined forces to become cofounders of the greater Boston chapter of ALDA. What could possibly go wrong? Well, while there were some bumps in the road, more went right than wrong, and this made for yet another interesting and telling chapter in Andrea's ever-evolving life with NF.

Marylyn was a hard-driving realist. She had a sharp edge and could be impulsive. She didn't back down from a confrontation. In fact, she seemed to rise up in contentious situations. People respected her, admired how she had overcome adversity, appreciated her perseverance, and were sometimes intimidated by her. When Marylyn was in the room, you could often sense her edge—like the lit fuse of a firecracker ready to ignite; you just didn't know when or why. In short, while she wasn't always warm and fuzzy, she certainly knew how to get things done. Marylyn was highly focused and goal oriented—she knew what she wanted to do and would run through a wall if need be to get it done.

Andrea was a dreamer. She led by example, was not a great manager, and was far from confrontational. She was happy when the people around her were happy. She learned to accept her deafness, dove into sign language without reservation, and ultimately came to grips with being "deaf" (although the Deaf world never accepted her). Andrea viewed the world through the lens of socialization. If she could engage you in conversation, she felt that it was going to be interesting, educational, and fun. She could always find some common ground, get you talking, and figure out how to connect with things that were important in your life. Andrea was also naive, and she jumped into this venture with innocent enthusiasm. "This is going to be a lot of fun," she said. And while it was fun, it also turned out to be a hell of a lot of work, sometimes frustrating, and more than a little challenging.

These two polar opposites moved forward with starting up a new franchise. They were trying to emulate the success of the mother ship in Chicago, but they faced several major obstacles.

First, they didn't have a Bill Graham. From the stories Andrea told me, and from the information on the ALDA website, it was clear Graham was a charismatic leader. He had the personality, dedication, and visionary skills to rally people together for this cause. He worked tirelessly, developed great relationships, and was able to deliver on his vision.

Andrea and Marylyn, combined, had a lot of the same qualities. But it's difficult for any coleaders, even if they're well aligned, to emulate what a Bill Graham created. And while these two women were usually on the same page, that wasn't always the case. They shared a common goal, but the path they envisioned to get there, based on their personalities and styles, was sometimes divergent. This led to occasional snipping that appeared to me to be based more on style than on substance.

As a start-up, Andrea and Marylyn also didn't have the infrastructure, connections, and organization that existed in Chicago. Over the years, Graham had built relationships with government agencies, vendors, companies, and various Chicago attractions. He also had an evolved organization that handled the finances, membership process, social functions, and employment opportunities. All of these things would have to be built from scratch into the new Boston. While Chicago was more than willing to assist and share their experiences and expertise, it was still a very challenging endeavor.

For the several years that ALDA Boston was in existence, there was a lot of energy, and a lot was going on. Its identity became primarily a social club and a support group, with late-deafened adults getting together to yak, share stories, complain a little bit about their situation, and be with people dealing with similar challenges. There were seminars, field trips and cookouts and parties. Andrea and Marylyn hosted the national ALDA convention. A great deal of informal counseling took place, and an internal aid system blossomed. Although the formal job placement/clearinghouse aspect of the Chicago model never came to fruition (which I think was the key to sustainability), a strong bonding and encouraging culture did.

For Andrea and her late-deafened cohorts, the support group aspect of the organization held real value. It warmed my heart when I'd go to pick up Andrea after an ALDA get-together and hear peals of laughter coming from the group. This was clearly a safe space where they could be themselves and be happy—free from the weighty chains that constrained them in the hearing world.

Andrea had a positive impact on almost all of the people she dealt with at ALDA. She was outgoing, easy to talk to, interesting, and interested in each one of their lives. With her big smile, bubbly personality, and bounty of hugs, she had a way of drawing people, whether hearing or late-deafened, to her.

Andrea also had a trait that really became the glue for this group. As I had learned when we were dating, she had an innate desire to know more about you, your family, your job, and your dreams. Our kids and nieces and nephews called it "holding court." She asked a lot of questions, but she wasn't nosy; she was interested. She wanted serious stuff, but she always made the group laugh. She demanded details and shared information, but it never came across as gossip. The nuances of life were important to her, and she knew they were important to you. It was her way of showing how much she cared.

This caring showed up at almost every meeting and interaction I observed. These late-deafened adults gravitated to Andrea, and she, through the force of her personality, became the ringleader for many of the sessions.

Almost every meeting ran late as they sat around conversing, strategizing, and consoling—with Andrea usually at the center of the clutch. As I sat waiting in the parking lot (wanting to lean on the horn to move the group along but chuckling to myself at the absurdity of doing it), I was constantly reminded how much Andrea meant to this group and how far her efforts went to improve the quality of their lives and bring a ray of sunshine into what was most often a gloomy situation.

She brought together a group of older isolated women and men who had little interaction with other people. She made sure they came to the meetings, personally picking them up and driving them home if necessary. She introduced them to the emerging technologies that made communication, safety, and socialization easier. ALDA, in many cases through Andrea, gave them something to look forward to every week and a better quality of life.

For the younger people in the group, Andrea (as well as Marylyn) were role models. Both had found success in the hearing world as late-deafened adults. Andrea spent many nights on the TTY talking to members of the group who were fractured and trying to put their lives back together. They'd lost jobs and relationships or were having financial problems, and some had become estranged from their families. Andrea took it upon herself to research job conflicts and issues, interact with the base organization in Chicago, and act as a mentor.

Andrea and Marylyn accomplished a great deal with ALDA Boston. They helped a lot of people who were orphaned by their disability, raised a higher level of awareness of their cause, had a good time, and Andrea made some lifelong relationships. They started out with a group of six members and grew the group to 100 plus. In 1992, they hosted the annual ALDA convention in Boston—truly a herculean feat for them to pull off. The amount of time, energy, effort, and caring these two women put into the effort of building this chapter was mind-boggling—almost every available minute they had was plowed back into ALDA.

What amazed me about this chapter of Andrea's life was how much she was able to give to the late deafened adults of ALDA Boston, who were struggling with their new identities, while she herself was dealing with the enormity of her own brokenness. Time and again in her battle with deafness and NF, she would find a way to dig down deep and put others first, burying her own needs for the moment, to support those around her.

At some point, ALDA Chicago began partnering with another organization called Self Help for the Hard of Hearing (SHHH), and the philosophy at that time shifted from how to support late-deafened adults to how to "fix" them. Marylyn told me she and Andrea were out of step with this approach and didn't feel as connected and committed to the cause as they were when they started the chapter.

As a result, the team of Andrea and Marylyn lost their enthusiasm, and the chapter waned. When their involvement ended, there wasn't a blowout or a lot of drama. Like a start-up business with two bright entrepreneurs who couldn't quite break through and take the company to the next level, ALDA Boston atrophied, and the air slowly came out of the tire. It didn't end badly; it just kind of fizzled and fluttered away in the cold New England sea-breeze. But ALDA Boston never died; some of the members kept it alive (although it was on life support for a while). The chapter was eventually revived and continues to support the needs of late-deafened adults in the Boston area today. Andrea and Marylyn were always justifiably proud that they birthed this important entity and that they built a strong enough foundation for it to survive, even in their absence.

For Andrea, this was the first major post-deaf challenge she'd undertaken out of her comfort zone. In her mind, it and she had been very successful. It gave her a lot of confidence. She and Marylyn built an organization, they hosted a national convention, and she traveled to Chicago with Amber, family, and friends to attend several other national conventions (where she learned a great deal about deafness in general and specifically about coping strategies). It was the first time she ventured away without me and stayed alone in a hotel since she lost her hearing. She developed the poise and backbone to speak at the national conference and was held in very high esteem by Graham and the ALDA national board. It was amazing to me how quickly Andrea was processing and using the knowledge and experiences she was gaining and growing as a result.

Andrea was learning that life, especially her new life, was a contact sport. This realization steeled her determination, but it didn't dull the loving side of her personality. She displayed her special ability to push through difficult circumstances with a smile while putting a smile on the face of everyone she encountered. She and Marylyn developed and maintained a high level of respect for each other, even after they stepped down from their leadership roles at ALDA. They continued to meet, brainstorm, and reminisce post-ALDA as they both moved on to new ventures.

Andrea's foray into ALDA was important for both her and us. It was a real building block in redefining who she was and who she might become. It gave her a focus, a goal, and a challenge. It was something positive that she could drive and that I could support. It made her feel needed and important. In this instance, for us, she was the CEO, not a junior partner. She was the boss. I was the driver, the cookout guy, and the sounding board. As meaningful as it was for her, it also helped create a positive counterbalance in our difficult-to-figure relationship dynamic.

Watching Andrea go through her battle with NF and, up to this point, four brain surgeries was not only inspiring, but incredibly painful for me. Not only was NF slowly stealing her mind and body from her, but it was also always trying to dominate and come between us. I watched Andrea's grace and silent determination – and tried to emulate her, subjugating my own fears and anxieties as I grappled with the here and now, as well as an uncertain future.

Foremost, there was the fear of the unknown. We never knew when, how, or to what extent NF was going to act or what the next medical tests, brain surgeries, rehabs, and the like would bring. NF also threatened to drive us apart by challenging our ability to communicate. Add to this evil bucket of circumstances some giant dollops of chronic fatigue, stress, and wild mood swings, and I realized what every partner in this type of situation eventually comes to understand: The disease not only threatened to destroy Andrea, but it was also taking aim at us and coming straight for me and our family as well.

To combat NF from besting me, I narrowed my focus. I realized that, as a family unit, the world now revolved around Andrea. I simply had to pick my spots more carefully. Golf on Saturday with my friends? Nope, it took up too much time, and I needed to get stuff done and be with my family. Instead, the kids and I formed "The Explorers Club," and we walked the woods and wetlands surrounding our house for hours every Saturday while Andrea rested. Basketball on Wednesday night at the local rec center? It only worked if I could be home early for dinner, spend time with the kids, and catch up with Andrea before going out. Impromptu gatherings after work to celebrate a big win or just the end of the week? I was much more selective.

I worked hard to keep my business trips to a single day, which made for some very long treks venturing on daily trips as far as Miami, Dallas, or Salt Lake City. We did a lot of business in Honolulu, and it wasn't unusual for me to fly out on Monday morning and be home for dinner Tuesday evening. I traveled back and forth from Boston to Honolulu seven or eight times for our client, the Bank of Hawaii, before I saw anything outside of a business dinner, board room, or data center. The highlight of my Hawaii adventure was ultimately getting lunch one day at the famous beach bar, Dukes Waikiki. My colleagues thought I was crazy as they hung around for an extra day or two to see the sights or relax, but I needed to keep my eye on the prize: holding NF at bay.

I did finally get my "Hawaii time" when Andrea and I visited the islands for our twenty-fifth wedding anniversary and saw all this lush paradise had to offer. When I hired a guide/driver to show us around, Andrea was perplexed: "You're blowing our money," she said to me. "You've been here a gazillion times. We don't need a guide!" File under: You can't win for losing.

This was also the point in time that I began to view NF as my evil mistress. I hated her, but she was an indelible part of my life; I wanted to ignore her, but she demanded attention; I wanted to fix her, but she was incorrigible. I now knew that I was going to have to continue this devilish Faustian dance forever—until one of us broke. I prayed that I had the strength to stay the course.

At work, I tried to work smarter and not just harder. I started delegating a lot more tasks that I wouldn't have dreamed of not doing myself a couple of years earlier. I was fortunate to have both a strong team and a great deal of flexibility, so I could, for example, finish up paperwork and emails at night after Andrea and the kids were in bed and catch up on weekends, if need be.

I stepped back and prioritized what was really important in the context of NF. Some of the things I decided to shed so as to keep order were easy; they just didn't interest me anymore. Music ceased to be enjoyable. Andrea had long since packed her guitar away, and if Andrea and I couldn't enjoy music together, it no longer brought me any pleasure. Every time I passed that old guitar sitting in the corner of the garage, I felt a pang of sorrow and resentment. Going to sporting events—once something I did with almost fanatical zeal—took a back seat. Although still entertaining, it was no longer a priority. As I mentioned, playing golf was something I'd always enjoyed, but it was too much of a time commitment, so I pretty much put it on the back burner until I retired.

To keep NF from getting to us, we had to work in partnership to align our relationship, goals, and strategies to make the most of the life we were now given. This was a delicate balancing act.

I felt I had to present the most optimistic perspective possible, delivering bad news only when it became necessary or bordered on ominous. I tried to balance positivity with practicality. Small stuff became just that, small stuff. As a colleague of mine told me many years ago, "Don't sweat the small stuff, and the older you get, the more you realize that almost all of the stuff is small." We didn't have time or energy to dwell on it. I learned to carefully pick my spots when a serious discussion was required about the next, new NF2 crisis—sometimes parsing bad news in manageable chunks. It was important to stay upbeat while not becoming delusional or Pollyannaish (as if NF would ever allow us to do that!)

At the same time, I was also trying to be careful about taking over too much of the decision-making process. Even while battling her health issues, Andrea needed to have both a say and a role in the finances and the household decisions, especially when it came to the kids. She needed to be their mom, not just their dad's assistant. This became more difficult as her memory and cognitive capabilities declined. However, as long as the kids lived at home, she never relinquished her motherly role, responsibilities, or love for her children. To Andrea, this aspect of her life was one thing that was even bigger and more powerful than NF2.

Finally, I had to tread carefully on my emerging caregiver role: Too little involvement and things could go sideways quickly; too much control, and it could negatively trigger Andrea's sense of independence and self-worth. Andrea was very sensitive to her diminishing capabilities, and I developed a sixth sense as to what issues needed to be addressed and when.

As our relationship with the disease matured, we learned that dealing with NF was not analogous to a knockdown, drag-out boxing match or even the war analogy that we had grabbed onto earlier in the progression of the illness, but rather, it was a high-wire walk across a tightrope, requiring constant focus and subtle shifts in balance with every step.

At this point, our life consisted of wild swings up and down, a roller-coaster ride of satisfying highs offset by unfathomable lows. In some ways, ALDA, for Andrea, was a stabilizing venture that helped balance this seesaw way of life. Ultimately, as we learned to understand and play the game better, there were more highs than lows, and at this point in our lives, that was pretty much all we could ask for!

CHAPTER 11

God Deals the Cards; It's Up to You How You Play Them

Life started to even out for us a bit in the late '80s. The kids were growing up healthy, ADS was thriving, and we felt like we were dealing with Andrea's NF2. We thought we were playing our hand well and were hopeful we'd weathered the worst of the storm. Our careers were becoming more established, and we had a great network of friends and family. In the early '90s, we bought a small Cape house on Cape Cod that Andrea named Driftwood. Over the next thirty years, Andrea rebuilt the old-fashioned, outdated house into an open, bright, and airy beach home that reflected her own personality and the ocean environs where it resided. A true retreat, we spent countless happy hours entertaining, swimming, and enjoying our little slice of heaven.

For all the positives we enjoyed, the specter of NF2 was always lurking in the shadows. That ensured that the next twenty-five years would be like a tale of two cities or a coin with two sides. On one side of the coin, we appeared to be living a pretty normal family life, albeit with a deaf woman and a service dog. On the flip side, Andrea had to deal with her deafness and NF2 every day, and she needed a brain operation every few years to keep the tumors from growing and incapacitating her.

Over time, we came to understand and appreciate two important lessons that helped us weather the yo-yo effect of Andrea's disease: (1) Life isn't fair, and (2) God deals the cards—it's up to you how you play them.

We learned that, if you expect life to be fair, you'll be continually distracted, disappointed, and confused, and it's difficult to play the game of life with that mentality. But once we accepted the premise that life was never going to be equitable, we never looked back and almost never again uttered those useless, draining words: "Life isn't fair!" It was the number one lesson we tried to impress upon our kids.

This is a lesson I learned, of course, the hard way, while I was in college. To make ends meet (meaning put gas in my car so I could get to school), I worked weekends and some nights at a local convenience store chain. I was a model employee: early to work, good with customers, conscientious, and hardworking. I had a great relationship with my boss, and I bailed him out whenever I could if, for example, someone called in and he needed a last-minute replacement. I was even held up at gunpoint one night! Although I was very skittish for a long time afterward, twitching every time the door opened, I stuck with it because I needed the job.

One Saturday night, I wasn't feeling well; in fact, I was really sick. I toughed it out. The store closed at 11:00 p.m., but by about 10:45 p.m., I was vomiting out the back door. No one had been in the store for at least half an hour, so I closed up shop and went home to bed.

I came in for my shift on Monday night, and my boss was there, with his boss. I had no idea why, but it didn't feel good. They escorted me to the back room and asked me what happened on Saturday night. I told them the story. The big boss said to me they received a complaint from a woman who tried to buy milk around 10:55 p.m. but the store was closed. I told them, yeah, I was sick and closed the store ten minutes early. My boss said, "I'm sorry to have to do this, but company policy is that no staffer is allowed to close the store early without calling their manager and getting approval. The penalty is termination."

It took a minute to sink in, but it finally dawned on me that I was being fired! I couldn't believe it; I reminded both guys that I was a model employee, that at one point I'd had a gun trained at my head, and that I *really* needed this job.

The big boss chimed in, "We understand, but that's company policy, and our hands are tied." To which I replied, "That's not right. That's not fair." My boss, who for sure didn't feel good about the way this whole thing was going down, got up to leave and said to me in a quiet voice, "Son, if you learn one lesson from this, remember, life isn't fair."

I hated losing my job. Over the next couple of months, there were times I had to hitchhike to school thirty-five miles away. That was okay; the tough part was hitchhiking home in the dark after basketball practice. But my boss was right; I learned a life lesson about fairness. I always tried to treat everyone whom I met, especially those who worked for me, fairly because I knew what it was like to be treated in a way that wasn't on the up-and-up. As painful as the experience was, it was a small price to pay for a lesson that would become a mainstay of my character and serve me well in so many difficult situations.

Andrea and I also accepted that we were dealt a bad hand. It was pointless to throw our cards in the air and shout, "This hand is lousy! I demand better cards!" We kept anteing up for the next hand, never getting too distraught, cocky, or complacent with the hand we were playing; always hoping (and praying) for the best, but preparing for the worst; gradually finding out that the deck, sometimes for better and worse, gets reshuffled and re-dealt at random intervals by the big dealer in the sky. Even when we were dangerously low on chips, we revived our spirits with scripture (1 Corinthians 10:13), paraphrased, "God will never give you more than you can handle."

At the same time, we began to more fully understand that NF2 was an insidious disease that not only dealt Andrea huge body blows in the form of complex brain operations and long rehab stints but also administered "death by a million cuts" daily. There were constant seemingly "smaller" issues that became perhaps more debilitating than even the more visible, high-profile events. Memory lapses, mood swings, balance issues, cognitive processing, eye problems, and throat and swallowing challenges all became more prevalent and an increasing impediment to everyday life.

To fully understand the breadth of the disease, you have to appreciate what one of Andrea's doctors told me early on when I asked her, somewhat naively, to explain NF more fully to me. Her response was as follows:

- NF is chronic; there is no cure.
- NF is progressive and gets worse with time.
- NF reduces your life expectancy.
- If NF doesn't kill you, it will take years off your life, and one of the conditions spawned by the disease likely will finish off the job.
- NF puts enormous stress on many major organs in your body, making them more likely to fail.
- NF can cause deafness.
- NF can cause cognitive disabilities.
- NF often causes eye-related issues.
- NF can cause mobility issues and lead to becoming wheelchair-bound or completely immobile.
- NF can weaken your immune system.
- NF creates significant stress (for both the patient and their families) leading to the potential for tension related maladies such as high blood pressure, head-aches, depression, stomach distress, and wight gain.

- NF can degrade your fine and gross motor skills.
- The surgeries necessary to try to control the tumors created by NF are high risk, with no guarantee of success.
- The outcomes from NF surgery are sometimes more severe than the disease itself.
- There are no FDA-approved drugs to treat NF.
- The chemotherapy and radiation therapies used to try to combat NF are experimental and can have major side effects.
- NF is hereditary: There's a fifty-fifty chance you can pass it on to your children.

She added, with a sad smile, "And she's lucky she didn't start getting the symptoms when she was a child. The disease is much worse for children, with a much shorter life expectancy."

Boy, was I ever glad I asked that question!

Between 1987 and 2011, Andrea underwent eight brain surgeries. Additionally, she had a shunt installed to drain fluid from her brain. This helped relieve the pressure buildup from a lack of space in there as a result of more than forty tumors in her cranium and spine (after a certain point, the doctors gave up trying to count them). In layperson's terms, a drainage release valve that kept her head from exploding.

From Andrea's perspective, she told me it was like facing your biggest, most extreme, phobia, battling your way through it, and being told you had to go back and do it again (and again and again.) Like a reoccurring nightmare she couldn't control,

N2F reappeared at will, causing her to not only face a torturous present, but relive the painful past while realizing the future promised no relief.

It reminded me of Sisyphus in Greek Mythology—NF2 was the rock that Andrea had to forever push up the steep hill, without ever being able to escape her fate by reaching the top of the mountain. As bad as that was, she also worried that as in the Greek myth, she was somehow being punished by God. This illusion of NF2 as a form of punishment for some sort of unknown sin, sinisterly lingered in the back of her mind in the form of psychological anguish as she tried to make sense of the "why me" question. Yet another piece of NF2 collateral damage callously created by the disease.

The brain surgeries were big-league operations, lasting anywhere from ten to more than fourteen hours, during which surgeons attempted to remove as many and much of the tumors as they could. At the same time, they tried to minimize any serious inadvertent damage. This community of tumors had become intertwined and integrated with her nerves and blood vessels. The surgeries were extremely intricate, and the slightest misstep could destroy a key function (sight, facial muscles, balance, and so forth), cause a stroke (which happened), put her into a coma (which happened more than once), or cause her to die. These surgeries were always on our minds and made it difficult (but also imperative) to try to ratchet down the stress levels.

The recovery and rebuilding process from the surgeries was brutal. After getting through the immediate surgical recovery for several hours, Andrea would spend up to a week in the hospital—in areas ranging from the neuro-ICU to a standard patient room, depending on how well she tolerated the surgery. During this time, her goals were modest—to clear her head, eat a meal, and get out of bed. The clouds lingering in her brain from the surgery and the anesthesia made sign language and communication challenging. From the hospital, she was transported by ambulance to a rehab hospital where she would reside for a period ranging from several weeks to a couple of months. Here, she relearned the basic functions of talking, walking, eating, and getting to the bathroom that we all take for granted. Once she got home, she required physical and occupational therapy almost every day for another three-plus months. She literally had to relearn every aspect of everyday living, every time, reconstructing herself physically, mentally, emotionally, and spiritually.

Then the hard work began—spending hours in the gym to build up her strength and endurance. Getting back behind the wheel of a car, first in a parking lot, then at the local cemetery, and finally on the road. She had lots of visitors, which simultaneously buoyed her and wore her out. We had to be very careful of her injuring herself by falling, stepping on a broken glass she didn't hear smash, or burning her fingers on the stove. Any of these things, all of which happened at one point or another, could land her back in the hospital and, worse case, back into the rehab hospital cycle.

Andrea pushed ahead, seemingly oblivious to the tirade of arrows being slung at her. To quote the writer Shel Silverstein, author of her favorite children's book, *Where the Sidewalk Ends*, "If the track is rough and the hill is tough, thinking you can just ain't enough!" When it came to recovery, Andrea was short on thinking and high on action. No lamenting or self-loathing, she got herself up and going every day—pushing herself to the limit, a day closer to her regaining her optimum capabilities. Andrea was simply amazing at being able to keep the constant internal stress from consuming her.

A big part of this self-motivation was because she needed to get back to being our children's mother. You might ask, what was it like to be a mother in her situation? I guess the easy answer is that it was like every other aspect of her life—challenging, unpredictable, and rewarding. Andrea was so instinctive and committed in this area that even during her darkest hours, she never took her foot off the gas when it came to being a mom. She told me that, unlike a lot of women, she loved being preg-nant, and it was clear that her children were her greatest joy. So while that surge of love always radiated from her, the practical matters were a constant trial.

Getting the kids up and going in the morning and out the door, coordinating their schedules, and dealing with the inevitable jousting and whining are part of every family's every-day routine. My sister-in-law terms it the "daily shit show." For Andrea, without the benefit of hearing, without the easy use of a phone, and often with physical challenges plaguing her, it required a bit more effort and focus. She got up and downstairs early, breakfast was already set up, and she stayed with the kids to get their jackets on and get to the bus on time. One of the keys was allocating the extra time necessary for her to get the job done.

Andrea always planned her day out the night before. She would spend fifteen minutes after dinner getting prepared—that was critical because, in her world, everything took a little bit longer, whether it was taking a shower, getting in and out of the car, returning a phone call, or going to a meeting at the school. She moved slower, and time moved faster. She overcame this reality with planning, prioritization, and brute determination—plowing through issues, changes in the plans, and misunderstandings.

Prioritization was an essential part of her strategy. She always put the kids first, and if some of the other stuff in life had to take a back seat, so be it. If taking care of an issue with the kids in the morning caused her to run late for the gym, that's the way it was. Taking the kids out after school and spending forty-five minutes with them talking about their day was important—cleaning the kitchen, not so much! Making sure they got where they needed to go to—be with their friends, go to a sporting event, or make it to a medical appointment—was a top priority; the garden could get weeded tomorrow. Getting their homework done never took a backseat to getting her nails done. In all those instances, it was a matter of priority.

Finally, because the kids were our prime concern, we tag-teamed this part of our lives, and worked seamlessly together. I spent a lot of time with the kids, but I also focused on doing the things Andrea couldn't or didn't want to do so she could be with them—like cleaning the kitchen and weeding the garden, but definitely not doing her nails!

I think that Andrea's mindset and will to be a great mother fueled her ability to persevere through many of the issues created by NF2. This is a woman who would ask me every time, shortly after waking from brain surgery, "How are the kids doing?" The old adage "Where there's a will, there's a way" embodied Andrea's outlook when it came to her children.

Being a mom brought Andrea great pleasure and satisfaction, and helped to offset other issues on the "bad side" of the coin; running the gamut from inconveniences to heartbreaking lifestyle roadblocks. One of the most difficult impacts of this side of the coin was our decision, after Peter's birth, not to have any more children. Andrea and I both loved kids and loved being parents. We would have liked to have had, as she put it, "a gaggle of children"—something far short of eleven, but more than two! We didn't feel comfortable with the hand we were holding in this area, so we folded and walked away from this part of the dream, never looking back. More collateral damage.

The loss and/or distancing of some friends and acquaintances weighed heavily on outgoing Andrea, and the impact of NF2 on her career was a bitter pill to swallow. She longed to be able to casually pick up the phone and grab a drink or dinner with friends, but in more and more instances, they were too busy, it was too much of an inconvenience to get her into and out of the car and the restaurant, or they simply had better options. This created an increased level of social isolation that would have become much more pronounced if she didn't have such a large, committed family and a small core group of wonderful friends supporting her.

These issues were the by-product of NF2 being a chronic, progressive, neurologic disease. While adapting to being deaf was job number one, and I don't think anyone could have done a better job with that "inconvenience," NF2 remained the constant elephant in the room long after she lost her hearing; and that elephant was not only large, but always on the move, capable of increasing levels of disruption and destruction.

As time went on, we aged, and Andrea's memory started to fail, her reasoning became blurred, she tired more easily, and her already shaky balance was increasingly unsteady. NF2 made even being deaf more difficult. Trying to read lips, follow a conversation, interpret ASL, or focus on the TV's closed captions all became increasingly heavier burdens.

All these symptoms became more severe over time, and as a result, they morphed into more significant, challenging daily impediments. Getting in and out of bed, going to the bathroom, bathing, and getting in and out of the car became a little more difficult every year. A constant reminder that NF's clock was steadily ticking down.

These issues were definitely on the abnormal or surreal side of our coin.

The "bad side" of the coin was ever present and increasingly filled her plate with new and troublesome obstacles. So Andrea became a master at pivoting—both at the macro level in the big picture and with micro-pivots in her daily life. We strove to offset these difficulties by spending as much of our time and energy on the sunny side of our life, the "good side" of the coin.

This part of our world included many happy, routine, and conventional aspects of life—made possible by playing our cards as best we could. Rather than fold, we kept our options open, throwing out cards, picking up some new ones, betting heavy or light, and bluffing when advantageous—trying to make those decisions with as clear and rational a mindset as we could, while attempting to drain as much of the emotion out of the situation as possible. We had a positive outlook, a desire to make life as good as we could for our children, and heaps of help from a lot of the great people who hung in with us.

For me, staying on the normal side of the coin meant keeping Andrea and myself busy, and I had no problem doing that. Supporting Andrea was my priority, and I put a lot of my energy into helping to make things go as smoothly as possible. Also, our two kids were active in school and sports. I ran the town basketball program and coached many of our children's soccer, baseball, and basketball teams. On top of that, I was working like a madman helping to manage our suddenly blossoming and successful consulting firm.

ADS was growing dramatically from its genesis in 1980 with four original members and a single contract, into a $65-million operation employing 350 people that went through an initial public stock offering (IPO) in 1998.

There was plenty here to help keep me engaged. As the executive vice president of operations, I was responsible for sales support, underwriting deals, and getting the work done after we won the business. When we were flying highest, about fifty million dollars of the operating budget was my responsibility. I oversaw a staff of almost three hundred, made up of highly skilled project managers, banking specialists, bank business analysts, and technicians.

I did a lot of hard traveling, and it took a toll on me. I was tired and occasionally burned out, and it seemed I had a constant backache. But I was young, and I loved my job, the people I worked with, and the clients I dealt with. I built some great, lifelong relationships and friendships.

I also went back to school. It nagged me for years that I never obtained my college degree (I had taken various, one off, courses over the years and was fifteen credits short). Completing this bit of unfinished business wasn't easy. In addition to the hour-long drive after work twice a week to the campus (at least, I didn't have to thumb a ride this time around!), there was the studying and the indignity of being, by far, the oldest student in all my classes. But I was determined, and over several years, I completed the program and was the proud recipient of a bachelor of arts degree in history (with an English minor). I never told anyone but Andrea that I went back to school, and when it was completed, we celebrated privately. I moved forward with a great level of satisfaction and personal pride—being able to fill out various applications and bios with the words "*Graduated* from Bridgewater State University," as opposed to "*Attended* Bridgewater State College." I'd been gone so long that my college had become a university! But being able to change that one word was worth all the effort.

On the "good" side of the coin for Andrea, she exhibited enormous energy while running the household and reinventing her professional profile. No matter how much she was battered by her surgeries/recoveries or took on and juggled, our two kids remained at the forefront of everything she did and every decision we made. We wanted them to be regular kids despite what was an irregular household. Although Andrea would eventually start her own business, go back to teaching, and also run evening sign language classes, she always saw herself as a mother first, with her kids remaining her top priority.

She also became a workout beast. As mentioned, we had a small gym in the house, she had her own workout trainer and Pilates teacher, and she went to the gym almost every day. This commitment to movement and exercise was a key component of not only maintaining her stamina, appearance, and strength but also helping her clear her head and keep a positive perspective.

Other components allowed her, despite her constant trials, to gravitate toward the positive. After Andrea became deaf, her other senses, over time, became more enhanced. Her sense of smell, for example, was legendary. She could smell and identify food in a restaurant while passing by it in a car. If Andrea smelled something that wasn't right, I didn't ask questions; I checked it out. If chocolate was involved, her range of smell seemed to have no bounds! Dining was important, with good food and wine serving as the catalyst for conversation, laughter and good times with friends and family. Over the years, we enjoyed many fine dining experiences at restaurants and in our homes in Cape Cod and Florida, where Andrea's evolved sense of taste and smell enhanced her pleasure.

She became even more in tune visually with nature, art, colors, details, and especially body language and facial expressions. She saw colors, patterns, nuances, and intricacies that went right over my head. It allowed her to pick up on and enjoy many interesting, beautiful, often overlooked little things in life. She also read body language and facial expressions almost to a fault. Many times, she would scold me and tell me, "It's not what your words are saying. It's what your face is telling me."

Andrea paid a keen eye to how she looked. She wasn't a "clotheshorse" or vain in any way. Her appearance was just one of those little details that she paid attention to and enjoyed doing. (She was an "earring horse," if there is such a thing. She had hundreds of pairs of earrings for every conceivable situation and event.) She fussed incessantly over her hair—ever conscious of the long scar lines on her skull as a result of hundreds of staples and stitches. She never wanted to draw attention to that darker side of her life. For thirty-five years, she trusted only one person, her hairdresser, Tricia, to touch a hair on her head, and her "do" always looked fantastic.

Andrea also paid close attention to decorating our houses around the things she loved: the ocean, art, and family. Our rooms were filled with sculptures created by her grandfather who had emigrated from Italy, paintings by her mother (who inherited her father's artistic talents), mosaics she herself made (inheriting artistic talent from two generations), and of course, photos of our family and keepsakes from our travels. The many pieces of artwork that we procured during our travels reflected our love for adventure and our proclivity for the ocean.

She vigorously maintained her beautiful gardens. When she was no longer able to tend to the gardens herself, she assumed the role of foreperson, directing my every shovel and prune. Her mosaics grew into a minibusiness. She also pursued her passion and strengths in education to start another business, Andrea Cahill Educational Services, or ACES, providing educational consulting, teaching sign language to hundreds of children of all ages and needs, many of their parents, as well as tutoring a wide range of children and teenagers (much more on both these topics in chapter 14).

Her sense of touch was another key part of her personality that brought her joy. She was a toucher, a hugger, and, most of all, a hand-holder—a trait that reflected her desire to make everyone feel at home. Cuddling babies was the ultimate high for Andrea. She would bounce them, kiss them, and squeeze them to the point of overindulgence. Nothing made her happier than to have a baby on her lap, squeezing their cheeks and tickling their belly. Andrea used touch in a very positive manner, but woe to the woman who patted me on the back or touched my arm! While Andrea would continue to smile, her eyes would turn ice-cold, and if it happened more than once, she wouldn't hesitate to speak up. Waitresses were her favorite targets and although I tried many times to explain to her that it was only about the tip, she refused to buy it!

People liked Andrea, and she liked people. She nurtured—and was nurtured by—a cornucopia of deep and enduring relationships with friends and family. Between our large families and diverse groups of friends, we had a lot of company. I remember one year when we didn't have five nights to ourselves between late June and Labor Day. While the places we lived in were special, Andrea was the real attraction. People loved her and wanted to be around her.

For forty years, she hosted the Cahill Family Christmas Party at our house for fifty of her crazy in-laws—all while not being able to hear a word or a joke anyone was saying or listen to a single note of the Christmas music that was playing. Every year, she'd complain about having the party, but when the show began, Andrea was in her glory—sitting in the center of the masses, squeezing personal stories out of nieces and nephews, and of course, kissing up every baby in sight. Everyone left happy, most with a humorous Andrea story or two to lighten their ride home.

She had a lively, albeit, unconventional sense of humor and was quick to make a joke or laugh at one, even if it was at her own expense. While she was more than willing to kid around about something you said or did, no one was quicker to notice something you wore or brought, or faster to compliment you about it, than Andrea. It didn't matter if you were an old friend or it was the first time you'd met her—you were going to get a compliment and a laugh, and you were going to feel comfortable in Andrea's presence. In short, she was pretty damn good company.

While we loved the company, it could be wearing, and within minutes, the bad, flip side of the coin could rear its ugly head. Andrea tired easily and usually took a good nap each afternoon. When we had people at the house, the combination of her not wanting to miss anything and not wanting to show any weakness often caused her to skip the nap. Fatigue created issues with her memory, balance, and stamina, but never her disposition. When she finally hit the wall, she would wordlessly sign to me, "I gotta get to bed, Petes."

Andrea was adept at consistently doing the little things that mattered, whether it was that quick compliment, making sure she always had just the right treats for her grandsons every time they visited, or being the keeper of occasions for our extended family. Decidedly old-school, she had every birthday and anniversary written down in her planning calendar. At the beginning of each year, she would sit at the kitchen table and rewrite them all into her next year's calendar.

We were spending hundreds of dollars a year on cards until I finally discovered the Dollar Store, and we were able to drastically reduce our yearly card costs! No emails for Andrea; she wrote a note on each card, and it was always something meaningful. I was constantly impressed by how she had just the right thing to say every time.

Our love of travel would lead us to visit all fifty states and twenty countries—by car, train, tram, plane, boat, ship, Vespa, bicycle, and on foot. I pushed that little travel wheelchair up mountains, across innumerable cobblestone streets, and into improbable situations that only we would get into. For example, late one afternoon in Bratislava, Slovakia, I had to pull Andrea down the stairs in the wheelchair to get to the bathroom on the lower level. As with many European public toilets, a small fee is required to enter. I didn't have any change, but fortunately, a woman was leaving, and we wheeled right in. However, when we went to get out, the door wouldn't open because we hadn't paid to get in! I had to leave Andrea locked in the toilet, crawl under the door, go upstairs and get change, and then release her from her Slovakian confinement. After I pulled her backward up the stairs, we stopped for a drink at an outdoor plaza and were rewarded with a gorgeous sunset and a wonderful juggler in front of us in an ancient courtyard. We toasted and smiled at our good fortune and ability to flip our coin of life from bad to wonderful in the blink of an eye.

One scary travel moment occurred in the crowed city of Krakow, Poland, when an adventuresome, but very deaf, Andrea wandered away from our meeting place. Krakow is a crowded maze of locals, college students, and tourists, congesting narrow cobblestone streets that lead out to a large plaza. That day, it was teaming with people, and Andrea was nowhere to be found. She didn't know the name or location of the hotel, had no way to communicate with me, and, as far as I knew, didn't speak Polish. As I surveyed the mass of humanity crammed into this beautiful, historic town, I was not optimistic about finding her anytime soon. At that point, it occurred to me to put myself in her shoes and think, *What would Andrea do?*

As I walked down the street, I thought about shopping, food, and conversation. While the conversation piece seemed ludicrous, I knew somehow, someway, Andrea would improvise and make a friend. And suddenly, I knew just where to look— the day before we'd been to a clothing store that was connected to a confectionary shop. I have no idea how, but like a homing pigeon, she'd found her way back, bought an outfit, and was sipping on a hot chocolate with a pile of fudge in front of her. Of course, she was carrying on a conversation with the owner. When I admonished her for wandering off in a foreign country with no form of communication, she turned to her new friend and said, "Isn't he a pain in the ass?" Rarely a dull moment when traveling with Andrea!

Back home, about once a week or more in season on Cape Cod and in Florida, we were on our boat, where Andrea was most comfortable. With no need to stand or walk on the boat, Andrea was free. The spray of the seawater, the wind in her hair, and the glint of the sun off the ocean waves invigorated her. She loved the ocean, the smell of the salt air, and the joy she felt on the boat. We often took friends and family out with us, and Andrea aspired to be both the entertainment director and the captain (although I'd try, to no avail, to explain that the highest rank she could attain was first mate—even to the point of getting her a hat that said "First Mate").

Andrea had a banner quoting the philosopher Joseph Campbell that read, "We must be willing to let go of the life we have planned, so as to have the life that is waiting for us." This gave her the inspiration to look forward, not backward, to not dwell on what might have been, but to accept, as best she could, the life she now had and the one that lay before her.

We came to learn over time that it couldn't always be about the destination with NF because there is no good endgame with this disease. Therefore, we reasoned that it had to be about the journey and making that as enjoyable as possible. Isn't that really true about life in general?

What Andrea came around to, and then would emphasize to me, is that you can choose to be happy. That attitude may not change your situation or circumstances, but it will improve your outlook, lessen your stress, make you a little more tolerable of the people around you, and make your day-to-day experience a tad more enjoyable. If you can smile when things are dark, still be supportive when you're exhausted, or make your partner laugh when you want to cry, then you've improved the quality of your life as well as that of the people you come in touch with.

We couldn't change the cards we were dealt and knew we would never win this game. But once we realized that it wasn't about *winning* the game, we focused on *playing* the game. And we found that the deck still had plenty of aces, and we also had a few pretty good cards of our own up our sleeves.

CHAPTER 12

Lucky Cards

In our hand, we held two high-value face cards: family and friends. There's an old Yiddish proverb: "God gave us burdens; also shoulders." We had strong shoulders, but we were also blessed with a bounty of family and friends who lovingly offered *their* shoulders to cry on or to help bear our burden.

Nobody should be on their journeys alone, but Andrea and I needed more support than others, and what we needed was not easy or obvious to give. Just as we had to make adjustments requiring a great deal of effort and patience, so did everyone around us. And not everyone could.

When Andrea became deaf, it was obviously much more challenging to communicate with her. As her NF2 progressed and she was more frequently tired, confused, or otherwise impaired, you had to work even harder to maintain a real connection with her.

One important aspect of Andrea's personality that NF2 was never able to seize was her desire to be with and around people. Andrea didn't want to be an island. She cherished her relationships with her friends. Being social was literally in her DNA. Against this backdrop, she felt the pain of friends who no longer wanted to be part of her new life.

Some of her closest friends drifted away or dropped off. Maybe they didn't know what to say anymore, or maybe they were sick of having to repeat themselves and find ways to help Andrea understand, or maybe they didn't want to be stared at in a local restaurant when they had to help Andrea to the bathroom. Whatever their reasons, they faded away and disappeared from our lives.

Andrea was more confused and hurt than she was angry. She'd say to me, "I haven't seen Sally for a while," or, "When's the last time you heard from Alice?" It had been longer than she realized since we'd had any contact with these people, and I sensed they'd "checked out" of their relationship with us. To them, it could have been no hard feelings; just too much work; they had better options; the relationship was not as strong as we thought it was; or they were uncomfortable. Like not seeing the end of a movie, we never knew for sure what actually happened.

One of her best friends who lived two blocks away only stopped by when she had friends in from out of town, and she wanted to show off her "deaf friend." When she sold her house and moved, she texted me, "The key you lent me to your house is under the mat." She never stopped by, contacted Andrea, or said goodbye.

Another close friend worked in a coffee shop a mile up the road. For years, I'd bump into her, and she'd lament, "I haven't seen Andrea in forever. I'm going to come over and see her next week and catch up." It never happened. As time went by, she'd see me in the shop, we'd catch each other's eye, and she'd quickly retreat to the back room.

Yet another friend left the state, with no goodbye, no explanation, and no contact. Text messages went unanswered. One couple, who lived up the street, simply disappeared. They just stopped coming around one day, and we'd go years without even a sighting (although their kids would stop by to see Andrea). Another woman, who was one of Andrea's best friends in Falmouth, didn't stop by anymore, but her morning walk took her past the house every day! We didn't see her for a month, then a summer, and then never again.

There were more, and it hurt. Andrea could sense she was being "ghosted," but she had her pride and dignity and wasn't going to chase after those fleeing her. What made it more painful was that these were people and their families who, over the years, had been in and out of our house, gone to the same parties with us, had kids that grew up with our kids, and, in some cases, had come on vacation with us. More collateral damage from the wrecking ball, NF2.

These disappearing relationships only served to make the people who stuck around more beautiful and precious. Andrea and I believed that God put all of us on earth for a reason, and on many occasions, God put people in our lives that can only be described as angels. Some seemed to materialize at just the right time and help us through the most difficult of times. Others came and remained in our lives, providing continual help and love.

What they gave took a lot extra and was needed even more, and as a consequence, it was more valuable and heartwarming. We considered ourselves blessed to be constantly surrounded by such love and dedication.

Our extended family—our two children, their spouses and children, my ten siblings and their spouses, and Andrea's two brothers and their wives—often seems too large to count. It's impossible to add up the countless times and ways they rode in like the cavalry to provide reinforcements and avert chaos and disasters. Amazingly, all of them stepped up to help us at some point along the way. To say we were grateful seems almost trivial given the importance of what they did for us. Thank you, all!

I can't list and acknowledge all the friends, neighbors, and acquaintances who gave us a boost at just the right time and made our lives just a little easier, our load lighter, and our path clearer. Momentarily or in the long term, they were all angels. But from the perspective of a caregiver and a person enduring these kinds of travails, let me illustrate a few examples of the value and joy good relationships can bestow.

Building relationships came naturally to Andrea because she innately understood the concepts of giving back and showing gratitude. She was outgoing and comfortable in her own skin. I was more reserved, especially until I became familiar with the people I met. I built relationships in more rational, less emotional ways: I warmed up to people slowly; I got to understand you; and we became closer as a result of mutual values, respect, and trust. This model worked very well for me in business and often in life too.

In reality, I didn't have a lot of time for new friendships. Outside of work and my group of high school buddies, my time was limited, and I was more than content to piggyback off Andrea and let her do the spade work of making new friends. I spent a lot of time at work, especially as we got the business off the ground, so it made sense that my support system started there.

My key relationships in the early days of NF2 were with my colleagues at work, specifically with the cofounders of ADS, Bob Howe and Bill Gallagher. Both were brilliant in their own ways, and both became great friends and mentors to me. Of course, they loved Andrea and would, and did, do anything they could for us.

These were also tough ex-military guys, hard-ass executives with a lot of their own money invested in this start-up. There was no room for slacking on the quality of the services or the delivery of the product (both primarily my responsibility), and I worked my tail off to make sure it happened. But they showed me that while business was business, there were far more important things in life.

ADS gave liberally to many different charities (including one we established to fund NF2 research at Massachusetts General Hospital, *The Andrea Cahill Foundation*), and both

Bob and Bill went above and beyond to make any accommodations I needed to support Andrea.

A great example of their commitment to us came over a six-week period one summer when we tried a radiation regiment to shrink Andrea's tumors. We had to get into MGH at seven-thirty every morning, Monday through Thursday, for the radiation treatments. This was a bit of a challenge, as we lived seventy miles away from the hospital. I needed to be with her, but the logistics seemed impossible.

Bob tracked down a limousine company in our town and cut a deal with them. They would arrive at our house every morning at five-thirty and take us to the hospital (with only one stop allowed: Dunkin' Donuts for Andrea's iced coffee), wait for the radiation to be completed, drop me at the office after the treatment, and take Andrea home to rest. At the end of the day, the limo came back to the office to pick me up and take me home for the evening. Bob also lined up caregiving, cooking, and cleaning help at the house for Andrea. It was a challenging and exhausting six weeks, but with ADS's support, we got through it.

And talk about the ability to build relationships; Andrea became such good friends with the limo driver that, after the radiation was finished, she'd stop by the house just to say hi and check in on Andrea's progress. She'd even bring lunch. The neighbors would rib Andrea about being a big shot with a white limousine seemingly always parked in the driveway.

Bob had the big-picture focus, while Bill was more of a detail guy, and he became intimately familiar with our situation. Bill had an uncanny sense for being able to see problems coming down the road before I did—sometimes logistical, sometimes stress related. He would regularly approach me with his thoughts and concerns, along with potential solutions or options that helped me avoid a great deal of trouble. There was nothing he wouldn't do to make our lives more livable.

Bill kept an eye on my work profile, knowing that I was prone to taking too much on myself. He insisted, sometimes demanded, that I get support and build out a network to ease my load. Bill and I would often get together after work for a beer and discuss life outside of ADS. Usually, it was just the two of us, but sometimes, our spouses joined. He and his wife, Penny, were personally close to Andrea and me, and these sessions gave me some breathing room and a chance to decompress.

Bill helped keep me centered during the early years of Andrea's illness. It was Bill who hired me back as a computer operator after I'd quit my old job in 1977 to head to California with my friend and later brought me on as one of the four original members of ADS. He was always somewhere in the mix as I tried to sort things out. He taught me how to use a chainsaw and spent many weekends helping me clear the land for our building construction. He and I bonded over our mutual love of basketball and would often meet at the YMCA at 6:00 a.m. a couple of times a week to just shoot around and work off some stress. And he always had my back at work.

One day when Andrea and I received bad news from an MRI, it was Bill who jumped on a plane to Los Angeles *that night* to stand in for me for a three-day series of key meetings—no questions asked; he was gone before I even had a chance to ask him. Whenever I needed a legitimate sounding board, not just someone to parrot back what I wanted to hear, Bill was there.

This relationship and these guys, during the most difficult times, helped me keep my head above water and not have to worry about the impact our situation was having on my ability to do my job and make a living (and, as every caregiver knows, make sure that I kept our essential health insurance intact). Angels, for sure, and ones I'm forever grateful for.

Andrea's main go-to person was her mother, Marian. I've never seen a mother-daughter relationship that was so close. Andrea was Marian's "miracle girl," but in many ways, Andrea was simply Marian's best friend. They gabbed and laughed and bickered more like BFFs or sisters than a mother-daughter tandem, and they loved each other unconditionally.

At a moment's notice, Marian would drop anything and everything to help her out. Whether it was sleeping overnight at the rehab hospital to spell me, taking the two babies into her house for weeks while Andrea was sick in the hospital, or jumping on two buses, the subway, and a cab to come stay with us so I could travel for my job, she was a pillar of strength and determination.

Too many times to count, she watched the kids while we went to a medical appointment, a test that invariably ran late, or a procedure that was more complicated than we expected. She was always there when we needed her—even if sometimes we just needed to go out to dinner or take a drive.

Reciprocally, we adopted Marian after her husband, Al, died in the late 1980s. She summered with us down on the Cape, came on trips and vacations with us, went to the kids' school events and sports games, and seemed always to be with us. I guess she needed us almost as much as we needed her. It was a wonderful, selfless, mutually beneficial relationship, with love as its foundation.

She was a constant companion for Andrea and a wonderful role model for the kids. Natalie tells stories to this day about staying with her grandmother when Andrea was recuperating in the hospital, with fond memories of going to the pond to feed stale bread to the ducks, reading at the library, and being pushed on the swings at the playground.

Andrea and her mother enjoyed the hell out of each other and, between the two of them, would come up with some crazy ideas. It was not unusual for me to come home from work and find all the furniture in the house rearranged. One day, on a whim, they decided to remodel the bathroom and had run up a bill of several thousand dollars before I got home from work and was able to shut off that spigot (no pun intended).

My favorite Andrea-Marian story was the day I came home on my birthday and saw a bright red Jeep parked in the driveway. I went inside to see who was visiting. Andrea shouted, "Surprise, happy birthday!" She had bought me a Jeep for my birthday because she said I never buy anything for myself. I was ecstatic. After I took the Jeep for a test drive, we sat down and had cake and ice cream. Shortly after I blew out the candles, Marian smiled at me across the table and said, "Happy birthday, and when you get a chance, can you write me a check for twenty-one thousand dollars?" Happy birthday, indeed!

When she passed away in 2013, some of Marian's ashes were spread in the Atlantic Ocean at the end of our street. Every day that we were on Cape Cod, for the remainder of her life, Andrea sat in the parking lot there to speak with Marian—sometimes just to say hi, other times to bring her up to speed on the family gossip, or ask her advice, but always to tell her how much she loved and missed her.

Andrea also had another mother figure, one she dubbed her "Jewish mother." One day, Andrea was walking back to the car from one of her mothers' group meetings at a playground in Hingham, and a woman approached her and began signing to her. She had seen Amber's RAF leash and was familiar with the farm. Leslie was a special needs teacher who also signed fluently. She and Andrea became fast friends that day. Leslie had a degree from Boston University in education and deaf studies, and with her many connections in the education and deaf worlds, she became a conduit for Andrea to spread her wings. Leslie was also the only person who both understood Andrea well enough and signed well enough for me to fully trust in any situation.

Boy, were we lucky that Andrea decided to take Amber for a walk at the playground that day!

Leslie gave Andrea an empathetic ear (along with signing hands), helping her better understand and negotiate with the Deaf community. Although she was around Andrea's age, Leslie behaved like a Jewish mother to Andrea. They would sit and talk for hours about life and death, relationships, their kids, hopes, and disappointments. She encouraged her, admonished her, and, most of all, worried about her.

Leslie was always there for Andrea emotionally. In addition, she helped with sundry practical matters. Showing her how to order something online, track down an answer to a nagging question, or find a therapist who worked with deaf patients and signed. Nothing was a problem for Leslie when it came to supporting her friend.

Leslie was also a fantastic knitter, and Andrea loved to knit before her fine motor skills stopped cooperating. Whenever Andrea got really frustrated, she would give me a pleading look, and I'd say, "Want me to call Leslie?" and she'd nod. Poor Leslie would come over time and, again, examine the patient (a blanket, a hat, or a scarf), diagnose the problem, and perform corrective surgery—usually undoing knitted sections to get back to the mistake and moving forward again. The knitwear Andrea-Leslie produced always came out looking pretty darn good. Leslie had unlimited patience and kindness. She never made Andrea feel inadequate and always found a way to build her up, even when she was redoing her knitting!

Leslie also had a great sense of humor, often laughing over the craziest of things. For example, she loved the nativity scene we put up in front of the house every year, but her Jewish heritage wouldn't let her take the setting too seriously. She nicknamed the three wise men—each a three-foot-high concrete statue—the "three wise guys." When I moved them to our Cape Cod house and had no room to store them in the shed, I simply left them set up in the backyard. When Les came down for a visit and walked out on the back porch, I heard a shriek and then the two of them laughing to the point of tears. I asked Leslie what was so funny, and she pointed to the nativity scene and said to me in mock indignation, "I can take the wise guys during Christmas, but now they're following me to the *beach*? Really?"

Leslie was the last person to text Andrea the night before she passed away and signed off with her usual, "It was so good to talk to you, hon." A friend indeed, to the very end.

Andrea was the only girl in her family, but she was blessed with a soul sister when her brother Peter married Rosemary and moved in with Andrea's parents while they got established and settled. Andrea knew Rosemary in high school, but during this time, they became much closer. When I came on the scene, the four of us became great pals.

I knew Rosemary was fun to be around—a wonderful mother and a good friend. But I soon came to appreciate the depth of her love and loyalty for Andrea.

Rosemary was one of the few of our family members who *really* learned sign language. She was quick and smart, and she took it seriously, but more than anything, she understood that it was the best way to keep her intimate relationship with Andrea alive. Rosemary was constantly asking me ASL questions—How do I sign this? What does that mean? Why is this gesture that sign?

Whenever Andrea was in the hospital, Rosemary was the first one to visit, often staying overnight to give me a break. When Andrea came home from rehab, Rosemary would leave her family for two or three days a week and stay at our house to help nurse Andrea back to health. Nothing was too much, and everything was done with a smile. She would cook, clean, do the food shopping and the laundry, and, most importantly, sit with Andrea for hours, reminiscing and helping her see that better days were ahead.

We also had a lot of fun. I loved taking Andrea to the beach with Rosemary, where I knew Rosemary was uncomfortable with yucky things like seaweed, horseshoe crabs, and pails of salt water. I would torture her by eating kelp, hanging strands of seaweed over her head, and pouring sandy water down her back. Andrea would admonish me with cries of "Stop abusing the poor woman!" while the look on her face said, "Do it again!" To this day, all I have to do is mention the word *seaweed*, and Rosemary recoils in mock horror! Thank God for family, and thank God for Rosemary.

If Rosemary was the sister Andrea never had and Leslie was her Jewish mother, our friend Paula in Florida was her self-proclaimed "Italian sister." When we bought our place in Florida, we became friends with Paula and her husband, Arthur, who owned the condo above us. Within days of moving in, Paula and Andrea had a special bond that ran so deep you'd swear they'd been friends since childhood.

They loved to laugh, cook, and banter. They shared a love for life, family (their mothers, kids, and grandchildren), and their heritage. They enjoyed each other's company, a glass of wine or Prosecco, and the most annoying habit of eating raw hamburgers when they were cooking.

Paula would often saunter down after dinner just to shoot the breeze. Inevitably, the conversation would take on a strange, humorous tone, whether they were talking about the condo association (Paula was on the board of directors, and Andrea was not happy with the two-inch-thick rule book), politics (Paula loved to talk politics, and Andrea just liked to be contrary), or fashion.

One night, Andrea complimented Paula on her earrings. Paula asked her if she wanted them, and Andrea said she'd love to have them. As Paula reached out to give them to her, she smiled her sweetest smile and pulled them back, and the following conversation ensued:

ANDREA. Hey, what the heck, you said I could have them.
PAULA. You can, but I want a pair of yours in return.

ANDREA, *lying*. Well, um, I only have a few pairs here.

PAULA. I've seen your jewelry box. You have dozens.

ANDREA. Is that the only way I can get yours?

PAULA. Yup.

ANDREA. Okay, I guess that's fair.

Paula would have given her the shirt off her back if she needed it, but she recognized that Andrea was used to being treated differently, and she was going to treat her simply as her good friend and "sister." To me, that was not only good enough; it was beautiful.

And speaking of good friends, I have a group of ten friends who date back to high school and junior high school and have remained close over the years. As a group, we go away once or twice a year to golf, and we get together for the holidays. Over the last half century, we've been to one another's weddings; celebrated the births of our children and grandchildren; talked a lot of sports, politics, and life; and consoled one another through family illness, tragedies, and death. When people ask me how many brothers I have, I reply, "Fourteen," because we're that close.

I know I'm being redundant, but I still have to say it: These guys and their wives loved Andrea. They knew her when she was healthy, and they fully appreciated the valor she showed during her fight with NF. They helped me immensely over the years when I needed some love, perspective, or sometimes a good swift kick in the ass.

Among this group are Rich and Mary, who forged a tight bond with Andrea. Mary came from a similar close-knit Italian family. With mothers who played central roles, their heritages, and outgoing personalities, she and Andrea could have lived parallel lives growing up.

Andrea's face would light up when Rich and Mary would come for a weekend visit. Mary and Andrea would sit around over glasses of wine and simultaneously revere and critique their families (honing in, especially on Rich and me as victims). But as long as we supplied them with food and wine, they didn't care if Rich and I were in the next room or on a distant planet.

Rich always made Andrea and me laugh out loud. One afternoon when we were driving, Andrea and I were having what we thought would be a brief conversation in ASL about which restaurant to go to. But in this case, the animated signed conversation went on for several minutes.

Finally, Andrea turned to the back seat and asked, "What do you guys think?"

Rich launched into a minute-long faux signing routine, mocking us with perfect facial expressions, exaggerated body language, and hands flapping wildly. While many a deaf person might have been insulted, Andrea roared laughing; so hard that she almost banged her head on the dashboard.

Suffice it to say we always had a good time. But without going into detail, Mary and Rich also have had their own challenges over the years, some of which somewhat aligned with parts of our story, and I think this shared experience made us a little more empathic toward one another's plights.

Rich and I had laughed our way through our teens and twenties together, but now we were both in the deep end of the pool, with serious adult issues. While we often still found a way to chuckle, we also cried, supported, buoyed, inspired, and pushed each other forward. Oftentimes, a short text or a single emoji would do because we knew exactly what the other was thinking and going through, and few or no words were necessary. Indeed, a friend in deed, especially when I was in need.

Finally, there were our neighbors. In 2002, our neighborhood on Cape Cod was changing. Many remaining widows on the street were either dying or moving to be closer to their families. A younger crowd moved in, and while that was good for the kids, we were curious as to what it would mean for us.

It was always a tricky thing for people to move next to or across the street from a deaf family. Some of our neighbors over the years shunned us (politely), some coexisted (nicely, but not necessarily warmly), and some (although not as many as I would have hoped) embraced us.

When the house next door sold, we hoped for the best but didn't have high expectations. The family we met across the yard was labeled by Andrea as simply the Nābs, two sisters and their husbands—Janet and Clay, and Nancy and Harry— bought the house together. We soon became fast friends, and they helped make Andrea's life so much better in so many ways.

They thought Andrea was a hoot, and she made them laugh at all of us, at our kids, and at themselves. Andrea would sway across our big yard to their house (her balance was still good enough to weave across the lot). Later on, after a few drinks, Andrea and one of the couples would stagger back together, and they would deposit Andrea on the couch on our porch. Sometimes they would call me on my way home from work to come and pick up Andrea to drive her the twenty-five yards home. When I did pick her up, I could hear an eruption of laughter as I drove up the street.

The Nãbs are kind, sensitive, laid-back, and funny. Harry, who had a brain tumor of his own removed, had a special connection with Andrea. They both were inclined to converse in the form of questions, and it never took too long before Andrea and Harry were the only two in the group who had any idea what the hell they were talking about!

Most of the time, it was pure frivolity. Andrea would give it to them, and they would give it right back to her. One time when they came to visit Andrea in the hospital, Clay was wearing a nice polo shirt and khakis. His usual attire was a T-shirt and cargo shorts. Andrea eyed him from her bed and commented, "Don't you look good all dressed up for me? I guess I must be in real trouble!" It was the last time I saw Clay overdressed.

Janet and Nancy would float in and out of the house, engaging Andrea in discussions about knitting, cooking, gardening, crafts, and almost anything else. Since there was often a glass or two of wine involved, sometimes the conversations turned silly as they used their okay-but-rusty sign language, and Andrea replied to them in "Andreaisms," resulting in a word salad that was often both incomprehensible and hilarious. It seemed like whenever they were around, the gravity of whatever situation Andrea was dealing with would dissipate.

In what turned out to be a final act of love, Clay recognized that Andrea was really struggling to get up the stairs to the house, and he proposed building a ramp. Clay is one of those guys who can build anything, so we agreed on the business terms, and he began. Andrea wanted no part of a ramp and complained about it throughout the process. Clay is a perfectionist, and the ramp, built during a steamy July, took longer than expected. It came out beautifully, looking more like a part of the house than a handicap accessory.

Once it was completed, Andrea loved it. It made my life much easier, and for the last seven months of her life, it kept her much safer. When I went to settle up with Clay, he wouldn't take a dime. That really pissed me off, but there was no way he was going to budge. "I did it for Andrea," he said. "You know I'd do anything in this world for her." I did, and I also knew any of the other three Nābs felt the same way, and that meant the world to us.

Scientific studies have proven what most of us know instinctively. People who have good relationships are better adjusted, more resilient, and live longer than people who are isolated. And that was certainly true for Andrea and me. We always strove to build bridges, not walls, and that mindset paid huge dividends again and again. Our relationships were the primary reason we were able to stay positive, deal with the insanity of our situation, and maintain an optimistic outlook (even if only guarded optimism was the highest level we could muster up on some days).

For a caregiver, relationships are essential. No one I've encountered in that role has been able to successfully be a sustained, effective caregiver without support. It may not take a village, but guaranteed, it will take more than you alone.

And by the way, having the village along for the ride turns out to be among life's greatest sources of joy.

CHAPTER 13

Smile When Your Heart Is Breaking

When we surveyed the cards in our hand, we found another one that made playing the game a lot more fun: a joker.

The old cliché is absolutely true. Laughter *is* the best medicine. It has actually been clinically proven that laughter reduces stress, improves the healing process, and facilitates better relationships. It certainly lightened the symptoms of doom and gloom and awkwardness that often permeated our state of affairs. The best kind of laughter we found was either (a) laughing at our latest quandary, or (b) laughing at ourselves. And Andrea was a mirthful jester. Andrea was genuinely funny without trying to be. It's not that she was a comedienne, but she was comical. It was in part because of the offbeat way she looked at the world and in part because she had a limited filter. Of course, she could always enhance any humorous situation with that trademark smile of hers.

What made her sense of humor so endearing was her ability to laugh despite her dilemma. People would be amazed and clearly impressed that someone in her position, with everything seemingly stacked against her, could laugh and enjoy life. But she could and did. Like a coach calling a timeout to break the other team's momentum, Andrea used humor to dispel the cycle of negativity that continually threatened to permeate any positive aspects of her life.

Her humor could be stinging, although she never meant it to be malicious (unlike yours truly, she found sarcasm to be, "the lowest form of humor".) She pointed out a lot of "duh" moments that made you break out laughing simply because Andrea seemed to say out loud what others might be thinking. There was a great deal of humor in her questions. Sometimes she would ask a question that was so bizarre, so outrageous, or so confusing that the person on the other end of the exchange would have no choice but to be taken aback and chuckle. Some of it was so cringeworthy that, to explain it (or soften it in some instances), I called it "tumor humor." It was the only explanation I could come up with for some of the things that came out of her mouth. Even if it wasn't true, it felt good to blame one more thing on the damn tumors!

Sometimes Andrea's humor—often I couldn't tell if it was intentional or unintentional—was so unorthodox and politically incorrect that it would make even *me* squirm. At one of her rehab stays, the attending physician was very short, maybe five feet tall. Somehow, he and Andrea got into a conversation about how difficult it must be to buy clothes for a man his size. While I was uncomfortable with the back and forth, the doctor seemed to be enjoying it. As he turned to leave the room, Andrea said, "Oh, Doctor, I have one more question. Is that a real tie or a clip-on like I buy for my son?" Thinking she was over the line, I stepped in and tried to move the doctor along, but instead, he came back over to her bed and, with a big grin on his face, untied his tie, put it around her neck, and said, "See, it's a real tie. It even fits you!" Touché!

During another hospital stay, the Catholic chaplain at the hospital was guiding Andrea in prayer. Her best friend, Leslie, was visiting and interpreting. Andrea was trying not to smile because Leslie was fingerspelling something and getting it all wrong. Leslie looked confused. Andrea turned to the chaplain and said, "She can't help it. She's Jewish." What she meant was, of course, "She's signing it wrong because she doesn't understand the material," but she found a way to light up the room with one of her classic "Andreaisms."

Another time was when she was away with her girlfriends for the weekend. Coincidentally, one of her friends, Sheila, had also had an acoustic neuroma removed and had a balance problem. After a few drinks, the two of them started back to the lodge, locking arms and swaying back and forth to stay upright. Andrea looked at the crowd staring at them and said to her friend in a robust voice, "Look at them eyeballing us. They must think we're a couple of drunken lesbians!" Sheila told me they did fall over, but not from the alcohol or the balance issues, but because Sheila was laughing too hard to stay upright.

Sometimes, her deafness created funny situations that allowed her to laugh at herself. One day, we went into a nautical store to find a ship's bell for the front porch. Andrea was confused as to why we were there and we were in a hurry, so I mouthed to her quickly, without signing, "We're trying to find the bell."

Andrea went off, I found the bell, and when I got back to her, she and the cashier were hunched over in the corner, moving along the wall together. Something wasn't right, and when I asked the cashier what they were doing, she replied, "We're trying to find the smell." Andrea had misread my lips, and for the past fifteen minutes, they'd been walking around the store trying to "find the smell."

Andrea erupted in laughter and said in typical self-deprecating fashion, "I have a great nose, and there was no smell. And I have no hearing, and you bought a damn bell!" Man, I thought, you can't make this stuff up.

Yet another time, she was with my brother Ed in Quebec, following me on our bike ride to Montreal to raise funds for Andrea's foundation. Between the United States border and Montreal, there are numerous small villages where little English is spoken. At a restaurant where they stopped to get a bite to eat, a young French-speaking waitress came over, and when Andrea told her their order, she just stared at Andrea and shrugged. Andrea waited and repeated the order, again getting no response. They simply stared at each other. Finally, after the third time, Andrea turned to my brother and said, "What? Is she deaf?"

My brother was dying laughing. He told me half the restaurant (probably the half who understood English) turned and glared at them. There were several seconds of dead silence when Andrea said to my brother in a loud voice, "So do you think we're going to get breakfast or not?" They eventually got breakfast—though nothing close to what they ordered!

I, of course, was often the butt of her jokes—usually, it seemed, when I was trying to help her. She loved to take advantage of situations where I was in a tough spot and she could mess with me.

One of her favorite times to do this was in public bathrooms. When Andrea was in a wheelchair, it was difficult for her to get in and out of the ladies' room. The handicapped stalls had wide doors, and it was hard for her to reach the door to close and lock them. We developed a system where we would wait (if we could) until the restroom was empty, and I would wheel us into the stall, lock the door, and turn my back until she was finished. I stood there, hoping no other women would come in before she was done. But inevitably, other women would come and go.

When Andrea saw another woman's feet in the stall next to her, she thought it was funny to start talking to me. I would try to shush her, but she thought it was hilarious that I was trapped in a ladies' room, couldn't speak, and couldn't escape! Sometimes a woman would ask, "Is everything okay in there?" Of course, I would have to sign this to Andrea, and she would reply, "Oh, it's fine. I'm just talking to myself in here." She would then sign to me, "Be nice to me, or I'll tell them you're in here!" It gave me flashbacks to being held captive in that closet at Wheelock College all those years ago! I'm surprised I was never arrested.

When the play *The Vagina Monologues* came to Boston years ago, Andrea convinced me to come along with her and about a dozen of her friends to interpret. I'm up for just about anything, but I must admit I was apprehensive about this—and it turns out, for good reason.

The Vagina Monologues is a one woman, episodic play that explores sexual experiences, body image, reproduction, vaginal care, and prostitution, among other things, through the eyes of women of various ages, races, and sexualities.

I was the lone male in a theater of several hundred wound-up women who were all ready for a fun-filled, rowdy afternoon of interactive dialogue on every women's issue there was—from mainstream to taboo. The only thing that could possibly make their day more enjoyable was a sacrificial lamb/man to torment. Andrea thought it would be funny to serve me up for just that purpose.

I stood in front of the stage, across from Andrea, interpreting what was a highly interactive show. There was a lot of give-and-take with the audience and many impromptu jokes. Many of the sexual signs are pretty graphic in nature, and it wasn't long before the actress on stage started to pick up on some of the more obvious sex- and gender-based signs. She would walk over to me and ask me to repeat certain signs for the now rabid audience.

As I would show them the signs for penis, vagina, or masturbate, women in the audience would mimic and chant the signs. I was teaching them sexual signs, and they ate it up. It was the dirty signing version of the film *Dirty Dancing*—complete with music and movement.

In what was an obvious setup, the actress asked for a volunteer to come onstage as a prop. Andrea, caught up in the moment and thinking this would be hilarious (and it was), jumped up and yelled out, "PETER!" I tried to respectfully decline, but energized audience members were on their feet, screaming, "PETER! PETER! PETER!"

I finally gave in to my newfound fans and went onstage. Not only did the actress use my body for the physical representation of anything phallic, but I had to interpret the dialogue as I imitated a penis, a tampon, and other more tawdry devices.

Andrea and her friends were doubled over in laughter. Andrea, having pulled off the coup of a lifetime, thought the whole thing was especially funny—and to be honest with you, so did I. Once again, Andrea had managed to embarrass me, in this case, humiliate me, and somehow have me come out of it thinking it was funny.

And here's a delightful footnote: After the show, the actress came over to thank me for being such a good sport and asked if Andrea and I would consider going on the road with her. She thought the whole sign language aspect of the show that day took the play to another level. Before Andrea could even open her mouth to speak, I thanked the actress and quickly replied that, as much as we appreciated the opportunity, right now we were going to take a pass. Then I almost knocked her over as I bulled my way to the bar!

Much of Andrea's humor was on display in medical facilities, which, of course, is the last place you would expect to find humor. But Andrea was nothing if not unconventional.

After her surgeries, a team of doctors would stop by every few hours to do a quick neurologic exam to make sure the brain was resetting properly. This was often a large group of very serious doctors, residents, and interns. They would check on Andrea and ask her a series of questions. One of the questions was, "Who is the president of the United States?" She glanced quickly at me and answered, "Tim Cahill." Tim is my cousin and at the time was the Massachusetts state treasurer. The lead doctor furrowed her brow, and a murmur rippled through the group. They asked a couple of other questions and moved on. Once they were out of hearing range, Andrea smiled and said to me, "That ought to buy me an extra day of rest in the hospital, you think?" To this day, I honestly don't know if she was pulling my leg. My cousin was extremely happy with his promotion!

She had a lot of doctors—at one time more than seventeen *active* doctors. It annoyed her that every time she saw a new doctor, he or she would ask her the same questions, sometimes more than once.

Andrea decided she would play a funny (in her mind) little game with them. The first question they would often ask her was, "Why are you here?" And Andrea would gleefully kick off her own version of a medical Abbott and Costello who's-on-first comedy routine:

ANDREA. I don't know.

NEW DOCTOR. You don't know why you're here?

ANDREA. No, aren't you the doctor? Shouldn't you know why I'm here?

NEW DOCTOR. Well, I do know, but why don't you tell me?

ANDREA. If you know, why do I have to tell you? Isn't it on the computer?

NEW DOCTOR, *increasingly frustrated*. Yeah, it's on the computer, but I want to hear it from you.

ANDREA. You don't know how to use the computer?

NEW DOCTOR. I know how to use the computer, but I want to hear it from you.

ANDREA, *now looking at me*. Petes, I'm not sure we can trust this doctor if she doesn't even know why I'm here!

While Andrea's use of humor may not have seemed like a good way to start a relationship with a doctor who's trying to help her, she made it work. It was her way to deflect some of the seriousness of the situation. She used humor to mask her fears and humanize the doctor. The next time we saw that doctor, she started off the appointment with, "Good morning, Andrea, and no, I'm not going to ask you why you're here today!"

Again, she liked using me as her prop. Often, I'd rephrase a doctor's technical response to my questions in my own words to make sure I understood what they were saying. Andrea, thinking I was trying to show off my newfound knowledge, would wait patiently until I finished, quickly roll her eyes, and reply, "Don't listen to him. He doesn't know what he's talking about." Like every accomplished prankster, her timing and delivery were perfect—no small feat for a woman who couldn't hear a word.

After some of these encounters, I'd say to Andrea, "You need to be a little careful with the doctors, especially the ones we don't know. You might piss them off."

She'd look at me and unhesitatingly replied, "Screw them if they can't take a joke!"

Andrea was so in tune with humor and the positive impact it created that she would be the first one to belly laugh at a joke. Because of the communication challenges (or the fact that the joke just wasn't funny), Andrea would sometimes miss the humor or not understand the punch line. No matter what, she'd tell me after the interchange, "I had no idea what she was talking about, but I could see she thought it was funny, so I laughed anyway."

Andrea's humor, while sometimes outlandish, was quite effective. Consciously or not, her jokes almost always had a positive effect on the room. Sometimes they cut the tension; sometimes they put people at ease; other times they emphasized something positive; and often they created a more relaxed, enjoyable atmosphere that countered the craziness of our circumstances.

Within our family and circle of friends, Andrea's sense of humor (and the often-accompanying eye roll) was legendary. But even many people who had casual interactions with her would tell me that the two things that stuck in their minds were her ability to laugh and make them laugh, followed by her big, broad smile.

Humor was something we were pretty good at, and we played to our strengths. That joker card always came in handy, especially when the chips were down.

CHAPTER 14

Play Your ACES
(or When Times Get Tough,
Get Back to What You Do Best)

A ndrea had a few more aces up her sleeve. Post deafness, Andrea did a lot of things right in a drive to take back some control of her life. Losing control to NF was, along with the uncertainty, one of the most dramatic effects of the disease. Through its controlling nature, NF saps your emotional and physical strength, and plays with your mind in ways that seem designed to constantly keep you off-balance. Andrea slowly developed strategies to claw back bits and pieces of control.

One of the best things that she decided on, consciously or subconsciously, was to resume her teaching career and feed her passion for working with kids, and ultimately adults, again. Later on, she also leveraged her artistic nature and her family's creative heritage and started a business with it.

It was yet another life lesson we learned: When things are not going your way, get back to basics and double down on what you do best. It sometimes works for your golf game, it can work for getting yourself in shape, and it worked beautifully for us at this point in our personal life.

Before NF2 struck, Andrea had been an excellent and joyful teacher. Teaching was her childhood aspiration. It was her career, her passion, part of her core being.

Fast-forward to 1986, and try to imagine this young mother, living in a new town with two young babies, having not only lost her hearing but also lost something that, short of her family, was the most important thing in her life from the time she was five years old: her teaching career. I don't know about you, but that scenario probably would have been enough to push me down a deep rabbit hole of depression or maybe further into an even more destructive cycle of pain.

Fortunately, Andrea was not me. She was about to show NF that she could still leverage the traits of the young high school girl who worked over her father in order to follow her dream. In the face of what NF tried to steal from her, Andrea was determined to reimagine her ambition.

Andrea reinvented herself and used her skills to benefit herself and others. She threw herself at so many different aspects of education that it was hard to keep track of what she was doing, and with whom, on any given day or night. When it came to teaching and educating, she was a ninja; even more so, she juggled so many balls she often appeared to be a "ninja-cator":

- She started her own business, Andrea Cahill Educational Services, or ACES (prophetic of the way she tried to play her cards). It began with Andrea teaching sign language from our home or the library. She did a lot of work with the parents of autistic kids who were struggling to find a way to communicate. She worked with people who had a sibling or parent who was deaf and had never found the right avenue to learn sign language. She also worked with junior and senior high school kids who struggled with foreign languages in their college prep curriculum and decided to learn sign language to meet their language requirements.
- ACES evolved into working with parents and kids on pure educational consulting, often drawing on her special needs background to assist with reading, speech, and comprehension issues. The business model expanded further to provide tutoring in a variety of academic areas. It was a sight to behold, watching a deaf teacher tutor hearing kids and doing such a phenomenal job that the word-of-mouth advertising became so great she had to start turning away business!
- She began teaching adults sign language. This was mostly friends and family who were close to Andrea and wanted to be able to communicate better with

her. Amazingly, almost forty years later, there are still people from these groups who've maintained a fair amount of sign language vocabulary and skill.

- On Thursday nights at seven, she taught a group of her closest friends to sign as part of a regular program that she labeled "Wine and Sign." This particular offering quickly became a victim of its own success. There was always a lot of laughter, not to mention a lot of wine. The group certainly learned some sign language, but every week, I had to go up at about 11:00 p.m. to kick them out and, like a bartender at last call, tell them, "You don't have to go home, but you can't stay here!"

- She taught sign language at night school with yours truly in four different area towns as part of their continuing adult education programs. In the later years, this was her bread and butter. Andrea developed a well-designed curriculum for levels one (beginner), two (intermediate), and three (advanced). We also developed a pretty good dog and pony routine, with Andrea as the straight woman for my sign language comedy act. We kept it light, but Andrea, ever the teacher, always reined it back into focus when I got too carried away. These groups always got their money's worth—in entertainment and education. Two of our students went on to become professional interpreters. We had so much fun with all of these ventures. Andrea was the talent—she had the brains, beauty, and personality. When I was involved, I was to her what Ed McMahon was to Johnny Carson—a dependable sidekick who could do the administrative stuff, throw in a joke or two on cue, and stand in once in a while, if necessary.

- As part of her ALDA program, she worked with late-deafened adults to teach them sign language. This greatly enhanced their level of communication with one another, which led to a higher degree of socialization and stronger bonds within the group.

- She taught full-time at a variety of public and charter schools. These were probably her most challenging gigs. Andrea was used to teaching elementary school–aged kids and eventually adults. These young adults were not always as focused or invested in learning as they could have been (what did we expect? They were teenagers!). There were definitely some behavioral issues—especially when they figured out that Andrea really was profoundly deaf, and when she turned her back or looked away, they could say anything with relative impunity. Administrators weren't always as supportive as I thought they should have been.

None of the extra work she had to put in or the added difficulties and complexities mattered to Andrea. The joy of teaching transcended these issues, and she carried on in several eastern Massachusetts schools: South Shore Charter School in

Hull, South Shore Collaborative School in Hingham, Norwell Middle School, and Marshfield High School.

In addition, hundreds of elementary school kids in Hingham received their first exposure to issues resulting from a disability, as well as service dogs, through the scores of talks Andrea gave over the years. She explained not only how deafness was not a disability but how a service dog could make life easier for someone who was deaf, blind, or had other physical challenges. While the kids loved Amber, Andrea taught them that Amber was a working dog, not a pet.

She met with the same group of kids at different times during the school year to demonstrate and teach them to speak and sing songs in sign language. They delighted in "talking" with their hands, and once a year the children at our kid's elementary school would perform for the parents, ending with a signed song.

Her students wrote her letters, created ASL art, and sent glowing testimonials and recommendations to her bosses, extolling the virtues of both Andrea the teacher and Andrea the person. Through these teaching endeavors alone, Andrea touched the lives of thousands of people. We would get stopped in the supermarket, the local papers did articles on her, and even years later, it was not unusual for an old student to come over and sign, "Hi, Andrea! How are you?" to us. Talk about gratifying!

Andrea certainly raised the visibility and awareness of what it meant to live and thrive as a late-deafened woman living with all the issues that were part and parcel of fighting a serious, chronic illness. In many cases, she was the first exposure to a deaf person her students had. The fact that she could relate to her hearing charges, while profoundly deaf, was an important part of her advocacy and ability to connect.

But Andrea brought something even more special into the interaction with almost everyone she met—she handled her situation with such positivity, grace, and panache that she inspired people to think differently about how they viewed disabilities, disease, challenges, and handicaps. About what it means to overcome the obstacles life throws at you—not in the abstract but in the flesh. Many of her friends, students, and even acquaintances told me that she inspired them to look deeper inside themselves; to be better people; to see the world through a slightly different, more compassionate, and loving lens; and to be just a little bit more caring and sensitive.

As much as what she did, it was the way she did it. She was never preachy, showy, or in your face. In fact, she was nothing—except Andrea. She demonstrated by example without even knowing she was doing it. She showed us how to overcome adversity without even acknowledging that she was dealing with it. She radiated faith without needing to ever bring up her convictions, her church, or her beliefs. This innate aura is what made her so likable, approachable, and ultimately so significant to so many people.

She changed the people she touched in a fashion that is hard to describe, but in a way that was tangible and, for many, profoundly meaningful. The best analogy I can come up with is how people talk about a special relative, who, although they might not have been in close physical proximity to, or see regularly, felt their influence in a way that was memorable, deeply ingrained, and lasting. Andrea's influence was also often deep and, in many cases, inspirational. Like that special family member, she had the ability to alter your life just a little bit for the better, bring a smile to your face, and make you want to be, or do, more.

As her friend Leslie told me, "What I need to say over and over is that my life was enriched by being friends with Andrea. She taught me about resilience, courage, fighting, and ignoring the hurt others can cause, and blowing off the small stuff. Andrea's endearing traits—the ironic ability to listen, being nonjudgmental, her positivity, and her ability to focus on you and your issues (regardless of how insignificant they were compared to what she was going through)—made you want to be a better person, to reflect Andrea's attributes and character for sure, but to also put them into action in your own life. Not just what I see but what can I do. Not only acknowledging the other guy's plight but also demonstrating real empathy, choosing to be happy, making those around you happier, and living your life to the fullest." Thank you Leslie, I couldn't have said it better myself!

These are some of the things that made Andrea's star shine so bright and light up the lives of so many. But if Andrea were a star, she would be a reluctant one. To her, any glory and acclaim were not the accolades she desired. It was the personal joy she received from interacting with people and, specifically, from teaching. Pretty much teaching anything, anytime, to anyone gave her the satisfaction she craved.

Boy, did I learn a hell of a lot from this amazing woman and gifted teacher. She was an A+ in my book!

Eventually, Andrea was asked to teach at Quincy College. I know she would have been a fantastic college professor, but by then, I think even she realized she was maxed out. As the relentless debilitating impacts of NF2 accumulated over the years, this vibrant chapter of her life had to close.

But she was far from finished. She pivoted once again to her next venture, which was a real nod to her family's heritage and skills. Her grandfather came to the United States from Italy and was a wonderful artist and sculptor. Her aunt and especially her mother were talented painters. Another aunt was an accomplished seamstress.

Andrea herself was extremely creative and "crafty." At some point, as if she didn't have enough going on, she decided to start another business, aptly named Dynamic Ceramics, making mosaic picture frames and mirrors. She did research, and it didn't take her long to figure it out and develop her own unique style. She started small, trying different methods, making mistakes, and honing her skills. At first, she kept her mosaics for the house, but as she felt more confident, she began giving them out as wedding and birthday gifts to family and friends. Well, they became a hit, and Andrea threw herself into this new venture with passion and drive.

Our house quickly took on the look of a factory. She had to acquire and finish frames for the mirrors and pictures. There was a constant smell of stains and varnish. The fragments of the mosaics came from old pieces of plates, coffee cups, pottery, and whatever kind of terra-cotta she could get her hands on. Her friends learned to be careful not to serve her coffee or snacks on something colorful or bright that might catch her eye, lest she would say slyly, "How much do you really like this tea set?" We scoured secondhand shops, yard sales, and her favorite: the swap shop at the dump.

Once the materials were obtained, the cups, plates, saucers, pottery, and the like had to be smashed up into the right-sized pieces. That was a great job for relieving caregiver's stress!

Eventually, these pieces would be glued to the frame with a special goop she developed that looked like and had the texture of sand, giving many of her creations an ocean-like flavor. Over time, we had to take over one of the extra rooms in the house and create a workshop for her quickly burgeoning enterprise.

Like a flash fire, her business took off. At first, it was word of mouth; then she decided to strike up deals with local cafés and coffee shops to display and sell her pieces. Eventually, she moved up to Starbucks. It was fun for us to get a coffee and watch people ogle over her art. As the business peaked, I started to deal with buyers on the Internet.

Finally, like most of her forays, there was a point in time when she had to decide if it was a business or a hobby and whether she wanted to take the venture to the next, more professional level. Of course, in Andrea's mind, it was always a hobby because she wanted nothing to do with the business aspects of pricing, cost analysis, negotiating, or profit/loss.

In many ways, she had a simple, almost childlike approach to life and especially to business. I would always chuckle when someone asked her what I did for a living. After watching me help start and be a significant part of growing ADS consulting from scratch into a sixty-five-million-dollar business culminating in its successful IPO on the NASDAQ stock exchange, Andrea would shrug her shoulders and casually answer, "I have no idea, but I think he makes pretty good money."

Over time, she ratcheted down her mosaic business until she only did a few a year. Eventually, her fine motor skills would not allow her to function in the particular way she wanted to with this art form, and she gave it up. Another piece of collateral damage.

We still had a bunch of her pieces in the cellar, and we slowly gave them away over the years as wedding gifts, thank-you presents, and mementos. In what may have been an omen, Andrea decided just before her last Christmas to give the remaining pieces away to family and her closest friends. I could see by the looks on their faces as they opened the gift that they were touched and honored. A month later, after she passed, these beautiful works became family heirlooms.

Andrea didn't exactly reinvent herself; she simply leveraged her talents in a different environment. It gave her outlets, hope, a sense of accomplishment, and avenues to connect with people. She allowed her personality to shine and her capabilities to touch many different types of people in special ways.

By identifying her aces and playing them well, she not only excelled at the game of life, but the "house" was a winner too!

CHAPTER 15

Down but Not Out (Trust Me, Miracles Really Do Happen)

It's a fine first step to buy into the idea that life's a journey, not a destination, and Andrea and I did. But inevitably, there came a time along that journey when the burdens got heavy, testing our strength and willpower to keep going. Just when we took a look at our hand and saw not even a pair of deuces, we found an ace in the hole: our faith.

My faith grew at a snail's pace until I encountered Brother André and Saint Joseph's Oratory on Mount Royal in Montreal. I'm not sure it fits the technical ecclesiastical definition, but going up to Montreal and experiencing the beauty, peace, and story behind the oratory transformed me. You could say I was born again.

I experienced a spiritual connection with Brother André and Saint Joseph that changed the way I viewed life and the way I lived my life, and it brought me into a much deeper relationship with God. That result was pretty amazing, but how it came to be was almost surreal.

I was raised Catholic by two parents who, while they ensured we went to CCD (Confraternity of Christian Doctrine) classes and to church every Sunday, were not very involved with religion. My father stopped going to Mass when I was young. My mother came from a devout Catholic family—her brother briefly attended the seminary, and two of her cousins were Maryknoll brothers. But she went to Mass only sporadically until my father passed away when she became a more regular churchgoer.

As a Catholic kid growing up in the 1950s and 1960s, I experienced the strictness of the nuns, became an altar boy, and learned a lot about the church, the Mass, and Catholic rituals. When I was an altar boy, the Mass itself was a reflection of my relationship with the church. Before the reforms of the Second Vatican Council, which allowed priests to celebrate Mass in the local language, the priest would say the Mass in Latin, and the altar boys would read the prayers and responses off a laminated sheet. We did everything by rote, not understanding even the words, much less the meaning behind the words. I went to church out of a sense of routine, obligation, and guilt until I got out of the house, and then I slowly drifted away.

I had no real spiritual connection to anything religious, except the Bible. Ever the prodigious reader that I was, I had immersed myself in both the Old and the New Testaments by reading a well-worn Saint James Bible my grandmother had bequeathed me. Unfortunately, I read the Bible to read—not to ponder, analyze, or deepen my faith. The Old Testament was full of fascinating stories—to me, lore, if you will—of ancient mythology. While I reveled in the tales of the prophets, Moses, Jeramiah, and Job, I did so out of intellectual curiosity and not spiritual awakening. Likewise, I read the New Testament as a part of history, not from a perspective of awe and adulation for what Christ went through and endured for us. I knew a lot about God, but I didn't know Him very well, and I wasn't much like Him in my own spirit and actions.

Meeting Andrea was the first positive turn in the road toward establishing a higher level of spirituality. She had a stronger faith and a deeper bond with the church. She attended Mass every Sunday and sang in the choir. She was active in the Catholic Youth Organization, taught CCD classes, and had a firm understanding of Catholicism. Holidays such as Christmas and Easter at her house had a much greater religious orientation.

After we married and had children, we became regular church attendees, and our children received all their sacraments. I was present and paying attention, but I still wasn't getting too much out of it. After all, we were busy with work, kids, events, friends, trips, of course, NF2, and the like, which all seemed to push religion and faith to the background.

Additionally, in a strange way, Andrea's deafness was an impediment for me. Because I had to interpret the Mass, often-times from the pulpit, I needed to focus on the ASL inter-pretation of the service. Much of the Mass was the same each

Sunday, but the Bible readings, including the gospel, the music, and the homily all required weekly study and attention. In my zeal to ensure Andrea understood the liturgy, it diminished my connection. I was paying more attention to her comprehension and less about what the Mass meant to me.

It was also draining. The Catholic Mass runs on average for about an hour. ASL professional interpreters usually work twenty minutes on and twenty minutes off. Interpreting is hard work, the idea being not to interpret what is being said word for word but to transmit the *meaning* of the words in a manner that the receiving party can understand. After interpreting music, biblical passages, prayers, and sometimes long-winded priests, I was less about reflecting on the service and more than ready to take a nap.

Fortunately, I had a small group of friends—my own personal "God squad," if you will—who never allowed the flickering embers of my faith to die out. This group, John, Charlie, and Al, constantly helped me put my NF world into a faith-based context. Our small-text chain was almost literally a lifeline for me in my darkest hours of despair. These guys would encourage me, provide me with relevant biblical passages, remind me of Jesus's suffering, and emphasize the context of what I was experiencing with the greater picture of Christ, the Holy Spirit, and the promise of heaven and eternal salvation.

We read Bible passages daily (especially my favorites from the *Notre Dame Press*), discussed worldly events, and kept each other grounded in times of despair. We prayed for the sick, the marginalized, one another, and those close to us who had gone before us. Together, we celebrated, mourned, cajoled, and especially prayed. This group was my rock, and as my faith deepened, I hope I was able to provide them some solace from my own fortified spiritual beliefs, which would be enhanced dramatically through our next medical trauma.

In the early 2000s, Andrea was going through a particularly tough cycle, and with the encouragement of her neurologist, we decided to try to avoid yet another brain surgery by using radiation to shrink her tumors. It was a disaster.

For radiation treatments, Andrea was placed on a flat bed with a metal halo tightened around her skull, holding her head perfectly still. The machine ran over the targeted area and transmitted a beam of strong radiation directly to the tumors based on coordinates derived from her MRI. The beam passed through her skull, aiming to destroy any abnormal cells in its path. There is no feeling, sensation, or pain. Andrea had stereotactic radiation, which even more precisely directs the beam to its mark.

That was the summer we went to MGH four days a week for six weeks. We left the house around 5:30 a.m. for a 7:30 a.m. treatment. The treatment itself took twenty minutes. It seemed to me that it took longer to get her head situated and locked in place than it did to "beam" her. The radiation room was cold and metallic, offset only by the warmth of the technicians, whose caring and support helped make the process tolerable. Andrea was back home by around 10:30 a.m.

When Andrea started the radiation therapy, she was invalid-level sick. She was mostly in a wheelchair, had blurry and sometimes double vision, and didn't make a lot of sense when she spoke. The radiation added a host of side effects on top of that condition. Much like the chemotherapy side effects that she would have to deal with later in her life, she was crushed with additional severe fatigue, headaches, and hair loss, along with the usual trio of nausea, vomiting, and diarrhea.

Because it was a ninety-minute ride each way, it quite literally became hell on wheels, with our driver often having to pull off the road so that Andrea could lean out the side of the car and get sick. When she finally arrived home, she was wiped out for the rest of the day. On Friday, Saturday, and Sunday, she would work to build back some strength and keep down some food so she could be ready for the next round on Monday. Like a staggered boxer, her only goal was to get through the round, "freshen up," and get back in the ring. Each week was more debilitating than the one before.

When the treatment was mercifully finished, she went hopefully back in for another MRI to assess the impact of the radiation and prayed it was worth it. The answer came back, and it was a stunning disappointment. The radiation had zero, nada, nil effect on her tumors. It was hard for us to fathom that she could go through this procedure and not get even the smallest benefit. These were truly times that tried our souls.

Even more disheartening was that she was in worse shape than when she started. It's hard to describe how bone-weary the radiation made her. Every action she took required a dispro-portionate amount of energy, and her energy level was totally depleted. To get her on and off the toilet or in and out of bed was like moving a hundred-twenty-pound sack of flour—dead-weight. She was too tired to eat, talk, or even get frustrated or pissed off. She would tell me, "I'm not tired. I'm so far beyond tired. I can't even see tired." She existed in a state of being, not living.

Andrea was quite sick when she started, sicker during the treatments, and unrecognizable when she finished. Other than that, Mrs. Lincoln, how was the play?

Her tumors were continuing to grow into an intertwined mass, making it difficult for the surgeons to even determine which tumors were creating which problems. She was physically compromised and frail, now fully relegated to a wheelchair, and her vision problems became so bad she kept her eyes closed most of the time. She was also having more trouble talking, and when she did, much of the time it was nonsense. Sometimes the sentences came out backward; if it wasn't so damn heartbreak-ing, it would have been fascinating. She was unable to function without constant support. Even on our bad side of the coin, this was extreme, truly one hot mess.

Slowly, the side effects of radiation began to wane, and she began to migrate back to her invalid level—pre-radiation stage. While that was still really bad, we figured we always had surgery as a fallback position. It wasn't a great plan B, but it was all we had. Of course, in the torturous world of NF2, any bad situation can always jump to worse. We soon found out that one of the side effects of the radiation went far beyond just making her sick. She was now at far greater risk for any brain operation.

Against this backdrop of deep melancholy—if there was ever a time when we jaded, discouraged, and resigned to our fate, this was our lowest point—we met with Andrea's neurologist, thinking we were going to come up with a plan, an approach to bring Andrea back to life. Instead, we received a figurative, coldhearted, open-hand slap in the face. The radiation hadn't worked, and in fact, rather than shrinking any of the tumors, it had shrunk some of the blood vessels in her brain, further complicating a surgical approach and increasing the already significant downside. In this doctor's opinion, surgery had now become too risky. There were no other new options or technologies available to us or on the horizon. She saved the biggest bombshell for last, telling us that there was really "no hope at this time" for Andrea and her situation.

We were stunned, frozen in her cramped office, and unable to respond because we were incapable of processing what she'd just told us. No hope? We'd been led to believe that, while there was no cure for NF, the disease would be manageable for many years, and with the resources at MGH, some support and accommodations, and hard work, Andrea would be able to have a life worth living. NF has an average diminished impact on the life expectancy of those with the disease of about eleven years, but we hoped that Andrea's good genes might offset that—many family members lived well into their nineties, and her mother had lived to the ripe old age of eighty-nine. Now we were being told there was no hope, at age forty-six. Shell-shocked, we departed the hospital in a daze—once again left on our own to digest, debate, and make sense of this latest sinkhole.

I felt like we were free-falling. It was our WTF, is-there-a-God, maybe-it's-time-to-throw-in-the-towel moment. We were dispirited, weary, and depressed. It occurred to me that maybe all our bravado about fighting/beating NF was nothing more than that, bravado—childish gibberish, fool's gold, or a pipe dream fantasy.

We met with her surgeon Dr. Barker, and although he was not as definitive as her neurologist (and nowhere near as insensitive as her), he did explain to us that he considered any surgery at this point extremely high risk. Too many tumors were too close together, and too many areas of her brain were being affected. He was willing to consider surgery, but he certainly wasn't champing at the bit to move forward.

Dr. OJ and Dr. Barker had always evaluated Andrea's situation through a risk/reward lens. In this case, they not only thought the risk likely outweighed the reward, but he couldn't even come up with a viable strategy regarding what tumors to attack and what impact removing some of the tumors might have. They were weighing Andrea's current situation against the most basic of medical ethos: "First, do no harm." From our perspective, we were beginning to think, *how much more harm could be done?* It was that bad.

I'm not sure how or why Saint Joseph's Oratory popped into my mind. In retrospect, I would chalk it up to divine intervention. Andrea and I had both been to Montreal, separately and together. Our trips together had been purely for pleasure. We went to the Montreal exposition, hung out in the Old Town, took in a ballgame, and visited the Molson Brewery, the Casino de Montréal, and other attractions.

But on one of my jaunts north many years earlier, I remembered that my buddy and I ended up in this huge church with an enormous dome. More specifically, I remembered seeing dozens of crutches and canes on the walls—implements that infirmed people had used to get into the church but discarded after being cured. Andrea then remembered it too. She had been there as a teenager with her parents. She even recalled the name of the church: Saint Joseph's Oratory.

What were the odds that I would pass through this holy site on a party trip and recall it twenty-five years later? More so, how crazy was it that Andrea, in a wheelchair, barely able to remember her own name, would not only remember being there but was able to come up with the name of the place? But it seemed that whenever our human capabilities fell short, God would reach across that chasm to help us find a path.

We took this revelation as a sign, did some research, found someone to watch the dog, and "jumped" in the car to head for Montreal and check out the oratory. It was a longshot, but at that particular moment, we were grasping for any type of direction and hope. At that point, we realized we didn't hold even one strong card in this hand that had been dealt to us.

It turned out to be the best thing we ever did. We drove the six-hour trip mostly in silent thought, amid a sense of gnawing apprehension and sorrow. Once again, we were hoping for the best, but we'd been ground down by bad news, Andrea's declining health, and the seeming inevitability that NF2 was about to finish off what it had started almost fifteen years earlier.

Cue the angels and the organ music! The entire mystical experience was far beyond anything we expected, imagined, or ever encountered. The oratory itself is physically imposing, situated atop Mount Royal, overlooking both the city of Montreal and the seemingly endless plains stretching out beyond the city as far as the eye can see. It's the tallest church in Canada and one of the largest domed structures in the world.

The church was built as a tribute to Saint Joseph by Brother André. André's life story is extraordinary and well worth reading about. Born Alfred Bessette on August 8, 1845, one of ten children in an indigent family in Quebec, he was so frail that he was baptized conditionally at birth in case he died. He was orphaned at age twelve and couldn't read or write, but after wandering through New England for several years as a laborer, he entered a novitiate and became a priest.

He first served as a porter at the Collège Notre-Dame in Côte-des-Neiges, Montreal. Across from the college was an empty, rocky lot, and Brother André's dream was to build an oratory there as a tribute to Saint Joseph, his spiritual hero. This diminutive, unassuming man of the cloth did just that and so much more.

Whatever journey you're on, Saint Joseph is known as a good companion to walk alongside you, and that was certainly the case for Brother André. As the building took shape, Brother André began to perform miracles in the name of Saint Joseph. The crippled and the lame walked again, the sick recovered, and demons were driven from the afflicted. Although he earned the moniker of "the Miracle Man of Montreal," when the sick would come to him for healing, he would point to Saint Joseph and say, "Go to Joseph." Through his sheer will and devotion, he built the greatest church in Canada, helped thousands of sick people get better, and became an internationally famous cleric. He passed away in 1937 and was elevated to sainthood in 2011.

Despite his fame, he remained eminently humble, often seeming confused that people would lavish such praise on him. Brother André often described himself as "St. Joseph's little dog," attributing all favors to the intercession of the great "Guardian of Jesus." To him, it seemed obvious that the source of his spiritual power was Saint Joseph. He saw himself simply as a vessel. From our position, as a bonus, it certainly wasn't lost on us that the name André is the male form of Andrea.

When we arrived at the oratory, it took us a while to get acclimated among the multitude of crypts, churches, displays, gift shops, and spiritual sanctuaries. We went to Mass (in French, but no matter), found the wall of crutches I'd remembered, lit intention candles, learned more about the man who conceived and built the complex, and met with a priest for a blessing. We visited Brother André's very humble abode on the edge of the oratory and marveled at his faith and devotion to Saint Joseph. The tiny, Spartan, one-room living space, situated above a small chapel in the shadow of the oratory, stood in stark contrast to the enormous, splendid, opulent monument to Saint Joseph. Brother André's room consisted of a bed, a night table, a sink and commode, and a small hotplate for cooking. It was adorned only with a cross on the wall and a Bible on the table. If the oratory was a tribute to Saint Joseph's magnificence, this room was a reflection of the faith, humbleness, and spirituality of Brother André.

Finally, we made our way up to the basilica, and it took away our breath. The Italian Renaissance-inspired design, the massive dome (over five hundred feet above street level), and a marble altar framed with long sheets of red fabric hanging from the ceiling combined to create an unearthly, holy structure. The centerpiece of this majestic setting was an enormous crucifix hanging from the apex of the ceiling and hovering, almost mystically, over the altar.

We spent a long time praying in the basilica. Pilgrims, attendants, and tour groups came and went. But for us, it felt as if time was suspended. Despite the loud echoes from the believers and the tourists, I was enveloped, along with Andrea, in a complete sense of spiritual silence. Andrea and I were comfortably alone with our thoughts in this giant building—finally at peace, with each other and with God. For me, all the anxiety

I'd been holding in drained out of my body to the point where I felt limp and light-headed. While I never received a definitive answer to my prayers regarding Andrea's future, I was filled with complete certainty that, regardless of what decision we made or where this disease took us, God had our back.

We had intended to go out to dinner that night, but by the time we arrived back at the hotel, we were physically and emotionally exhausted. We agreed that while we weren't sure exactly what happened at the oratory that day, something very powerful and special had occurred. I slept that night like I hadn't in a long, long time.

Andrea woke up the following morning and said to me immediately, "I want to have the operation." I had the same feeling but was glad to hear her say it first. My mind flashed back to our decision to have Peter years ago when Andrea awoke early that chilly New Hampshire morning and said out loud, "I want to have the baby." Could we expect God to grace us with a second miracle?

We went back to the oratory and thanked everyone we could find—the priest who blessed us, Brother André, Saint Joseph, and even the woman at the gift shop—for allowing the word of God to penetrate our human defenses.

That night, we went to Le Keg, our favorite steakhouse in Old Montreal, and celebrated. Our French waitress must have thought we'd completely lost our minds when, after we opened our second bottle of wine, she asked us why we were rejoicing. Andrea, from her wheelchair, gave her a crooked, drunken smile and shouted out, "I'm having brain surgery!" The waitress, clearly confused, smiled politely and scurried off. I'm pretty sure it was a first for her. Celebrate a baby, a birthday, or a new job, for sure, but brain surgery? *Fous Americanins!* (Loosely translated: "Those crazy Americans!")

For all the good feelings and spirituality generated by our pilgrimage to Saint Joseph's, Andrea still had to go through a dicey, high-risk, and complicated surgery. The surgeon came on board, and we proceeded to surgery against the vocal protests of Andrea's neurologist. She didn't like it, and we didn't care. It would be the last time we spoke with her; we canceled her as our neurologist, and not too long after the surgery, she left the hospital.

This was, by far and away, Andrea's toughest challenge to date. While I might have described her bravery as a combination of courage and denial, there was no denying her courage as we sat in the pre-op meeting. Even in her diminished state, I could see the worry in her eyes as we reviewed the procedure and especially the risks, which included loss of functions such as walking, talking, and seeing, facial and more expanded paralysis, seizure, stroke, and death.

Clutching the small statue of Brother André that we'd brought back from Montreal, Andrea faced her choice and fears head-on, signing off on the surgery, risks, and potential consequences. We were at the point of no return, with only our surgeon and God to protect us.

The operation itself was an exercise in endurance for Drs. OJ and Fred Barker, who tag-teamed as co-surgeons. Since they had no clear or defined targets, their general plan was to weave their way through the mass of tumors, avoiding blood vessels, arteries, brain matter, and the like, and extract as much as they could. The goal, and our hope, was that they would somehow be able to remove enough of the tumors that were causing Andrea's problems to improve her quality of life—without hitting something that could further degrade her capabilities, or worse.

The surgery lasted for fourteen hours. By now, I had adopted a well-worn surgery-day routine, but this time felt different. More than ever before was at stake, but I felt confident we had the necessary support from Brother André. As I prayed in the small, beautiful chapel in the hospital, I didn't ask for a successful outcome this time—just to be able to accept God's will. I felt a curious inner peace that gave me hope and comfort.

In the surgery waiting room, I received periodic short but positive/neutral messages from the operating room throughout the day: "We're getting what we can." "No surprises." "No show-stoppers." As the day dragged on, some of our family joined me in the waiting area.

By 8:30 p.m., we were the only group remaining when an exhausted-looking Dr. Barker appeared in the doorway with the first piece of good news: Andrea had survived the operation and was being wheeled down to the neuro-recovery room. As for the degree of success, he wouldn't speculate beyond "We got a lot of tumors out of there." He looked relieved, and off we went to the surgery recovery room where our faith would be tested one more time.

Andrea arrived in recovery pretty drugged and tubed up—more than I'd ever seen before. It was evident by the brigade of doctors and nurses accompanying her that this was a big deal. As they got Andrea situated, we basically stayed out of the way. I knew it was going to be at least half an hour or more before Andrea would wake up enough to even recognize me.

At some point, I realized I'd forgotten my leather jacket down in the waiting area. My sister-in-law Rosemary was there, and she was a solid signer, and I'd only be gone for ten minutes, so I rushed down to retrieve it before they closed for the night. I was lucky to grab it just as they were locking the door. I scooted back to the elevator and up to the floor where Andrea was being tended to.

As I reentered the recovery room area, I saw a swarm of nurses running into one of the rooms and my in-laws being pushed into the hallway. I heard, "Stat, Bay 17," being repeated over and over on the intercom. It took me a few seconds to connect the dots and realize that they were talking about Andrea! Are you kidding me? After all she had been through and having survived the operation, she was going to die while I went to fetch my jacket? As I bolted down the hallway and arrived at her bay, there were plenty of loud commands, clamoring, and tension, but there was no doubt in my mind that we were in the right place, surrounded by the right people, in our moment of extreme need.

She was having a seizure. Shit! That was one of the potential risks we signed off on yesterday. All hell had broken loose in a matter of seconds. Medical personal enveloped Andrea's gurney and swept in and out past us like we didn't exist.

The nurses and doctors moved into action like a well-oiled machine. Although the curtain was mostly drawn, through the opening, I could see pumps, paddles, computer screens, and needles being utilized simultaneously—an uber-high level of urgency, but absolutely no panic. It was like watching an Olympic synchronized swimming team through the lens of time-lapse photography. While the crisis only lasted for a couple of minutes, it reminded me of Gordon Lightfoot's ballad "The Wreck of the *Edmund Fitzgerald,*" when he sings, "Does anyone know where the love of God goes when the waves turn the minutes to hours." If NF turned those couple of minutes into hours, it was God Who reset the clock.

Then it was over—as fast as it began. She was back. Her vital signs began to recover slowly. The crazed beeping became more rhythmic. The pace of the attendants slowed down. She was out of danger. She'd been to the brink and back in a matter of minutes. It was breathtaking and frightening. It was also an incredible display of professionalism and skill by the MGH staff that left us shaking and in awe. As we hugged each other, I remember thinking to myself, *and she'll never remember anything that happened here tonight.* Yet another reason to thank God.

This episode was Andrea's greatest Houdini act. It was a long road back, but she slowly recovered her strength, and to all of our amazement, she got herself back almost to where she was before this round of tumors blossomed. She no longer needed a wheelchair, her eyesight improved, and her mental faculties returned. I knew she was all the way back when her trademark humor and biting comments to me reemerged!

At our follow-up meeting with the doctors, they had no explanation for how things that were so bad turned out so good. It was both refreshing and disturbing to hear one of the attending surgeons tell us, "We have no idea what we did to create such a positive outcome." Even the follow-up MRIs didn't show enough tumor retraction to explain Andrea's amazing transformation.

Of course, *we* knew exactly what happened. We'd become entrenched in the belief that Brother André had intervened and not only literally saved Andrea's life but also gave us her life back. We made sure that when Andrea was strong enough, we went back to Saint Joseph's yearly and later testified to this miracle as part of Brother André's canonization process. In 2011, much to our delight, Frere (Brother) André was canonized and became Saint André.

You gotta have faith, right? Of course, faith alone didn't bring Andrea back to her old self. She once again put in a tremendous amount of hard work to get there. It was, however, faith that provided her the opportunity to work her way back and the motivation to get there.

For me, my spiritual transformation was complete. There is no doubt in my mind that our journey to Montreal changed the trajectory of Andrea's sickness and the direction of my life. As we testified, to us, this was a clear sign, a miracle that God wanted Andrea to remain on this earth for reasons we still didn't fully appreciate. At least in the immediate term, we decided we could do good by being good, by professing our faith, and by giving God control over our lives. Our focus would be on living a life of joy, giving, and gratefulness.

This altered perspective is what allowed me to stop worrying about money, bigger houses, and shiny toys. I wanted to be more like Brother André and live a simpler life. While I've tried and am still trying to do that, what my deepened faith ultimately gave me was a better relationship with Andrea and, as a result, a better life. I became more patient, tolerant, and caring. I slowed down and began to, in Andrea's words, "enjoy the journey." Fewer things bothered me, and I was happier. I stopped counting everything. Andrea prodded me with a wall hanging that proclaimed, "Everything you can count doesn't necessarily count, and you can't count everything that counts."

Most importantly, I came to believe with absolute certainty that God has a plan for all of us, and what Andrea was going through was a part of that plan. God's plan doesn't mean that everything is going to work out right in this life, where suffering, pain, agony, and death are a given. Nothing that Jesus didn't endure on the cross for us. Rather, to me, it means that *ultimately* all is going to be all right—there is eternal peace and salvation for those who find the way. That our earthly existence is a small part of the plan, paling when measured against eternity. Jesus never promised that our journey on earth would be easy; he did, however, promise it would be worth it! Our faith is what allowed us to cope with the ever-dominating NF. It has helped me immeasurably in dealing with Andrea's passing.

I happen to be a devout Catholic, but it seems to me that God's love and grace transcends any specific religion and that, when you boil it down, most religions believe in a higher power, encourage goodness, and promote love as the greatest of virtues. Believe me, I'm no saint or Holy Roller—far from it—a recovering sinner at best, but because I have faith in God's plan, I'm at peace with what happened to Andrea and me. I still believe in hard work, strong relationships, and good luck. The difference is that now I see them encapsulated within this concept of fate, which, in my mind, is under the direction of a higher power who sees all, knows all, and ultimately judges all. My focus here on earth has become to be more like Brother André, with the hope that I end up in the right line at the checkout counter on Judgment Day.

One final footnote: While we were in Montreal testifying on Brother André's behalf, we also went back to Le Keg for a double celebration. We found the same waitress who we thought we spooked all those months ago and tried to explain to her that the surgery had gone very well. She looked bewildered, and we thought perhaps she didn't even recognize the new and improved Andrea. As we sat down to dinner, we assumed the language barrier was just too great. At that moment, a complimentary bottle of champagne arrived at our table, and our new friend was smiling and waving to us from across the room.

Fous François! Crazy French!

Montreal was good. The doctors at MGH were extraordinary. Brother André is our spiritual mentor forever, and God is great!

CHAPTER 16

Stuck in a Lion's Den? Then Fight Like a Gladiator

We had just gone through Andrea's toughest surgery to date and experienced our spiritual awakening at Saint Joseph's Oratory. But despite these monumental successes, a feeling kept rattling in our hearts and minds: There had to be more to life than surgery, recovery, preparation for the next surgery, surgery, rinse, and repeat. We were desperately searching for a way to make sense of the questions, "Why Andrea?" "Why is this happening to us?" and "What, if anything, can we do?"

That line of thinking evolved into "Why NF," and what can we do to make a difference for those suffering from this disease?

One warm June day, we walked down to the end of our street to watch a charity bike ride for Best Buddies, an organization that provides support services for individuals with intellectual and developmental disabilities. The riders flew by us. As they waved to the cheering crowd, there was a sense of exhilaration in each pedal and purpose in their eyes—as there should have been: They were working hard to raise money for a great cause. For whatever reason, the positivity and obvious camaraderie were glued into my mind. The following week, I read a newspaper article that covered the ride. It was a pretty straightforward piece, but one fact that I hadn't fully processed caught my eye: The ride had raised a boatload of money! At that moment, it dawned on me that this was the salve we'd been desperately searching for. This was a way to address our sense of emptiness and helplessness: raising money to help find a cure for NF2.

We were almost instantly energized. We sat down with Dr. OJ who strongly encouraged us to develop a game plan. He connected us with fundraisers at the hospital who explained to us that undertaking big research projects relied on government grants. But to get access to those grants, scientists at funding agencies had to see enough preliminary research that showed promising evidence of progress toward the causes and cures for the applicable diseases. We learned that fundraisers worked on a 1:10 ratio model: Every dollar of privately raised funds could leverage up to ten dollars of grant money. This insight into the medical fundraising game was educational and exciting to us. Within this model, even small fundraisers had the potential to generate large sums of money for research.

We then met with MGH researchers who were studying NF, and they filled us in on some of the impressive efforts they were working on to help find a cure. They opened our eyes to the fact that while we were naively looking at raising money for a capital-*C* Cure, the researchers knew that it was a painstakingly slow process, marked by some successes encapsulated within many failures. This lowercase-*c* cure process, while frustrating, still produced incremental progress that often translated into improved quality-of-life results for those fighting NF while moving the ball forward. We were impressed with their commitment and perseverance in playing the long game.

Against this backdrop, and in Andrea's honor, Andrea and I created the "Andrea Cahill Foundation (ACF) for Neurofibromatosis 2 Research at Massachusetts General Hospital" for the explicit purpose of providing the NF clinic at MGH with funding for NF2 research. Of course, we had no idea what we were getting into, but when had that ever stopped us before?

Setting up and managing a charity foundation proved to be a multifaceted juggling act. There were definitely times when we thought we might have bitten off more than we could chew, but we leaned on our determination, the support of our family, our hatred of NF2, and our faith, and with unwavering assistance from MGH, we jumped into the deep end of the pool and started figuring how this fundraising thing worked.

Fortunately, MGH guided us through the real pain-in-the-ass part of our fundraising effort: the administrative requirements. We glommed on to MGH's 501(C)(3) charity status, which saved us enormous amounts of time, aggravation, and money. All of the donations, tax accounting, reporting, and questions were managed by the hospital. Two representatives in MGH's fundraising office were assigned to us, Keith and Sarah, and they've been and continue to be phenomenal (dare I indispensable). They helped us set up a website that I customized with our message and photos to give it a real feel for what we and the charity were all about. The website managed the processing and tracking of donations, handling transactions by checks, credit/debit cards, and occasionally cash. (In recent years, we followed in the footsteps of our grandsons, ages eleven, nine, and six, who were taking Venmo payments at their summer lemonade stand to raise money!)

Then we brainstormed around the fundraising event. We had promised Brother André we would visit the oratory every year to give thanks, so why not combine our spiritual and fundraising aspirations? For our fledgling charity event, I would make the 335-mile trip over four days from Mass General Hospital to Montreal/Saint Joseph's Oratory by bicycle. Including Brother André in our effort gave us just a little more confidence and a ton of motivation that we could make it happen. And it happened. In 2022, we completed our eleventh bike ride for the ACF.

Before the first ride in 2002, Natalie and I drove the back roads of Massachusetts, New Hampshire, Vermont, and Quebec during her spring break from college to scope out the most suitable route. We had a great time going up and down country roads, occasionally coming to a dead end in the middle of nowhere, seeing old farms and barns, stopping at funky shops and pubs, and taking in the majesty of the Green Mountains. Naturally, we viewed the excursion from very different perspectives. She'd say, "These mountains are so beautiful." I'd think, *Holy crap, look at that incline!* She'd say, "Look at those cute shops," and I'd note, *Looks like a good spot to take a pee.* She enjoyed the winding roads that seemed to go on forever, while I thought about how sore my butt was going to be by the time I got to this spot.

Next came the crucial part—actually raising the money. I'd been selling in the business world for two decades, and if I learned anything, it was that the hardest part of any sale is "the ask." This is where the rubber meets the road. Asking people to part with their money takes some getting used to—even if you know it's for a worthy reason. I've read that 64% of all sales *professionals* have a difficult time asking for business (Action Selling, May 2018 – issue 168). A lot has to do with how much you believe in your product or service, your relationship with the buyers, and your organization's ability to deliver on your promises. Of course in this situation none of this was going to be a problem for me.

Andrea immediately distanced herself from the fundraising. She didn't like to ask for money, and she didn't like to draw attention to herself. I, on the other hand, embraced the role of CFO (chief fundraising officer). In addition to my day job, I'd also worked extensively in the fundraising role for my cousin Tim when he ran for local, county, and state offices. Fundraising for the ACF was easy for me because I not only believed wholeheartedly in the goal, but I was also dealing with people I knew and who cared about Andrea.

In the beginning, we were decidedly old-school. We sat around the kitchen table and came up with a list of family and friends who we hoped would be interested in our cause. We designed a flyer to mail out (yes, snail mail!), explaining what we were doing and asking them to donate. The first couple of times, we threw a party and put a basket on the buffet table, so people could toss their checks in on their way to grab a sandwich or a beer.

Of course, we had fun with the events. At our first fundraising party, one of our friends showed up in full traditional Scottish garb, including a kilt. He took it upon himself to harass the partygoers into making larger donations—threatening to "show more leg" if they *didn't* cough up what he considered a suitable contribution! We found that more margaritas could drive more/larger contributions—we moved up quickly to serving from a pitcher. We also learned that when people care, they *want* to be a part of something they feel is special.

Fundraising, like so many aspects of life, comes back to relationships. If you've built strong relationships in your personal and professional lives, fundraising can be a piece of cake. If you haven't, it's probably too late in the game to come knocking on the door and asking people to donate to your charity. There are a gazillion charities out there, and many people are locked into ones for personal reasons. When you run a small, personalized foundation, people have to want to give to *you,* even more than the institution or the cause. Of course, even as reluctant a poster child for the ACF and NF2 that she was, Andrea elicited tremendous love and affection for our cause.

As CFO for ACF, my job was to identify as many people as possible who might donate and then craft and distribute the right message across the diverse, ever-expanding media channels of newspapers, emails, websites, and social media. It takes thought and finesse to gently remind potential donors, without being annoying, that you're still out there and that the fundraising clock is ticking down.

Enmeshed in the fundraising effort was training for the ride itself. For me, this meant two things; first, staying in reasonable shape all year long by eating right, exercising, and doing most things in moderation most of the time. While my athletic career was generally undistinguished, I was always a gym rat and *considered* myself an athlete. It's more of a state of mind than a résumé. That mindset kept me in pretty good shape and gave me a good physical base level for more strenuous training. Second was the high-intensity training necessary to prepare your body to be abused far beyond its normal limits.

To undertake a marathon ride (approximately eighty-five miles per day for four days), there is no way to avoid long hours pumping on the bike. I start in earnest about six weeks before the event—too early, and I'd peak too soon or burn out; too late, and I wouldn't be prepared. I have two bikes: For the first month, I use a sturdy, heavy, hybrid bike; for the last two weeks, I switch over to my sleek, French-made road bike. I can pick this bike up with one finger. The tires are so skinny they look like strands of spaghetti. Most importantly, it flies—especially after training on the heavier bike. My best day of training is always the day I switch over to bikes for the duration.

As with any longer-term training effort, at some point, the exercise becomes more mental than physical. Spending up to four to five hours a day on a bike as the training evolves becomes routine and tedious. The hardest part is making a schedule and sticking to it. It's a lot easier to convince yourself to do almost anything rather than hop on a bike day after day, especially when it's cold and raw, beat yourself up physically for a good part of your day, and end up sore and tired. But once you get over that mental obstacle and actually get on the bike, every ride is an adventure.

Along with these challenges and mind games come plenty of physical troubles. Working up to two hundred miles a week on the bike, along with plenty of hill work, doesn't come without strains, stiffness, and aches and pains. I've been lucky to have been cycling "professionally" for all these years without sustaining any serious injuries. Many thanks go out to my chiropractor. Father time, of course, is my biggest enemy. Every year, the aches get a little deeper, the mountains seem a little higher, and the recovery time a bit longer. The overused cliché, "No pain, no gain," is still one of my best motivators.

Given all of the energy and time we put in to get to the starting gate, the rides themselves should seem like an emotional release, almost anticlimactic. But they aren't. At this point, I am literally oozing with energy and adrenaline. Like a caged beast ready to be released back into the wild, I'm bursting to get on the bike and out of the starting blocks.

For each ride, we put together a support crew who would meet me each night and be available during the day if I had a problem. Over the years, this group always included Andrea and my sister Chris (who did most of the driving), as well as Andrea's mom, our kids, my brother Ed, and others who jumped in on different rides to help when necessary.

For the most part, this worked out well. There was one time I lost my cell phone in the mountains of Vermont. Without any way to communicate, I had no choice but to keep pedaling and hope the team would see me by driving up and down the route. But Andrea was hungry and sick of being in the car, so they went to a pub near the end of the route for a burger and a beer. I was lucky I saw the car in the parking lot on the way by! And perhaps only in Vermont would the person who found my cell-phone be nice enough to track me down and mail it back to me.

Initially, we stayed in low-budget motels to keep the costs down. At the end of one particularly long day, I came up to the motel to see Andrea, her mother, and the kids standing in front of a ramshackle building. They informed me they'd been in the room, and it was great—except for the cockroaches, bedbugs, and rusty water. The owner refused to give us a refund until I got the board of health in this tiny town on the phone. He quickly changed his mind, and we found more suitable accommodations not far up the road. When that owner heard our story, he gave us a room for free. On another ride, a postal worker offered to drive me, in a driving rainstorm, twenty miles out of his way to the next dry spot—a small restaurant that he swore I'd never find (I eventually did, and they took pity on my saturated state and gave me a free meal and wrung out some of my wet clothes in the kitchen!).

I met so many wonderful people on the road. After each ride, I'd reflect on all of the amazing people I'd encountered on the way—some who helped me, some who offered encouragement, and others who were simply welcoming. These interactions always renewed my confidence in the goodness of man- and womankind.

Training for hours, I'd allow my mind to drift off into the much pursued "riders' high" where I could cover many miles without realizing I'd even been pedaling. Often, with my head free and clear, I'd come up with brilliant and creative ideas, and things I could do to be better to improve the foundation. But unfortunately, at my age, these earthshattering cerebral revelations were often lost in space by the time I finished the ride (on occasion, I'd pull a pad and pen from my backpack and jot down notes while riding hands-free—not recommended or smart!). On many rides, the scenery, especially along the ocean, was breathtaking. I'd often be able to focus on things I'd normally miss: beautiful wildflowers, an osprey with its prey dangling from its beak, and awe-inspiring sunrises and sunsets. What I was always left with as I dismounted at the end of my ride, imprinted in my brain, was the stunning beauty of nature and the greatness of God's artistry on His canvas—the sky, the ocean, and all the earth.

In addition to this contentment and serenity, I've encountered a host of humorous and sometimes downright scary situations. As all seasoned cyclists know, it's wise not to get lulled into a false sense of security. A pilot friend of mine told me that for him, a cross-country flight consists of six hours of boredom bracketed on each end with fifteen minutes of potential terror. A long bike ride along various types of roads and byways has a similar texture: protracted periods of tranquility punctuated with brief and sudden life-threatening incidents. At various times, like any cyclist, I have had to deal with cars, idiots in these cars, potholes, small animals, other bikers, glare from the sun, weather conditions, getting lost, and other human-made and natural hazards, including my greatest natural peril: sand.

Cape Cod, where I live and train, is literally a big pile of sand dropped into the ocean. That sand forms our beautiful beaches and connects the Cape with our most desirable asset, the cool, clear Atlantic Ocean. Sand looks so passive, romantic, and beachy, but it can wipe out even the most experienced rider in a nanosecond. Hit a patch of sand at the wrong angle, or when you're accelerating or coming to a sudden stop, and you could be going down hard. I've had many near disasters, but the two times I've actually taken a dive have both been sand related. Both times, I bounced my head hard off the pavement. Other than a minor concussion and a lot of cuts and bruises, I was fine. But I feel compelled to offer this biking safety public service announcement: Respect nature's impediments—wind, rain, and sand—and always wear a helmet. Disaster on a bike happens fast—done before you realize it's happened. If you ride enough, you're familiar with the far too many "ghost" bikes that punctuate the landscape—memorials to bikers who were killed while riding. Whether they represent seasoned pros or casual day-trippers, these memorials serve as a stark reminder of the inherent dangers that are lurking every time anyone jumps on a bicycle.

Many a biker has taken a tumble over the handlebars as a result of a chipmunk or squirrel lodged in their spokes; it's bad for the cyclist and rarely ever ends well for the animal. Potholes, rain, and bad judgment, such as cutting across traffic or going too fast, are constant hazards. But by far the most serious and lethal aspect of biking is—you probably already guessed it—human beings. There is something about a bike moving on the side of the road—it matters little if there's a bike lane, a wide road, or a sign that pleads, "Share the road with bikes"—that brings out a primal rage from some drivers and their passengers.

I've been yelled at, spit on, had objects tossed at me, and had drivers try to run me off the road. One guy looped around and came back for a second try! Some wild-eyed teens took a swipe at me with a small bat. Drivers think it's hilarious to come up slowly from behind and scare the crap out of you by screaming obscenities in your ear (less of a problem now with the advent of ear buds). If there's a puddle to be had, there's always someone in the crowd who gets a thrill barreling through it and playing the always entertaining game of "soak the cyclist."

While these "games" are, I guess, enjoyable to the occupants of the car, they are really dangerous for the cyclist. Often, I have had only inches between a swerving car doing forty miles per hour or more and an unyielding curbstone or steep drop-off on my right. It takes full concentration not to flinch even an inch while these antics are at play.

While I seek out the safest routes, sometimes there is no alternative to getting yourself into a dicey situation. You can only hope that you have the skill, training, and focus to overcome the ever-present distractions.

Of course, some cyclists create their own problems and give the majority of safe, careful riders a bad name. You can usually spot them by the speed they're traveling, their entitled attitude that screams, "I own this road," and their garb: tight bike shirts and shorts and fancy riding shoes. They cut off cars, take wide turns, ride double- or triple-file and block traffic, and swarm roads and intersections with their large groups. To them, even a casual Sunday morning ride is an excuse to speed, swerve, and ignore signals in an attempt to emulate Lance Armstrong. Just so you showboats know, it's not only the drivers who can't stand you; many of your fellow cyclists don't care for your antics either!

The ride itself encompasses many different elements and emotions. The first day consists of euphoric filled highs followed by painful realities. My preferred route starts in the relatively flat terrain of eastern Massachusetts and takes me through the rolling hills and beautiful scenery of central Massachusetts. With an early start, fresh legs, and my adrenaline pumping, the initial five hours are glorious. Every time, it leaves me smiling to myself. *This ride is going to be a piece of cake!* In time, however, those endearing rolling hills morph into the daunting and challenging Berkshire Mountains. The roads narrow, the big trucks seem to materialize out of nowhere, and these mountains sneer at me as I attempt to maximize the downhills and fight through the steeper and steeper inclines.

As I cross into New Hampshire, I am greeted by a huge climb at Mount Monadnock but then rewarded with a three-mile slope that allows me to glide into the parking lot of my hotel. Usually, I arrive at dusk with just enough energy to shower, grab a burger, and climb into a warm bed. Day two is the toughest. It's important to get an early start, and the Green Mountains (the most difficult topography on the trip) await. With the adrenaline and excitement from the previous day pretty much spent, it quickly becomes a grind. My spirits rise as I cross over the Connecticut River from New Hampshire into Vermont and indulge myself with a large breakfast at my favorite diner in Bellows Falls, Vermont. It takes everything I have to get over the daunting Okemo Mountain, through Ludlow, Vermont, and into the gritty city of Rutland. Because there is a half-hour steep descent into Rutland, it's a refreshing conclusion to a difficult day. Day two is in the books.

Day three brings more mountains and also the breathtaking scenic beauty of central and northeast Vermont—Brandon, Middlebury, and Burlington, where I meet my brother Ed and take a relaxing boat ride across Lake Champlain—we're three-quarters of the way done. Ed always takes good care of me. As he's cooking out, I indulge in my first cold beer in over a month, soak my aching muscles in his hot tub, and take in the sunset over the Lake. On this night, I sleep like a baby.

For the final leg from Plattsburg, New York, to the oratory, the terrain is as flat as a pancake. The sixty-five-mile run into Montreal feels like a cakewalk after three days in the mountains. At the halfway point lie the US-Canadian border. Dealing with customs officials is always a delicate dance. On occasion, they wave you through with minimal interaction. Other times, they have a seemingly endless barrage of questions. Why are you coming in on a bike? You really came from Massachusetts? Where did you stay last night? How are you getting home? Where's your car? I've learned, over the years, to just answer the questions asked and don't volunteer anything more.

Case in point: One of our funniest, did-that-really-just-happen moments came when we were coming home crossing the border with the bike on the back of a rental car. The customs agent wanted to know how I got into the country without driving, what the bike was all about, and why I kept talking about Saint Joseph's Oratory. We chatted for a while, and I explained about the ACF and the purpose of our visit. He seemed impressed when we told him we'd raised twenty thousand dollars and waved us through and wished us luck.

About one hundred yards past the booth, I looked in the rearview mirror to see the customs official sprinting down the middle of the highway, frantically waving his arms. I pulled over, and the out-of-breath agent sputtered, "Did you tell me you have twenty thousand dollars in your car?" While it's legal to carry any amount of money over the border into the United States, anything over ten thousand dollars must be declared. The customs official panicked when it occurred to him that he thought I said I *had* (as opposed to *raised*) twenty thousand dollars. Once we got things straight, he exhaled, and we were back on our way. I suspect it was a long walk back to his station to explain to his supervisor why he had to leave his post to chase down a car that had already been cleared for entry!

Once we passed through customs, it was a sprint to the finish! Just across the border coming into Canada, the landscape is littered with quaint, French-speaking villages not far outside Montreal that give you the feeling that you're coming up through the French landscape into Paris. Finally, glimmering in the distance, even before you can see the skyscrapers of Montreal, Saint Joseph's Oratory atop Mount Royal emerges. Like Oz, it appears to be surreal, and in many ways, it is to us. I'm inspired and motivated every time I see the basilica—and it's a good thing I am because I'm still thirty miles out, and I have to push myself and what has become my appendage, my bike, to the summit and across the finish line.

When I hoist my bike over my head and get my congratulatory bear hug and kiss from Andrea, I can finally exhale and truly take in the moment and savor our accomplishment. We did it—again. It's a remarkable feeling, one I try to hold onto and savor for at least a few hours before we get to our hotel room and collapse!

In Montreal, we always splurged and stayed at the Montreal Marriott Chateau Champlain, where they came to know us and gave us the same room every trip, overlooking the park and downtown. The hotel's valet supervisor, Henri, would even have a homemade sign that read *"Bienvenue, Peter et Andrea!"* It felt good to be welcomed and welcomed back. At that point, all the logistical, administrative, and physical machinations felt more than worth it. With the assistance of so many people, we were able to channel our energies to support not only the researchers but also the unfortunate victims of NF2. We popped champagne at Le Keg restaurant, made the long drive home, and finished up the fundraising and *thank-you*s. More than one person has asked me if I rode my bike back home—my reply: "I might be crazy, but I'm not insane—yet." (but if the money was right I'd definitely consider it!)

For me, this is truly a labor of love. One of our earliest, largest donors said he would contribute only if I completed the ride—and he wanted a time- and date-stamped photo as proof! Given the size of his donation, I assured him that if I had even a breath of life left in me, I would drag my ugly carcass across the finish line and secure that donation. Over the years, happily for us, he and many of our family, friends, colleagues, and even complete strangers choose to donate again and again.

After we established a base of donors, we explored new contribution streams. We've been able to connect with more businesses and tried to enlist larger corporations with large charity budgets. ADS was always atop my fundraising partners. I recall one year after I stepped away from running operations at ADS, Bob Howe approached me about returning to that role. We went through the normal negotiation banter, but Andrea was skeptical. Finally, he came back with his best, last offer: If I came back, ADS would match the first five thousand dollars we raised for the ACF. The bastard knew how to reel me in. I took the job—and the matching funds.

One of the largest donations we get every year is through a man I've never met. Believe me, I've tried. He's a friend of a friend who believes in his friend and, through him, our cause. On our travels around the world, we (mostly Andrea) made friends and received donations from Canada, Indonesia, Japan, Ireland, Poland, Italy, and elsewhere. We've become good friends with a vintner and his family at his winery in Quebec, who has donated not only money but also cases of wine. Before we left the hotel for home, Henri always had a small remembrance for Andrea. We have been touched by every contribution and every thoughtful gesture, large and small, because we know they all came from the heart.

We've received donations from hundreds of individuals and many corporations. After my ride in 2022 and golf tournament in 2023, the cumulative total of funds we've raised reached $250,000. We cover all the expenses and administrative costs ourselves, so we can brag that 100% of every dollar donated to the ACF goes directly to MGH. Monies have been controlled solely by Andrea's doctors—initially her neurosurgeon, Dr. Ojemann, and when he retired, her neurologist, Dr. Plotkin. There are no stipulations on how these funds should be used. Our feeling from the beginning was that while we all approached this effort with the same general goal, the specialists would know best how to allocate the monies most strategically.

Over the past twenty years, the foundation has indeed helped leverage over two million dollars in funding for research initiatives that have tested experimental therapies, improved the quality of life of NF sufferers, and moved the needle toward finding a cure. A big success occurred when researchers identified genetic markers that allowed for a relatively simple test for children of NF-afflicted parents to learn definitively if they had inherited the gene for NF2. Those who were NF negative could exhale and begin to make long-term plans. Those who were NF positive could be tracked more closely to ensure they got the best possible, proactive NF care available. Every bit of knowledge gained about NF, even as small and spotty as it might be, incrementally inches us closer to the endgame. Even the failures cross possibilities off the list, so researchers can move on quickly and pursue other, more unexplored or promising, pathways.

A well-worn, inspirational quote by Nelson Mandela reminds us, "The difficult always seems impossible until it's done." This is the type of inspiration that keeps us pushing forward for a cure. While the ACF has certainly fulfilled Andrea's and my desire to do something practical and help make something positive happen, it was also an outlet without which we ourselves may have gone down a pathway to greater despair. A real win-win!

The genesis for starting the ACF really occurred that dismal day when our initial MGH neurologist told us, "There is no hope" for Andrea. While she could have been right (thank God she wasn't), it was her attitude and delivery that rubbed us the wrong way. No one should ever rob people of hope, regardless of their position, the number of degrees they hold, or their institutional knowledge. We can attest to the fact that hope extends beyond the bounds of medical science and human understanding and that miracles really do happen.

Doctors don't always get to have the final say; diseases can change course; unexplained events can occur; and as we came to appreciate at a very personal level, those miracles do happen. We have good friends whose daughter was diagnosed with inoperable and irreversible stage IV breast cancer. Her doctors (coincidentally or not, at MGH), her parents, her friends, and most importantly she herself never gave up hope. If that ship was going down, they were all going down with it, fighting with every ounce of energy they had. Through perseverance, modern medicine, faith/many prayers, and undoubtably a little luck, the doctors came up with a never-tried-before chemotherapy cocktail that not only reversed but also eradicated her cancer.

Not only did this woman live, but she also thrived and today lives a healthy, cancer-free life.

To give up hope means to give up trying, and that's what we felt this doctor was telling us to do. The ACF gave us hope when we felt hopeless. It gave us a way to wage a good-versus-evil struggle against an implacable foe. NF2 could slow us down in any number of ways, but it couldn't stop us from fundraising, or the doctors and clinicians from using the funds to search for therapies and chipping away to find a way to beat it, or take away the pleasure we derived from helping others.

Faith, hope, and charity are considered the three central theological virtues, and that's what the ACF represents to us, now, and hopefully, until a cure is discovered.

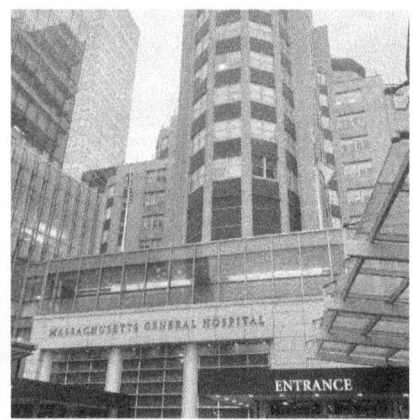

Andrea's hearing dog, Amber, helped her adjust to her new world of deafness.

Massachusetts General Hospital; Andrea spent countless days here as she endured twelve brain surgeries and recoveries.

Poland

Ireland

Her desire to travel was a testament to her perseverance; pictured here in Poland, Ireland and Italy. Travel kept her energized and always looking forward to the next adventure.

Italy

Andrea was happiest
around family—especially
at our beach house.

Peter's annual bike rides from
Boston to Montreal have helped
raise hundreds of thousands
of dollars for NF2 research.

CHAPTER 17

The Biggest Collateral Damage (or Handling the Kids with Kid Gloves)

As laser-focused as we tried to be on Andrea's situation and the enemy, NF2, other aspects of our lives simply couldn't be ignored. We had to manage our jobs, medical bills, family obligations, and trying to plan ahead when anything more than a few months out was a complete wild card.

I think we did a pretty good job by using the strategy of compartmentalization. Basically, when we found ourselves in any of the above boxes, we tried to block out all the other stuff that was going on in our lives and operate in a vacuum. If we hadn't done this, I couldn't have run an operations division at work, Andrea couldn't have taught, and we'd never have been able to even go out to dinner to relax and have a drink and forget about the cyclone usually swirling around us.

This strategy worked very well for us in almost every aspect of our lives, with one notable exception—our kids, Natalie and

Peter. Our kids' lives, emotions, concerns, and activities leaked into almost everything we did, so raising them in this challenging environment was, well, a challenge. There is no way I know of to compartmentalize bringing up your children unless you choose to raise them in an Israeli kibbutz.

We addressed this issue with the premise that Andrea's health and the well-being of our children would be our primary focus. Their activities, education, independence, and growth had paramount importance. But the severity of NF2 and the unpredictability of Andrea's health made for an uneven road for both of them.

They were dealing with not only a deaf, but also a weirdly sick, mother who would seem fine for a time and then, every few years, would get really sick, have to "go away" for a while to undergo major surgery, and sometimes end up on the verge of dying. She would recover, to some greater or lesser extent, and then repeat the process—again, and again, and again. It was a strange and difficult environment to grow up in and try to make sense of.

From my point of view, it was more than strange; it was unhealthy and potentially traumatizing. Our instinct, therefore, was to try to normalize the abnormal. For a long time, our children simply didn't fully grasp the situation. To me, bringing up the kids in this environment was analogous to driving a car in dense fog: You know where you're trying to go, you sense danger all around you, and you try to convince yourself and everyone in the car that everything is going to be fine, while everything you experience is somewhat distorted. We tried our best to keep the car on the road and shield the kids in the back seat from the ever-present dangers. Our best bet always was, to quote a Paul Simon song, to "believe that God keeps his eyes on the road."

But kids are very aware and intuitive about their surroundings, and they knew things weren't right. The atmosphere of uncertainty and impending calamity kept them constantly off-balance, and they acted out in a number of ways. Some of it was typical sibling rivalry stuff—pushing each other's buttons, bickering, pouting, and yelling. But some of it was not quite as normal.

Our children had a curious mix of many of their parents' characteristics. Natalie, the oldest by two and half years, was more of a quiet bookworm, not particularly interested in social activities, and a determined student who was capable of anything academically when she put her mind to it. Natalie was reading at the age of three, became an expert signer, and excelled in school. Language was her thing, including eleven years of advanced Latin.

Peter was loud, didn't have much of a filter, and loved to socialize and be around people. He also was a very smart kid but didn't particularly care about his grades. Sports were his passion and outlet. For a long time, Peter's desire to raise hell, especially in school, overshadowed his intelligence and stunted his academic accomplishments.

Although different by nature, the kids did have one other thing in common: They both developed a great deal of anxiety. They grew up in an environment of what Natalie termed "normalized dysfunction." They didn't feel comfortable asking their mom about NF2, and felt I had too much on my plate and didn't want to add to it. They knew things were always percolating in the background, and they were right. Even when things were going smoothly, like a greasy film that's impossible to remove, there was always the specter of NF2 hanging around.

When NF2 did rear its head and put Andrea in the hospital and rehab, different family members and friends would help take care of the house and the kids, and I was in and out at all hours of the day and night. Sometimes people they barely knew were in *their* house, telling them what to do and where to go, making decisions on their behalf, and providing them updates on their mom's condition.

At some point, they came to understand that the disease their mom had was hereditary, and they each had a fifty-fifty chance of getting NF. Watching their mom must have been like sitting through a futuristic horror movie—a potential window into their own ultimate destiny, complete with deafness, tumors, hospitals, and surgeries. As they got older, the impact NF2 might have on marriage and children began to play on their psyche. Andrea and I were saddened beyond words that the kids had to go through this. It was truly the most extensive collateral damage brought on by NF2.

The social aspects of school were sometimes challenging for our quiet, bright daughter, Natalie. Like her father, she would much rather stick her nose in a book than join in group activities. She never got into trouble and always received very good grades.

At home, she was similarly disposed—packed into a corner of her bedroom, reading, often walled off by a stack of books. When she was happy, she would flash a big, toothy grin that was a carbon copy of Andrea's radiant smile.

She wasn't challenged in the public school system, and as a result, she continued to turn inward. Eventually, we transferred her to an elite private school. This move, made with the best of intentions and love for her, was less impactful than we had hoped. While the academic environment was top-notch, the makeup of the student body was far from diverse and heavily weighted toward children of upper-class families beginning their educational journey, which targeted boarding schools and Ivy League colleges. There's nothing wrong with wanting the best for your children, but coming from my blue-collar background, it was not a space where I felt particularly comfortable. Natalie persevered, and as a result, these couple of years became a great educational experience that I think was the foundation for her future academic successes.

Although some of the social aspects of this timeframe were formidable, with the help of some extraordinary teachers, a lot of guts on her part, and our endless support, she managed to get through this taxing experience. She went on to an all-girls

Catholic high school (Notre Dame Academy, or NDA), where there were (in some ways) diminished social pressures and a high focus on academics, athletics, and structure.

She excelled as a student and made friends. She displayed a quirky sense of humor, and developed into a more independent young woman.

Unlike our sports-nut son, Natalie had zero interest in sports. Her high school, recognizing that sports were part of a well-rounded education, required each student to play a sport in the spring and the fall. For her fall sport, Natalie chose fall field hockey as the lessor of all the other evils. Not really grasping the nuances of the game, she gravitated to the position she could understand, and she became the backup goalie.

It was the perfect spot for her. Other than having to wear the heavy pads in the hot weather, all she had to do was sit on the bench behind the first-string, world-class goalie. We went to the matches for a while, but between us not understanding the game and the fact that Natalie didn't get a single minute of playing time, we stopped going. I'd ask her after every game how it went, and she'd always reply, without any discernable enthusiasm, "Good." Usually, I couldn't even get the score out of her.

One morning, after I dropped her off at school, I was listening to the local radio station, WATD, when the sports came on. The sportscaster ran down the local high school scores from the day before (her school, Notre Dame Academy, won their game 3–0), and then he announced the high school star of the week (who was usually a football stud who scored five touchdowns the weekend before). I almost drove off the road when the announcer barked out, "Natalie Cahill from NDA. She stepped in for the injured all-conference goalie and pitched two shutouts against highly ranked teams."

That night at dinner, Andrea and I made a big deal of it—because it was a big deal. Peter was constantly getting trophies and accolades for his sporting exploits, but Natalie had never been recognized at any level (unless you count when she was seven and was removed from the soccer field for sitting at mid-field and picking clovers).

She said to us, "I would have told you, but I didn't think it was that important!"—and it wasn't to her. The first-string goalie returned that week, and Natalie happily took her preferred seat back on the bench, seemingly oblivious to her fifteen minutes of high school fame.

She attended the University of New Hampshire and, like her mom, was drawn to teaching. She got a master's degree—completing her studies at the University of Arizona (perhaps the fact that her then-boyfriend, now-husband, Marc, was in the Air Force and stationed in Tucson had something to do with the school she attended).

Despite all the fears, uncertainty, and frustration, she loved her mom dearly. While Natalie was in Arizona, Andrea had a surgery that went sideways, and she ended up in a coma. She was distraught that she wasn't there when her mom needed her. Undaunted by not being able to get a flight back, Natalie put together a cross-country train ride that took her from Tucson through St. Louis to Chicago to Boston. She was present to help Andrea through her recovery. Just like Andrea would do anything for her children, the feeling was entirely mutual.

Unlike her mother who loved teaching first grade, Natalie taught at the high school level and is now a middle-school English/literature teacher. As had happened to her mother, after several years in her school district, Natalie was asked to become a team leader. She jumped at the opportunity—maybe for a little more recognition, responsibility, and/or money. But after two years, frustrated and disillusioned, she declined to continue in the role because it involved too much politics and conflict and too little benefit. I smiled to myself as I watched history repeat itself forty years later!

But history had also positively repeated itself with her passion for teaching and education, which are tributes to both her and Andrea. Her students, school district, and family (her husband and three terrific boys) are blessed to have her. I'm so grateful and proud to have her as my daughter and my most loyal friend.

At the luncheon after her mom's funeral services, Natalie spoke about the five lessons she learned from her mother.

- Never, ever give up.
- There is no more important job than being a mom.
- Talk to strangers.
- When you find the right person, you stay.
- Always eat dessert first!

Her heartfelt, beautifully delivered speech brought smiles and tears to the assembled crowd. I believe most people in the room left vowing to use one or more of these lessons in their own lives. Once again, the world was a little bit of a better place because of Andrea and, in this case, her daughter, Natalie!

Our son, Peter, experienced the same chapter but different verses. He, too, was troubled, but he lashed out, especially in elementary and junior high school. He had difficulty focusing and, in some ways not unlike his mother, was very outspoken— probably a nice way to say that he'd yet to develop a filter!

Though he was often in trouble and had little remorse, Andrea vehemently defended him. Often, she had a point. When a fourth-grade teacher announced to the class that they were going to have "a better day today because Peter Cahill was out sick," Andrea confronted her like no one else had in her thirty years of teaching. By the end of the lambasting, I was thinking, *I bet she wishes she went into engineering instead of education.* The school principal, district superintendent, and school committee all got an earful as well. The message was clear: Don't mess with Andrea's boy. The teacher retired the next year. When it came to her children, Andrea had endless love in her heart, with venom in her veins.

While I think that Peter had a lot of happy, normal moments as a kid (he loved video games, had a great sense of humor, and, like his dad, would play or watch any kind of sport), some of the scars ran deep. The time I mentioned when he was four or five and he was playing down in the basement when Andrea inadvertently locked the cellar door was devastating for both him and his mother. He wouldn't go behind a closed door by himself for many years.

Years later when Peter was a young teenager, Andrea lost her balance and struck her head on a steel spiral staircase and went down hard. Peter was really shaken up as he watched the EMTs come and position his mom on a stretcher, preparing to take her to the hospital. That night was particularly difficult for both Peter and me as the EMTs seemed to believe that some sort of domestic abuse may have contributed to her falling. While they grilled me and tried to interrogate a deaf, semiconscious Andrea, Peter and I tried desperately to explain her situation and pleaded with them to get her to the hospital.

As resilient as I think kids are, these types of things tend to stay with you forever and leave a lasting impression on young psyches. We couldn't control it, and we tried our best to offset it, but it certainly made us despondent to have to watch our kids suffer as a result of NF2.

In junior high school, I spent a lot of time with Peter's principal. We actually developed a pretty good relationship as we tried to corral a sometimes out-of-control young man. Nothing seemed out of bounds to Peter, physically or verbally. It was as if he woke up looking for trouble and ready at any moment to pick a fight.

Andrea and I recognized early on that Peter wasn't a bad kid. In truth, he was a good kid living in a bad dream. We never gave up on him, weathered some crazy behavior, and slowly managed to help get him back on the rails. Of course, with some justification, not everyone saw things that way, and Peter developed a reputation as a kid with a real chip on his shoulder who could lash out at any moment.

Peter figured it out in high school, cleaned up his behavior, improved his academics, and became a good athlete. He used sports as his hedge against his situation at home, playing every sport he could. In high school, he lettered as a freshman in wrestling, started on the varsity football team for three years, and was a part of two state championship lacrosse teams.

He also made a lot of friends through athletics. He went on to have a good, if somewhat eclectic, college experience and graduated from Suffolk University in Boston. It took him a while to find his way, but he has excelled professionally and has settled into the roles of a great husband to his beautiful wife Ali, and fantastic father to his own Bam Bam, Lou. He is, and always has been, my best sidekick.

Andrea, of course, continued to defend his ongoing but vastly diminished transgressions to the day she died.

Peter also spoke at his mom's funeral luncheon. He had the crowd roaring in appreciation when he told the story of one of the many days he came home from school suspended. The suspension didn't seem to faze Andrea at all, but the fact he was in the principal's office during the lunch period did. All this very Italian mother wanted to know was why the school didn't feed her son and what could she make him to eat.

Appreciative as he was, he said, "Thanks, Mom. I am hungry, but we have to focus. I got suspended again, and when Dad gets home, he's gonna be pissed," to which Andrea answered, "Don't worry about Dad. Was it cold in that room they kept you in? Let me get you a blanket and sweater to warm you up."

I *was* pissed when I got home, but Andrea could have cared less. I got over it, and again, she showed us the lessons of love and loyalty. Her love was genuine, boundless, and unconditional. She was going to protect her son, just like she did in fourth grade and like she would when he was a grown man. She also intuitively knew the depth of what her children were going through, and she was willing to give them the benefit of the doubt, sometimes to a fault. I would react, where she would respond. Thank God for mothers like Andrea.

It would have been disingenuous to tell the kids that everything would be all right when they could clearly see that it wouldn't. It was tough to say to them that they shouldn't worry about their mom when they knew better. It was useless to try to convince them that even though their mother was sick, they would be okay when they knew NF was a hereditary disease.

They experienced real trauma—neighbors yelling at them and getting away with it because their mom couldn't hear, and kids whispering that their mom was different, and knowing it was true.

Case in point: I often interpreted for Andrea, especially in public settings. In church, in particular, members of the congregation would gawk at our family, making us feel like we were part of a show. This was not malicious, and in almost all cases, it was a form of admiration, but that's not how it always felt, especially to the kids.

But they persevered. They learned sign language. They made friends. They got help when they needed it. They learned early and lived the lesson that life wasn't fair. They also learned the lesson of determination, from both watching their mom and dealing with the world around them.

The kids gave me an enhanced perspective on their childhood years when I asked them, for this book, what it was like growing up in this environment.

Natalie told me she was very uncomfortable, especially in the beginning, about her deafened mom. She was embarrassed because, like most kids her age, she wanted to fit in and not be different. One of her earliest memories was when Andrea started to go into the town elementary schools to educate the kids about service dogs and deafness. She had already gone to a couple of schools when she asked Natalie if it would be okay to come into her school and classroom. Natalie, horrified, told her, "No!"

Andrea decided she was going to do it anyway. Natalie said it all went fine, but it was the beginning of a lifelong battle with deafness, NF2, and being different.

There were other situations, at church, in stores, and at restaurants, or when friends and family came to the house to visit, where she felt like she was on display when she interpreted for Andrea. Later in life, she realized that most people were in awe of her signing capabilities, but at the time, it was a little too much attention for a girl whose goal was to fly under the radar whenever possible.

Andrea was sensitive to her children's plight. In one of her newspaper interviews, she mentioned one of the reasons her hearing dog was so important to her was that she didn't want her kids to have to take care of her and act as interpreters. As much as she tried, some of that was inevitable.

As Natalie got older, it upset her that so few people actually tried to learn more than the manual alphabet and a few common signs to communicate with her mother. While I understood that, and I tried to explain to her that like any language, it was difficult for most people to grasp a second language, especially if they didn't use it on regularly, the kids saw it as a lack of caring. Our family had the advantage of using it every day.

In Natalie's eyes, it appeared that people were more than happy to let her or Peter interpret. She became resentful. She logically wondered how were people going to improve their signing skills (especially Mom's friends and some of her family) if they didn't try and always allowed the kids to interpret.

Also, it didn't help that her mom was not only deaf but also impulsive. One time, Natalie told her mom she had a best friend in college who she thought was beautiful—much prettier than her. Her mom, of course, told her she doubted it and that, to her, Natalie was movie-star gorgeous. Well, when Natalie brought her friend to our house, the first thing Andrea said was, "Natalie, she's pretty, but you're much prettier!" Natalie was mortified, but her friend broke out laughing and thought Andrea was a riot. She and Andrea remained good friends throughout the years.

Natalie, as did Andrea, eventually made peace with deafness. Natalie got a better appreciation of what her mom was going through. And the fact that all her high school and college friends loved coming to the house and thought Andrea was funny, interesting, interested in them, and delightfully quirky helped create a different perspective.

NF2, however, was another slithering, mutated can of worms altogether. Natalie dealt with her mom's NF2 by blocking it out. It was simply too big, too much, and too scary to deal with. For a long time, Andrea and I didn't go into a lot of detail regarding NF2, trying to gauge how much and at what point the kids could absorb the sobering reality. Natalie was perfectly fine with the ignorance-is-bliss mindset until it got to the point where NF2 refused to allow her to sweep it under the rug.

Eventually, we had to address the realities of the disease with her and take some active steps to see if it was beginning to impact her well-being. Before the advent of genetic screening, we subjected Natalie to full-body scans, EKGs, hearing tests, and CAT scans to try to determine if she showed any signs of NF. She didn't, but rather than giving her any kind of comfort, these actions pushed the situation more to the forefront of her mind.

Genetic screening became available to test for the mutation when Natalie was in high school, but she resisted. She didn't want to know. As unsettling as this approach seemed to us (not knowing if you have the disease and living each day waiting to see if symptoms surface), we respected her decision. Our doctors told us that this strategy was not unusual; many offspring of parents with hereditary illnesses simply can't take that step and are willing to live with the constant apprehension that they could eventually be affected.

Only when Natalie entered into a serious relationship with her future husband did she decide to get tested. She tested negative and, at about the same time, also found a therapist who helped her begin to unravel the knots NF2 had created in her mind and heart.

NF tried to turn her life upside down, and for some time, it did. Her panic about doctors, dentists, and needles grew to the point of avoidance. To try to calm her fear of the house burning down, I put one of those infant identification stickers on her bedroom window in an attempt to reassure her that, if there was a fire, the firefighters would go to her room first.

The combination of testing negative for NF2, getting help, and having an understanding partner to bounce things off was huge in getting Natalie's anxiety under control. However, a lot of damage had been done. One example was when her mom was in the hospital on her first high school prom. While all her friends had their mothers helping them with dresses, flowers, and advice, Natalie had me. I was a poor substitute for Andrea (although I met a lot of very nice people who helped us get through it).

The beat went on. When Natalie got engaged, her mom was in a coma. Natalie called me late one night from California to tell me the big news. She was so excited, describing in detail the moonlit Coronado beach in San Diego and how romantic it was the way her fiancé had proposed. I grunted something positive into the phone and hung up; Andrea was in a coma, and I hadn't slept in three days. I had told Natalie that Andrea hadn't woken up yet from her surgery, but she had misunderstood and thought it was part of the usual reentry process. With the brilliance of her engagement now on the back burner, she took that five-day cross-country train trip to get to the hospital, worried sick that she might not get there in time to see her mom alive.

Peter, it seemed, never had to make peace with Andrea's deafness—as he told me, "It felt normal. It's all I ever knew." Like Natalie, being in public with a deaf mom was sometimes a challenge, and he didn't like to have the attention focused on him when he had to help Andrea understand conversations. There were times he was traumatized when he was locked out of the house or in the basement, but in my conversations with him, he seemed to take the deaf aspect of NF pretty much in stride. It appeared to me that both kids viewed Andrea being deaf as a completely separate issue from the disease itself, likely because deafness was always there, while the NF steadily progressed as they got older.

In fact, for many years, NF2 never really registered with Peter. He knew his mom had brain tumors (or rocks in her head as he visualized it as a kid) and knew that somehow the fact that she couldn't do things we took for granted such as jumping or down or hearing was connected to this condition. He told me that his first appreciation for NF, and that it was a serious disease, happened in middle school. It made him anxious, especially knowing that he could get it himself at some point. As time went on, he had a harder time pushing NF out of his head and began to obsess more about the possibility that what was happening to his mother could happen to him. It's easy to see how this constant concern had an impact on his behavior as a teenager.

But he fought the increasing concerns about NF2; he was going through puberty, and as such, there were lots of changes, and he had plenty on his mind to keep him distracted. While he was aware when things were going south for Andrea—operations, tests, radiation, and the like—he didn't ask a lot of questions. He said talking about it made it feel more real, and unless we were dealing with a specific issue, we all seemed content, for the most part, to ignore the growing elephant in the room.

The first operation he remembered was when he was in the seventh or eighth grade—lots of tension, hush-hush conversations, and many different people coming and going to help take care of him and Natalie while Andrea and I were away. From that point forward, he simply remembered Andrea often being in post surgery comas and rehabs; he knew it was bad, but he continued to play hide-and-seek with it because he felt that talking about it only made it worse. The lowest point for him was Andrea's five-day coma when they were about to cut her head open to relieve the pressure. That was the point in his young life when real got a whole lot more real.

At age twenty-two, encouraged by a girlfriend, Peter decided to get tested. The six-week waiting period for the test results where "brutal." He was working nights as a security guard and began to get sharp pains in his head and neck. He started to see a therapist and take medication. The day he was finally told he didn't have NF was one of the happiest days in his memory.

He worried, stressed, and acted out as a result of the fear of getting this horrific disease, and while waiting to find out, he watched his mother slowly sink into her own personal NF hell. As he told me, "I grew up with the disease, while the disease was growing up inside Mom." Not the way you wanted to watch your son develop, but he most definitely became a stronger man as a result of it.

Growing up, Natalie and Peter dreamed their mom would come home one day and she would be all better, but it would never happen. There was no beginning, middle, or end to this bad dream. They were trapped in a real-world snow globe that was shaken violently every couple of years by the crazed, maniacal NF2.

But despite all of the turbulence they experienced, one certainty they could cling to was how much their mom loved them. They, in turn, loved Andrea unconditionally despite her challenges and their situation. They represent to me a marvelous example of the human condition overcoming adversity and thriving in the face of obstacles.

I learned a lot from my kids as a result of Andrea. I learned to be more caring, more sensitive, and less judgmental. I learned there are two sides to every story, and both sides have a back story that we usually don't know or recognize. I learned (most of the time) to take a breath before I react.

I also learned that you can't shelter kids from the real world forever. At some point, kids need and deserve to understand what's going on around them. In hindsight, I think Andrea and I made the mistake of trying to protect our kids for too long. We loved them and wanted to shield them from the monster NF2, which was always nipping at our heels. We knew we couldn't outrun it, so we bobbed, weaved, and feigned to buy as much time as possible—even with our own kids.

I came to appreciate that we were all victims of our horrors: Was their mom declining more rapidly? Was she capable of making rational decisions? Would she suffer more in the future? Were we exploring all possible treatment avenues? Was there new technology that could help? What if I passed away before Andrea? Their life, in these areas, seemed reflective of the title of Tom Clancy's bestseller *Sum of all Fears*.

The last issue weighed heavily on their minds. They knew how much I did for Andrea, and they felt ill-equipped to carry that burden. They certainly didn't want to see their mom in a nursing home, likely unable to understand everyday interactions, lonely, and confused. Once again, the feelings of uncertainty, helplessness, and guilt all reared their ugly heads. Even after they had been absolved of having NF2 itself, the disease satanically found new ways to haunt them.

Andrea and I had learned that making life-changing decisions with limited and shifting information in real time required an ever-evolving perspective and the willingness to lay our bets down and accept/live with the outcomes. We certainly made our share of mistakes when it came to dealing with NF2 and our kids. One mistake we didn't make was that we always treasured them above everything else. We did everything we knew how to do at any given point in time, and we loved them dearly.

I know Andrea would agree that when we finally turned all these cards over, love trumped all!

CHAPTER 18

Can't Shed a Tear about
Not Being Able to Cry

Although we were fighting the good fight and because Andrea was so strong and resilient, even we didn't fully contemplate the completely corrosive and insidious nature of NF. That was the result of us constantly battling the disease and taking precious little time to step back and acknowledge the enormity of the hell we were dealing with. Psychologically, we didn't want to give in an inch, so all our drive and will went into the war. We couldn't let up, lest we lose our focus and be more susceptible to the next NF2-related curveball.

But in the game inside the game, Andrea had a lot of strange stuff going on all the time. Without a doubt, the brain tumors were the most prominent feature of the disease, but like a cat burglar, NF slowly and steadily robbed her of different capabilities—both overt and subtle. Amazingly, it wasn't until I sat down and wrote this book that I came to a fuller understanding and deeper appreciation for what she went through daily, increasingly so as the disease progressed. This realization and clarity have given me an even higher level of respect and admiration for this amazing woman who handled the everyday small things, the ongoing "routine" (by NF standards) issues, and the big-time, life-and-death moments all with such courage, grace, and dignity.

A day in life presented constant hurdles to overcome, adding up to a long and winding road that led to even more challenges. Her condition, at any given time, was a testament to the voracity of the disease, the will and skill of modern physicians to try to provide relief, and Andrea's unwavering perseverance.

While the doctors continued to focus on keeping Andrea's tumors at bay, Andrea was working overtime dealing with NF's many prickly tentacles.

For her, the answer to the question, "Where did NF2 strike her?" was, "Pick a part, any body part." Her eyes were one of many huge issues. One of her surgeries left her facial muscles weak, so Andrea couldn't shut her left eye all the way when she blinked or slept. The eye couldn't fully close and replenish its moisture, so her cornea began to dry out. To prevent this, she had several stitches in the corner of her eye to help it close. When this stopped working, she had a ghoulish eye surgery in which a metal weight was inserted inside her eyelid to bring the lid all the way down.

Even with these "modifications," she had to apply both expensive prescription eye drops (Restasis) and a prescription ointment to her eye every night and then tape the eye shut. Of course, she had to have a specific kind of hard-to-find tape to secure the eyelids. If the tape was too light, it wouldn't keep the eye shut; if it was too heavy, it would rip off her eyelashes and skin on the lid.

This issue was considered a minor side effect, and Andrea treated it as such. But try to imagine it: two delicate surgeries around your eye, applying two expensive drugs every night, taping your eye each night (a process that in total took at least twenty minutes), and visits to a cornea specialist several times a year to be told that you weren't following the process carefully enough and that you could possibly lose your vision in that eye. How heavy does that weigh on a deaf person?

She also had a pair of bionic glasses that had to be custom-built by the geniuses at Massachusetts Eye and Ear Infirmary (MEEI). These glasses balanced the vision capability from one strong "good" eye to the other eye, making her vision equal in both eyes. It was really a space-age piece of technology and provided her with better-than-average vision.

Of course, she had to see an ophthalmologist twice a year, and if her vision changed, new glasses had to be ordered. It was all wonderful until she inevitably sat on them or misplaced them and had to wander around in a fog until the new ones could be remade. Every time we had to go to any eye shop other than MEEI to have them adjusted or tightened, the entire operation would stop while the eye doctors and technicians analyzed Andrea's glasses with fascination and awe.

At another point, the doctors decided that she could benefit from a specialized, custom-made contact lens to protect her cornea. This process required numerous trips to the clinic to evaluate her eyes, take lens measurements, and synch them with her high-tech glasses. With Andrea's clumsy hands and forgetfulness, we dealt constantly with dozens of dropped or lost lenses and imperfect saline for soaking and cleaning. And the process added at least another half hour of preparation for her at the beginning and end of each day.

To top it off, Andrea stopped being able to cry after one of her operations. Now for someone like me who doesn't cry much, that doesn't seem like a big deal. But for Andrea, it was a very big deal. Crying was emoting for her, and this SOB disease had even taken that away from her. She lamented about this problem often, and although we looked at potential solutions briefly—there was some discussion of some sort of implant— quite honestly, it never made it onto our priority list.

She felt guilty about the cost it took to keep her working. It certainly wasn't cheap. For her eyes alone, the glasses were about one thousand five hundred dollars a pop, the drops and ointment about one hundred fifty dollars a month, and the specialty stuff like the custom lenses (thousands of dollars) was all out of pocket. We weren't independently wealthy, but we could afford it. I had stopped fretting about costs and money a long time ago, but Andrea was saddled with the guilt that she was a financial burden. Every time we'd stop at the pharmacy, she'd rehash how much she was costing us and would question if it was worth it (it was!).

That was just one eye. Andrea's valor was not confined to the big stuff; it was on display to me every single day. There were so many nasty minefields that came with the NF territory.

Another example was Andrea's mouth. One of the surgeries left her with facial paralysis, with no feeling on one side of her face or mouth. No matter how long she brushed or flossed, she could never quite get it clean. If a piece of food was stuck way down between her teeth on that side, she simply didn't know it. This led to many cavities, followed by many root canals, extractions, and implants. Unfortunately, this was an ongoing issue—just another cost of doing business with NF2.

As was the case with every aspect of her life, her deafness made these procedures more difficult. Trying to translate tricky dental verbiage, teeth numbers, and various options often didn't make any sense to Andrea, especially when she was tired or worn down. She was greatly frustrated because she felt she was doing all the right things and still getting bad results.

It didn't help that I was lucky to have pretty good teeth. That really ticked her off and was one of the few times she'd complained to me about the unfairness of her situation. "It's just not fair," she'd say. "You never even have a cavity, and I have every possible dental problem!"

It wasn't true that I had perfect teeth, but when I heard her complain, I wished there was a way to make her dental problems mine and give her one less cross to bear. At one point, I did need a tooth extracted and an implant. The oral surgeon must have thought I was crazy because I was ecstatic to have this work done. Finally, I would have some ammunition to counter Andrea's dental arguments!

Andrea also suffered from a condition called dry mouth. No matter how much she drank, swooshed, or gargled, her mouth was constantly parched. We tried every available treatment, but none of them had any meaningful impact. Andrea told me that her dry mouth was one of the most debilitating problems she had to deal with because it never went away and was always front of mind. Later, when Andrea went on her chemo treatment, this issue went from bad to worse, and for many years, it drove her to the brink of madness. She often lamented, "I feel like I'm living in the Sahara Desert."

In addition to her eye and mouth, Andrea faced a myriad of other physical issues: facial weakness, a shunt put in her skull to drain fluid from her brain to keep the pressure regulated, a frozen vocal cord, swallowing problems, severe headaches, muscle spasms, chronic fatigue, ovarian fibroids, balance issues, neuropathy, vertigo, a propensity for infection, memory and cognitive lapses, and ongoing weakness in her legs, to name a few. This list doesn't even begin to take in the side effects of the radiation and chemotherapy she was subjected to.

Her overall endurance and stamina were worn down by the magnitude and frequency of her brain operations. Mostly every time she had surgery, she bounced back strong, recovering maybe 90% of her pre-surgery capacity. That sounds pretty good, right? But if you start to do the math and factor in the number of brain surgeries she had, 90% of 90% of 90%, and so on, starts to add up pretty quickly to diminished capacity.

We made dozens of accommodations to try to stay ahead of NF2 and maintain the best possible quality of life—larger TVs with larger captions, TTYs (telecommunications devices for the deaf), self-lifting chairs, adjustable beds, innumerable grab bars, a handicap ramp, eventually redoing the master bed and bath to make them fully handicapped accessible, and canes leading to walkers leading to mobility scooters, to name a few. NF scoffed at our efforts and, with each modification, created new sets of obstacles that dramatically affected our daily lives.

Over time, getting in and out of a chair or bed became impossible for her to do by herself, and it frustrated the hell out of her. Simple things for you or me—the ability to get up and get a drink, answer the door, or at times make it to the bathroom—moved beyond her reach. When she did get up, usually with my assistance, she was unsteady, and that exasperated her. The walker she used slowed her down to a crawl and created many problems. As the disease progressed, falls became more frequent, and with her diminished balance and strength, getting her back on her feet became more difficult. We were late for everything, something I had to accept, and we started to refer to our pace as "on Andrea time."

"Andrea time" had a component beyond physical limitations. Andrea developed what I referred to as "dead spots" in her brain. We all get senior moments when we forget names and lose track of things. Andrea had all of those, but as a result of her many brain surgeries, she had other weird disconnects. She developed a distorted concept of time that was maddening to both of us. If it took her forty-five minutes to get out the door every day, she thought it took ten minutes. If it took twenty minutes to get from the living room to the car, she thought it took five minutes. Most bizarrely, if we had to be at an appointment at 3:00 p.m., she thought we had to *leave* at 3:00 p.m. No matter what strategies I employed to get us going, out the door, and on time to our appointed place, they usually failed.

Another related issue was her memory. Some memories were clear and sharp, but others were just plain gone, bleached away, and never coming back. Andrea accepted this as an aspect of her condition, although it was still very vexing. She was very self-effacing, especially when it came to trying to remember people and names. In some instances, she not only couldn't remember a person's name but also couldn't recall the person at all—even people she knew well. We'd play all kinds of name association games—the short woman always wearing the floppy hat who was named Bunny, the tall guy named Larry who looked like Larry Bird, or the tipsy couple Gene and Tina who we always saw at our favorite restaurant we labeled Gin and Tonic (although Andrea always wanted to call her Tipper, which, in Andrea's mind, became her name). No matter how we tried, there were some people that just never stuck.

This led to some predictably funny exchanges:

ME. Here comes Sally.
ANDREA. Who's Sally?
ME. Our neighbor at the end of the street.
ANDREA. Do I know her?
ME. Yeah, she's very short and has a nice smile.
ANDREA. Oh, shit, no idea.
SALLY. Hi, Andrea, how have you been?
ANDREA. Hi, Sally, good! Great to see you! And you?

This scenario would play out every time we saw Sally—or many other people. Much to her credit, Andrea was unfailingly polite and always found a way to make conversation and sometimes connect the dots on the fly. At different times she would remember the specifics of the conversation, but not the person, other times vice versa. It was curious how her brain worked (or didn't sometimes) and incredibly difficult to even imagine what she had to deal with.

Restaurants and trips were much the same. Picking a place to go to dinner was often like an Abbott and Costello who's-on-first routine:

ANDREA. Where are we going to dinner?
ME. I was thinking we would go over to Josh's Restaurant.
ANDREA. Where's that?
ME. A couple of miles up the road.

ANDREA. Have I been there before?

ME. Yeah, several times.

ANDREA. Did I like it?

ME. A lot.

ANDREA. Then let's go!

ANDREA, *after dinner.* I really liked it there!

The next week.

ME. Want to go back to Josh's? They have that special you like.

ANDREA. What's Josh's?

ME. Josh's Restaurant, up the road over by your brother's house.

ANDREA. Really? I don't remember it. Did I like it?

ME. Yes, very much.

ANDREA. Well, let's go back there!

This not only happened with people and restaurants but also with entire trips to the Maine coast, California, Canada, and even Europe. I started putting travel photo books together of our trips, and she loved going back and reliving them, but the next day, it was gone. These photo books helped bring her back to the pleasure of the event, even though she didn't remember what we did or when.

This was a great example of Andrea enjoying the journey. Rather than getting upset by the fact that she wasn't going to or didn't remember the adventure we were on, she basked in the moment, even reveling in the fact that we could do the same thing more than once, and she would enjoy it as much, or even more, the second or third time.

In public, Andrea could block out her plight, and being with other people energized her. When people would ask her how she felt, it was always, "I feel good!"; when they would tell her how brave she was, she would reply, "No, I'm not. Not at all." But bravery can take many forms. It's not just about running into a burning building to save the day. It can be putting your own struggles aside every day so as to not make people uncomfortable, looking for ways to help others as opposed to seeking or wallowing in pity, or internalizing your fears to keep them from your children. Andrea did all these things on a daily basis. Her public persona was carefully airbrushed and cropped—it was a mirage, but not in any way phony or fake—rather carefully crafted to put others more at ease and take the spotlight off herself and her predicament. She needed to do this, not just for others but for her own diversion and well-being as well.

Part of her bravery came from willful denial. Andrea knew, although she wouldn't allow herself to admit, until the very end, that NF would win the war. It slowly pulverized her mind, body, and will. But she found the inner strength to block out her situation when she was outside the house and with other people.

For example, whenever we would go to the NF clinic for her frequent checkups, she'd spend a good portion of the time with our wonderful nurse practitioner, Christina, cracking jokes, talking about babies, and poking fun at her neurologist (and Christina's boss), Dr. Plotkin. As I sat there and watched, the scene reminded me more of two neighbors sitting on the front porch and sipping coffee on a Saturday morning as opposed to a very sick woman chatting it up with a neurospecialist about life-and-death issues. Christina always made sure we eventually took care of business, but there were times when I had to chime in and say to them, "Hey, ladies, sorry to break up the conversation, but I actually have some questions that are germane to our appointment!"

In the same way, her appointment every six weeks for thirty-five years with her hairstylist, Trish, was more about people and friendship than about hairstyle. Before each cut, there would be a long discussion as to what style Andrea wanted. Eventually, she would decide she wanted to keep the *same* style she had. During the cut, there would be comedic discussions about whatever topic was on Andrea's mind—anything from gossip in town to something she saw on the cover of *People* magazine. The two of them would be roaring with laughter; sometimes Trish had tears in her eyes from laughing so hard.

Finally, the haircut would be finished, and the moment of truth arrived when Trish asked, "Well, how do you like it?" Occasionally, Andrea would say, "It's okay," but most of the time, characteristically unfiltered, she would say, "I hate it!" Trish would feign disbelief and then tell Andrea how hurt she was. By the time we arrived home, Andrea was telling me how much she liked her haircut and that I should text Trish to let her know she was sorry for her harsh remarks and that she loved her "do." Every six weeks, we would do this dance again, and everyone would play their roles perfectly.

Trish also cut my hair, and Andrea was generally equally displeased with the results: either too long or too short, or too much or too little on top, or the length of the sideburns didn't match. But Andrea had an obsessive fixation on my eyebrows, always encouraging Trish to trim them up more, lest I look like Andy Rooney! Well, the eyebrows were never trimmed close enough for Andrea's liking, and that led to an "only in Andrea's world" story that Trish continues to repeat to her customers to this day.

One morning, I awoke to the specter of Andrea hovering over me with a pair of scissors, attempting to "style" my eyebrows while I was asleep! Startled, I jumped up, causing the tip of the scissors in Andrea's unsteady hand to scratch my cheek—an inch away from my eye. Andrea recoiled and, in keeping with the Andy Rooney theme, went into full *60 Minutes* denial mode. She didn't have any explanation, just pure repudiation.

The next time we went to get our haircuts, I recounted the story to Trish, who had stomach pains from laughing so hard. Andrea proclaimed that she had no knowledge of what I was talking about and, anyway, didn't see what was so funny. At the end of my cut, Trish brought Andrea over and offered to teach her how to professionally style eyebrows. At that point, Andrea didn't appreciate the joshing at her expense and continued to disavow any knowledge/involvement right until her last visit. But the story lives on and has become a part of "Andrea-lore," a tribute to the zaniness and unpredictability of Andrea's personality.

As unfiltered and straight-to-the-point as Andrea could be, her empathy was like a sixth sense. That empathy was a big part of how she connected with people. She never wanted you to be uncomfortable with her situation (or even her words, as evidenced by her having me call Trish to "apologize" for complaining about her haircut). Whether it was chatting it up with the hospital staff about their families, asking about the kid's well-being the moment she woke up from surgery, or dragging herself to a wedding so the bride wouldn't feel disappointed, she was constantly locked in on what was going on around her, seemingly not concerned about what was happening to her.

A great illustration of the depth of her empathy happened one day outside our condo in Florida. I had been at softball for the morning, and Andrea was with a neighbor, visiting. They were headed out to an early lunch, and Andrea's friend was pushing her in the small, travel wheelchair (it's called a rollator). In our complex, like many places in Florida, there are small concrete rain gullies to collect water from the downpours and channel it off the road. To push Andrea over this culvert, you had to go backward to keep all the weight back against the seat. If you went forward, the downward angle of the gully would cause the weight to shift forward, and the person in the wheelchair would be quickly and unceremoniously splattered face down. Somewhere, I recall hearing the term "face-plant," which is actually a perfect visual.

Her friend had no idea about the aerodynamics and physics associated with a rollator (why would she?), and while trying to get up over the edge of the gully, she caught the lip and dumped Andrea face down on the street, with her head bouncing off the asphalt before she could get her arms extended to break her fall. As I was coming around the corner, I saw a frenzied group attending to Andrea and attempting to get her back in the chair. We eventually did lift her into her buggy, and aside from some scrapes and scratches and a nasty headache, she was fine.

As I approached the group, Andrea pulled me aside, and despite the blood dripping from her forehead and a big lump above her eye, she said to me quietly, "I'll be fine, but my friend is really upset. Will you go over and make sure she's all right?" I did, and she was, eventually. That pretty much summed up Andrea's empathy, always worrying about the other guy; and, at the risk of being redundant, in Andrea's state, a fall was more than a fall—it could trigger a seizure, require another MRI, or touch off some other set of dominos falling inside her brain. That was never a concern to her; she always put herself second when it came to helping, supporting, or consoling others.

But in private, Andrea had to battle her demons in a different fashion. Andrea had always been a smart, independent woman, and her cognitive decline was a real source of frustration and embarrassment to her. But while everyone who knew her admired her, she saw herself as a shell of her earlier, vibrant, smart self. Depending on the day and situation, she could be sharp as a tack or completely adrift. The longer she was out of the house, the more energy she exerted; or the bigger the crowd she'd been out with, the more dramatically her resistance suffered when she got home. I really tried to manage the situation by keeping the number of people we associated with small. But many people simply didn't get it, and they had no reason to; they'd bring another couple with them or turn a small, intimate gathering into a larger event that was no good and no fun for Andrea.

Despite Andrea's great lip-reading skills, it seems fairly obvious that if you want someone to read your lips, you should look straight at them so they can see your lips. The tricky part was that even when there were multiple people in the conversation, the person talking had to look at her, even if they were addressing someone else. If they weren't looking at Andrea when they spoke, she would be out of the conversation pretty quickly, even with me translating. Oftentimes in a group, multiple conversations would take place at once, and even the most proficient and skilled interpreter (which wasn't me!) couldn't help Andrea in these instances.

I could tell when Andrea was out of it, sometimes not even understanding the topic of the conversation, much less the flow of the dialogue. Often, she simply bluffed, smiling and nodding without a clue about the topic of conversation. As much as I tried to protect her, this aspect of the disease broke my heart.

Andrea took her frustrations out on herself and then on me. The more progressive the disease, the less she liked herself and the more she reiterated, "I don't want to live like this." With me, she vacillated between admiration and disgust with whatever I was doing to try to support her.

Our new cleaning lady (who, of course, became Andrea's friend) was aghast the first week she started when Andrea casually mentioned to her, "I hate him." It was not unusual for her to tell people she wanted a divorce. Other times, she called me her savior. It felt like being the disk on a yo-yo, controlled by the unpredictable bully NF2, at times lulled into a peaceful "rock-the-baby" mode before being violently jerked up and spun down.

Over time, I came to more fully understand and accept Andrea's dilemma. The underlying issue was that she was unhappy with herself and what she'd become. We were both pissed off at NF but, at times, would take our grief out on each other. As my appreciation for Andrea's tenacity and my faith evolved, I became much more tolerant of her outbursts. I tried my best to stay on an even keel and, more importantly, to keep Andrea centered. Intellectually, I knew this wasn't her doing, but emotionally, it was too easy to take it out on the easiest targets, each other. I reminded myself that, as Kanye West sang, "Even on her worst day, the good outweighed the bad."

We worked hard at managing the eight-hundred-pound gorilla, but it was difficult to cope. I felt Andrea, or both of us together, would have benefited from counseling, but she pretty much refused. She did see one person at the NF clinic for a couple of months. Dr. Plotkin and I talked her into it. She really didn't want to do it, and it didn't end well. Andrea was predisposed not to like this woman, and the therapist's style didn't mesh with Andrea's personality. She also didn't sign. That experience reinforced Andrea's perspective that therapy wasn't for her and had no value. Even when I found a therapist who signed, Andrea wanted nothing to do with her. This swing and miss was a big-time lost opportunity for us.

Oh, and sleep was a constant challenge. Andrea was never able to sleep through the entire night. Whether it was headaches, chemo related issues, or incontinence, we were up a minimum of two or three times a night. A trip to the bathroom was at minimum a twenty-minute excursion, wrought with many potential pitfalls. For at least the last eight years of her life, we never had a good, full night sleep. In Andrea's fragile and compromised state, this created obvious, as well as indistinct, physical and mental impacts. A fatigued Andrea was more prone to everything from falls to melancholy moods to illness. This resulted in mood swings, accidents, trips to the ER, and a generally unpredictable day to day existence. Everything bad was exaggerated, and everything good was harder to get to and maintain.

I'm certain Andrea was deeply depressed at times, but she never allowed herself to wallow in it. Many times, she was upset with me and came out with some scathing stuff, but she never held a grudge for long. Her short-term memory problem both helped and exasperated the situation. Often, she'd forget why she was mad at me, but like the movie *Groundhog Day*, it was only a matter of time before the same issue came back around again.

In the end, Andrea's behind-the-scenes life and her relationship with me became one of love and frustration. Our life was different from other people, but we were happy in a way that most would not understand. We had each other, and we drew strength from our now well-worn mantra of "happiness is a choice." Though we were continually swimming upstream against a powerful current, we structured our world in a way that allowed us periods of joy and tranquility.

Dealing with Andrea's cognitive and memory-related problems and watching her trying to figure things out reinforced yet another valuable caretaker lesson: to live in the moment and be present. I watched this wonderful woman savor joyful times with friends and family and revel in all sorts of sights and places from delicious meals to basking in the glow of her beautiful grandchildren to marvelous sunsets cruising down the Danube River—all with the awareness that she was not going to remember any of it. Rather than dwell on that painful reality, we soaked in all of the beauty, majesty, and love in those moments.

I learned from watching her that it's the doing that's important. It's the joy of living that, while it may never have left an imprint in Andrea's memory, etched a lasting impression on her soul.

I would often think that for any of the rest of us, any one of these ailments Andrea managed would be a major lifestyle issue. Some of them were life-threatening. All of them had a significant, often daily, direct impact on the quality of her life.

My reason for even detailing them here is not to make you feel bad for Andrea; she would want none of that. Rather, I hope that I was able to provide you with a glimpse into the world of someone living with NF—a torturous, treacherous, unnerving dark space.

But for Andrea and everyone battling NF, this was her life. These were the aspects of it that very few people knew about. She didn't want pity; she was a proud, dignified woman who made the choice to deal with her realities head-on and, despite them, live a full and fulfilling life.

CHAPTER 19

Brain Surgery Is…
Well, Brain Surgery

Amid the ongoing "small stuff" that Andrea had to endure regularly, there was also the "big stuff." No matter how many times we dealt with Andrea's diminished capacity and knew where it was leading, it was always chilling to hear the words *brain surgery*. They conjure up horrible images and life-changing, potentially life-ending prognoses. My buddy jokingly referred to these surgeries as "tune-ups." And while Andrea may have approached and handled her operations in a somewhat matter-of-fact fashion analogous in his mind to auto maintenance, they were no laughing matter.

Andrea's first three surgeries were the most straightforward she would have. In these cases, a tumor was sitting on each acoustic nerve and needed to be removed. Although scary, it was a clean shot for the surgeon. To Dr. OJ, these were pretty routine surgeries.

The next eight surgeries in the 1990s, 2000s, and 2010s were anything but routine, even for a world-class surgeon such as Dr. OJ, or upon his retirement, his extremely capable protégé, Dr. Fred Barker. By this time, Andrea had dozens of tumors growing in bad places, including her cranium and spine. Some of these tumors were large, while others were clustered, like bunches of grapes. Before Andrea's last surgery, the doctors were giving us estimates that she had somewhere in the range of forty to sixty tumors (and the large ones were likely comprised of many smaller ones). They were so intertwined and numerous that, even with the most sophisticated medical scans and technology, it was impossible to get a clean count. If my son once thought to the tumors to be like rocks, I now envisioned her brain to be like a Boston cream doughnut—so full that the insides were always threatening to not only fill the cavity but also overflow and spill out beyond the bounds defined by nature.

In some places, tumors of various sizes, shapes, and densities formed a complex mass interwoven with blood vessels, arteries, and nerves. Worse, they were located on or near her spine and in parts of the brain that controlled critical functions, from facial expressions, sight, and walking to memory. As Andrea said to Dr. OJ after one less-than-uplifting appraisal of her brain, "Boy, we have a real problem up there, don't we?" Leave it to Andrea to get this serious, world-renowned brain surgeon, delivering devastating news, to break out into a wry smile and deadpan, "Yes, we do."

Each surgery tackled a different set of targets and circumstances, but they all had common threads. Andrea would generally begin to show symptoms as her tumors grew; often, it was her balance or her cognitive reasoning. Sometimes, it was her eyesight or random sharp pains in her head. We would then go into MGH for an MRI and follow up with her doctors to review the MRI and discuss alternatives. We occasionally explored options like laser surgery (which didn't fit her situation) or radiation, which we tried with very limited success and serious side effects.

At some point, our doctors, Andrea, and I would come to the conclusion that surgery was the best option, and we'd schedule a date. For the next four to six weeks leading up to her surgery date, Andrea and I would fake staying in our routine (especially when the kids were younger and living at home) while thinking of little else but the countdown to the big day.

Finally, painfully, the day we dreaded would arrive. Andrea would decide she didn't want to go ahead with the operation (who would?). She'd vent for a couple of hours, I'd talk her through it, and eventually, we'd get in the car for a long, mostly silent, agonizing ride into Boston. Before we left, Andrea would give the kids a big, big hug and tell them not to worry and that everything would be fine. Of course, she didn't know if everything would be fine, much less if she'd ever see them again.

Usually, the tumors grew so slowly that there was no immediacy to the surgery. There were even times when the doctors decided to put off surgery until the tumor or tumors they were targeting grew larger and would presumably be easier to attack. But occasionally, NF would devilishly throw us a curve ball (although it often felt more like a knuckleball!)

One year we were vacationing in Florida and Andrea began to fail rapidly. We began to make plans to get her back to Boston to be evaluated over the next couple of weeks. But Andrea started to deteriorate so quickly that we needed to move immediately. She abruptly regressed into a semi-comatose state, needing assistance for everything from getting dressed and eating to bathroom visits. In this case, we theorized that one of the tumors reached a tipping point—the minuscule increase in size, just enough to push into the wrong area of her brain function, causing all hell to break loose.

After discussions with her doctors at MGH, we agreed that bringing her to a hospital in Florida was not a viable option. Unfortunately, we were not going to be able to get her on a commercial flight. We evaluated a private medical flight, but that was prohibitively expensive.

With the clock ticking, I decided to pack Andrea in the car and make the drive north from Bonita Springs, Florida, to MGH in Boston. It was about fifteen hundred miles, and I surmised if I could average around sixty-five miles per hour and throw in a couple of naps, I could do it in about thirty hours. I knew it was going to be bad, but I thought it was the right, maybe only, way to go.

I got Andrea up the next day at 4:00 p.m., and by 5:00 p.m., we were on the road. I figured it would be faster and easier to start the trip overnight. Andrea had no idea how bad her condition was or even why or where we were going as we embarked from Florida.

Everything went smoothly for the first five hours or so until Andrea had to go to the bathroom. We stopped at a gas station and parked as close to the ladies' room as possible. It took me the better part of a half hour to get her from the car to the bathroom and set her up on the toilet and then back to the car. The gas station attendant was looking at me like we were shooting the sequel to the movie *Weekend at Bernie's*. It must have looked to him like I was in the process of disposing of a dead body.

Our third bathroom visit was in rural Virginia. I got Andrea into the bathroom and waited outside. After five minutes, I went to open the door to check on her and realized it was locked. How Andrea was able to lock the door was beyond me; somehow, her sense of privacy overrode her physical limitations. We were very lucky she didn't fall over and smash her head.

Now I had a really sick, lethargic, deaf woman locked in the gas station bathroom. I tried to get the door open myself, to no avail. Several angry women came to the door with full bladders and went away less than happy with me when I told them it might be another twenty minutes.

Finally, I went to the gas station clerk, but she couldn't find a key. We tried to get it open, but no luck—so she went to call the cops. At that point, I put my shoulder into it and popped the lock open; I'm guessing Andrea hadn't fully clicked the lock shut. I pulled the car up onto the sidewalk, poured Andrea in, stopped at the office, apologized for the door, and threw fifty dollars at the attendant, and then made a beeline for Boston. As far as I know, I may still be wanted for the destruction of property in the Commonwealth of Virginia!

We trudged through traffic and the big East Coast cities. Andrea was in real distress, drifting in and out of consciousness. She was babbling incoherently, and the only thing that was keeping her from falling out of the seat was her seatbelt. I stopped one last time for gas in Connecticut, but it was me that was just about out of gas. I reached down deep, and fueled by continual cups of coffee and scads of adrenaline, I decided to push through the final three hours.

We arrived at MGH at about 1:00 a.m.—only a bit longer than the thirty hours I targeted when we'd started. *Not bad*, I thought, *given Andrea's condition, the traffic, and the agonizing pit stops.* I'm pretty sure the nurses and orderlies who met us at the door to admit Andrea looked at me and thought I was the one who should be seeing a doctor. I was a real sight.

The attending doctor gave Andrea a quick evaluation and, to my amazement, kind of admonished me for dragging her in so late at night. He ordered a full workup for the next day, convinced that Andrea had a blood or urinary tract infection. He indicated that she'd be likely treated at the hospital for a day or two and then sent home.

Although I was an exhausted mess, I tried respectfully to tell him that we'd been in this position more than a few times, and I was pretty certain her symptoms were consistent with her NF and rapid development of her brain tumors. He disagreed, saying that the slow-growing nature of the tumors made that unlikely. He believed it was probably a treatable medical issue coupled with sleep deprivation from the trip.

He was quite certain he had it under control, but I wouldn't let go. I don't know if it was my own sleep deprivation, adrenaline, or stubbornness, but I pushed back hard. It was now early Friday morning, and with the weekend shift coming on later that day, I couldn't take the chance that somehow Andrea would be discharged from the hospital and something traumatic would occur. In my mind, lots of bad things fit that category. Anything from a fall to a stroke, seizure, or coma was a real possibility.

I implored him to get in touch with someone in the NF clinic (Dr. Plotkin was out of the country) and get some background on Andrea and her condition. He didn't commit to it, but he didn't say no either. Exhausted, Andrea and I fell fast asleep in her hospital room.

If you've ever stayed overnight in a hospital, you know it's not the place to get a good night's sleep. Between the checking, poking, and prodding every couple of hours during the night, the continual beeping of medical machinery, and the daytime operation coming to life at about 5:30 a.m., any real sleep is hard to come by. So, as we groggily ate breakfast, now slightly more than thirty-six hours after we left Florida, the same doctor walked through the door of Andrea's room at about 7:00 a.m.

He couldn't have gotten much sleep either, but he looked pretty good. Maybe it was the contrast of standing next to Andrea and me, who looked like zombies.

He apparently had been able to get in touch with Andrea's surgeon and sheepishly informed me that he had been directed to get Andrea an MRI ASAP. Later, talking to Andrea's doctors over the phone, we learned that a few large tumors had, in fact, grown, and one of the bigger ones was pushing into some very delicate nerves. Andrea had her next brain surgery on Monday.

My instincts had been right, but it wasn't at all about that. I learned that none of us, including medical professionals, are infallible. I have the utmost respect for all the institutions and doctors who have treated Andrea over the many years. There's not the slightest doubt in my mind that without the skill, experience, insights, and compassion of the nurses and doctors at these institutions, Andrea would not have survived anywhere near as long as she did with NF. That said, doctors and nurses are humans. They can get tired, stressed, and overwhelmed with caseloads, paperwork, and technology. You have to be willing to engage as a caregiver, and that can be overwhelming and damn scary. We're all humans, and as you'll see in a couple of chapters, the one time that I let my guard down and ignored my instincts to push back and advocate had catastrophic consequences.

Other surgeries were more—dare I say—conventional. We developed an uneasy routine; after arriving at MGH the afternoon before the scheduled operation, we'd go through the pre-op process and check into the hospital for the night.

After settling into our MGH Airbnb (that was a joke), we went to bed knowing, but never saying, that this could be our last night together. Andrea slept fitfully in the hospital bed, and I in the chair next to her, holding hands and praying for one more miracle.

Going through this process brought back a lot of memories for me—most of them bad, not only with Andrea but also with my father. In 1965, when I was only eleven years old, my father was diagnosed with type 1 diabetes. Much less was known at that time about what caused diabetes, how to treat it, and its impact on the patient and their families—not unlike my experience three decades later with NF.

On the day of the surgeries, Andrea and I were always awakened early—usually around 5:30 a.m.—although it's a good bet we were never really asleep. It took a while to prep for the anesthesia, and I would stick around to interpret until Andrea was completely under. Under the bright operating room lights and the heartfelt gazes of the surgical team, I'd squeeze her hand until it went limp, and I knew she was down for the count. A couple of times, Dr. Barker asked me if I wanted to stick around and watch the surgery. He was kidding, I think, but in either event, I wanted no part of it.

These surgeries were all day events. I would go through my waiting paces, usually (by choice) alone. Occasionally, Andrea's mother, or one of the kids when they were older, would come in for a few hours, but I really didn't want any company, and I certainly didn't want to make idle chatter with whoever was with me. Andrea never understood this; with her personality type, she always enjoyed the company and couldn't understand why I wouldn't, even in this situation. What she didn't get was that I needed this time to look inward for strength, pray to God, and contemplate the future, regardless of the outcome.

We did this enough times for me to develop my own little process: Grab breakfast and read the newspaper, stop in at the chapel, go for a long walk, have lunch in the cafeteria, attend 12:10 p.m. Mass at Saint Joseph's Church, blast out updates to interested parties, read for a while, go back to the chapel, have dinner in the cafeteria (I kind of liked the food), and then sit in the surgical waiting room to await the call from the doctor. While it was comforting to know what to do and expect, it's not a good sign when you've developed a routine around your wife's brain surgeries.

The surgical waiting room is the area within the hospital where families can go, wait out the surgery, get updates on the patient's progress, occasionally meet with a doctor, and then be called up to the recovery area once the operation was finished. It is a place, as you might expect, laden with nervous tension so thick you could cut it with a proverbial scalpel. Most of the time, the doctors' calls and meetings were met with an "Oh, thank God. Thank you, Doctor. I'm so glad it all went well." Every now and again, rarely but not never, someone would start sobbing on the phone, break down, or be led out of the room by a doctor or an aide. It was a stark reminder of the seriousness of the situation and the fragility of life.

I'd register at the waiting room first thing in the morning, which allowed me to come and go during the day. There were very few people there when I first arrived. During the day, I would walk by, but I usually didn't go in. A lot of people were there for day surgery, and it felt a little frivolous to me—like they weren't in the big leagues like Andrea and me. Silly, but the mind plays a lot of silly games under stress.

I'd usually get back after supper. The room would be thinning out, with only the serious players still under the knife. As the minutes and hours dragged on, the feeling of dread increased, until one by one, we were all contacted, and regardless of the news, we made our way out to wait in a different area for our loved ones to be brought down from the operating room. I was often the last one out as they shut the lights and locked the door.

After her surgeries were completed, Andrea would be transported to the recovery room. This phase of the process could be as scary as the surgery itself. The first question was, is she going to wake up? Several times, she didn't for a while, and a couple of times, she lapsed into a coma for multiple days. Two other times, she had seizures in the recovery room, resulting in "code blue" medical emergencies.

At first, it was an issue about how well the recovery room nurses were going to tolerate my presence in their protective, sometimes chaotic ten-by-fifteen-foot world. The one time they tried to ban me from being in the room with Andrea, she got sick, was unable to communicate with the nurses, and almost choked on her own vomit. After that, there was no question: I asked my hospital contacts to pass down the word that I had full access in the future in order to interpret.

Over time, I got to know the recovery room nurses and them me, and they were fantastic—dedicated, caring, and doting on Andrea and me. They made a most unnerving part of the process as good as it could be. They even noticed when it had been hours since I'd had anything to eat or drink and made sure I had lots of graham crackers and cranberry juice! Every one of them had a warm heart and a welcoming smile, and they endeared themselves to an always-freezing Andrea with toasty heated blankets. We managed to make the ordeal pleasant and congenial. If it weren't for the fact that Andrea had just been wheeled out of brain surgery, we could have all been huddling around the campfire, toasting marshmallows, and singing kumbaya.

In the recovery room, Andrea dealt with all kinds of post-op maladies—seizures, comas, infections, choking, vomiting, and fevers—and fought through them, all the time not being able to understand a word that was spoken and totally dependent on her ability to understand my sign language, while functioning in a groggy, drugged, bone-tired, and semiconscious state. It was both inspiring and depressing to see her like this, seemingly helpless, but slowly fighting her way through the fog and exhibiting an exalted level of valor.

When she finally came to, her first, barely comprehensible question to me was always, "Is it over with?" I always got a big, tired smile when I answered in the affirmative. Her follow-up question, in a barely audible whisper, was, "How are the kids?" Ever the loving mother, the kids were front of mind, even when she had precious little mind.

I had made a vow to Andrea when she lost her hearing after her third operation that I would never leave her alone overnight in the hospital. Of course, it was because I loved her, but I also felt it would be too overwhelming, sad, and, quite frankly, too dangerous, given the potential for miscommunication for a deaf person to be alone, especially after a major surgery. There were rare times when I took a break and slept at home, but even then, I made sure I had a trusted friend or family member who could interpret for Andrea while she slept in the hospital. Without that link, I wouldn't have been able to sleep, even in my own bed! Little did I know when I made that promise that we would cumulatively spend well over a full year of our lives sleeping nights in hospital beds (Andrea) and in reclining chairs (me).

I never broke that promise, and I'm glad I didn't. Not only did my presence give Andrea a consistent support system and friend, but it also gave me unfettered access to the doctors and nurses treating her.

If you truly want to advocate for someone in a serious health situation like major surgery, knowledge is power. Not only do you have to get smart about the illness and procedure, but you also have to be present. For all the structured elements that make a hospital run effectively, there are dozens of unplanned events every day: decisions that doctors make during their rounds, specialists who stop by, sidebars in the hallway, information from the nurses (the most connected people in the chain), news from the outside world from the flow of visitors, and interactions with the surgeons, which, as I came to find out, often happen late at night, even after midnight. If you're not physically present in these instances, not only are you not in the know, but you're out of the loop and never current.

Staying current in the hospital is critical. New news can become old news in a matter of minutes. Situations arise, complications set in, plans shift, schedules change, and when that happens, yesterday's perspective is useless. Staying current—even to the point of real time—is the best currency.

By way of example, one evening at about ten, with Andrea safely asleep in her room, I went down to the twenty-four-hour café to get a coffee and bumped into one of Andrea's nurses who was getting off her shift. She casually mentioned that they were taking Andrea down for an MRI that night—actually right as we were talking. I had no knowledge this was going to happen.

Andrea had been through so many MRIs under anesthesia that we basically had our own personal anesthesiologist, and there was a preanesthetic drug protocol because Andrea was allergic to the contrast dye. But this was after hours, so I knew our guy wasn't on duty. By the time I got back to the room, it was empty, and Andrea was gone. Fortunately, I knew where to go and shot down to the MRI room. Sure enough, they were unaware of Andrea's allergy and premedication requirements. A potential disaster was averted.

Being present also offered me the opportunity to mix in some spiritual balm as well. On occasion, I could flag down a Catholic priest to stop by and pray with us and give us communion—that always lifted Andrea's spirits. She would take the opportunity to engage him in conversation about her opinions on what was right or wrong with the church, a biblical passage that had her confused, or a philosophical discussion about life, and life after death.

Other times, God found us. Andrea's second post-surgery coma lasted for five days, and the doctors were concerned about the brain swelling and building up pressure in her skull. My daughter was en route from college in Arizona, and my son rushed back from a vacation in California, very worried for their mother's well-being. They were right to be concerned.

It was a quiet Saturday (the fourth day of her coma) at the hospital when one of the junior surgeons casually informed me that they were going to take Andrea down for surgery that afternoon to perform a craniotomy (remove a portion of her skull to relieve the pressure on her brain). I threw a tantrum and told him before any procedure took place, I needed to speak directly with her lead surgeon. I got on the phone with Dr. Barker, and he assured me that this type of preemptive procedure was fairly standard. He reviewed Andrea's charts and said that he'd hold off until Monday morning and do the procedure himself.

Despite the reprieve, things weren't looking any better. Andrea was motionless, her breathing seemed labored, and with apologies to Procol Harum, she was "a whiter shade of pale." Her brother John stopped in to see her and was taken aback by her condition. Knowing she hated anyone touching her feet, he grabbed her toes in a loving but futile attempt to rouse her.

Saturday turned to Sunday, and late that afternoon, my son came to sit with his mom and hold her hand, while I went to 5:00 p.m. Mass at the Saint Joseph's Catholic Church. After Mass, I caught up with the priest and asked him to pray for Andrea that night and at daily Mass the next day. He said he would, and as a matter of fact, he had a prayer group meeting starting at 7:00 p.m., which had a robust prayer chain with spiritual connections all over the world. He promised to ask them to channel all their prayers toward Andrea and her recovery.

Back at the hospital we talked to the docs, and they indicated that they were going ahead with the surgery on Andrea early the next morning because the pressure on her brain was now dangerously high, and she continued to be unresponsive. My sister came in to visit, so Peter and I could go up the street to get pizza. My son, like his mother, is a lively conversationalist, but that night, we sat quietly trying to process what was taking place.

At 7:55 p.m., my phone rang. It was my sister, and I braced for the worst, but it was anything but. Andrea had woken up and even recognized my sister and tried to say her name. I remember looking up at the sky as we walked back, and as I thanked God, I thought, *never underestimate the power of prayer and the strength of faith*. Although we had no way of knowing it at the time, this would not be the last time that Saint Joseph would intercede on our behalf.

Andrea always impressed almost everyone she met through all her trials—seasoned nurses, veteran doctors, therapists, hard-nosed administrators, and the staff who delivered the food, changed the linens, and wheeled her down for an MRI or for surgery—with her courage, humor, caring, and forthrightness. The first three attributes often brought tears to the eyes of the people who cared for her. They forged genuine connections and admired how she handled her situation and all of the adversity life had thrown at her.

The last trait, forthrightness, often (but not always) brought waves of laughter from whoever her target was. As you now know, sometimes she literally had no filter, but very few people ever took offense at some of the crazy stuff she said. Her favorite go-to line when she thought someone wasn't being straight with her was, "You're full of shit!"

She became a legend at Spaulding Rehab Hospital when, on her first day of one of her rehabs after surgery, with probably two dozen patients and therapists working in a big open room, the young physical therapist said encouragingly at the end of the session, "You did great," to which Andrea screamed back to him, "You're full of shit." As I pushed her out of the room, I looked back at a stunned, silent room, watching us walk out with looks that said, "Did that really just happen?"

She particularly hated the hospital food (I actually found it to be pretty good and would sometimes finish what she didn't eat). The dietitian would come up to ask her why she wasn't eating, and after Andrea asked her about her age, boyfriend, and living arrangements, she would answer, "Because it's crap!" When the dietitian regained her composure and pushed back at her, Andrea would ask her, with a smug smile, if she brought her own lunch or if she ate this "crap." Andrea already knew the answer, and without fail, every one of them always brought in their own lunch!

My sister-in-law tells a funny story about Andrea. Shortly after surgery and on a restricted diet, Andrea spotted a bag of Hershey's Kisses across the room. Andrea asked for, requested firmly, and finally demanded that my sister-in-law bring the bag to her bed. Worried whether the chocolate was inappropriate or worse, but more concerned about Andrea trying to get out of bed with all her monitor and intravenous connections (or screaming out, "You're full of shit!"), she gave her the candy and prayed for a good outcome. Andrea tolerated the chocolate just fine!

But it did get a little weird when she developed a little crush on one of her young, strapping PTs. The conversation (again in front of a large audience) went like this:

ANDREA. I don't want outpatient PT when I go home. Why don't you come and live with us?
YOUNG PT. I kind of need my own space.

ANDREA. Not a problem. We have a spare bedroom.

YOUNG PT. Well, I have a dog.

ANDREA. No problem. I love dogs.

YOUNG PT. Well, I have a baby.

ANDREA. That's fantastic. I love babies too!

YOUNG PT. Well, I'm married.

ANDREA. You're still welcome, as are the baby and the dog, but your wife stays home!

When all was said and done, she pulled it off because she was real. In spite of the seriousness and potential consequences of her many brain surgeries, she didn't want sympathy or even empathy. She didn't want platitudes for her brave front. She didn't want any special treatment or pampering. She just wanted to get to know you, for you to be straight with her, and for her to get better. Unfortunately, her last desire proved to be unattainable, forever hanging out beyond her reach, or the reach of anyone unfortunate enough to be knotted to this ghastly disease.

CHAPTER 20

This Is the Poison
that Will Make Things Better
(Maybe, Maybe Not; the
Chemotherapy Trials)

D r. Plotkin was (and continues to be) relentless in his quest for ways to cure NF as well as improve his patients' quality of life. His obsession led to one of our last, perhaps most surreal, battles in our war with NF: experimental chemotherapy clinical trials. Oh, boy, was this a wild ride. We were about to get another master's degree, this one in the medical/pharmaceutical industrial complex, and learn that there's a fine line between medicine and business, success and failure, and heaven and hell.

By this point, our lives seemed like we were living the famous saying about Russia—"A riddle, wrapped in a mystery, encapsulated by an enigma." There were so many moving parts, so much we knew, but still much more we didn't. NF had become so dense and complex as to be totally indecipherable and impossible to foretell. Within this context, we searched and scratched for glimmers of hope.

Dr. Plotkin knew, as we came to appreciate, that curing or preventing NF was the long game, from which many of his current patients like Andrea would likely never see the benefit. There was, however, also a midrange game. That aspect of research involved using chemotherapy and other tools with the goal of stunting the growth of, or even better, shrinking, existing tumors. This could reduce the number of surgeries required, and would represent a significant step forward for the Andrea's of the NF world. The short game was finding ways to make life a little better every day for Andrea and her fellow NF2 sufferers—the ever-critical quality-of-life aspect of the puzzle.

Attempting to play all three games simultaneously was an exceptionally delicate balancing act. Although physicians take a vow to "first, do no harm," in the real world of NF2 research, this seemed to us almost impossible.

Chemo is both a dreaded and esteemed procedure in the medical community. Esteemed because it's among the strongest tools physicians have to fight certain diseases, primarily cancer. Dreaded because it generally has bad, sometimes devastating and debilitating, impacts on patients in the form of side effects.

Back in olden days (pre-2000), chemo was comprised of toxic chemicals designed to kill or disrupt cancer or tumor cells. The chemo targets were (and are) abnormally and rapidly dividing and fast growing—which, by definition, is exactly what cancer or tumor cells do. Because cancer cells divide much more often than most normal cells, old-school chemotherapy was much more likely to kill them. Some drugs killed dividing cells by damaging part of the cells control center. Others drugs interrupted the chemical processes involved in cell division.

Because chemotherapy drugs traveled throughout the body, they often affected normal, healthy cells that are fast growing too. Damage to healthy cells caused side effects.

The field has evolved, now focusing on targeted therapies. These drugs are specifically designed to block signaling pathways within cells. The concept being that the tumor cells are "addicted" to specific growth signals that are turned on when the tumor cells develop.

The concept of chemo never entered our thinking until early in 2014, when Dr. Plotkin approached us and indicated that a drug called AZD2014 was showing some significant success in shrinking NF tumors in lab experiments. It appeared to work by blocking the growth pathways in leukemia patients. Dr. Vijaya Ramesh, through research at MGH, showed that AZD2014 blocked these growth pathways in human meningioma cells (a type of tumor found in NF2 patients) in a dish. This set the stage to try this medicine on people with growing meningiomas like Andrea.

This was big news in the NF world. While the holy grail was always to figure out a way to outsmart the genetic aspects of the disease and thus keep the tumors from ever forming, the next best thing was to use medicine to slow the growth of tumors, or better yet, shrink them. Dr. Plotkin asked Andrea if she would be willing to be the initial human subject to try to see if AZD2014 might work on NF tumors in humans.

Andrea's initial reaction was, "No F——ing way!" Fresh in her mind was her experience with her mother who had passed away from cancer the previous year. When diagnosed at the age of eighty-eight, her mother opted to undergo a chemo regimen in an effort to prolong her life. It didn't go well. She suffered greatly and died a slow and painful death. Andrea was with her through the whole excruciating eighteen-month process, and as one would expect, she was hardly a fan of chemo.

But Andrea kept an open mind and agreed to think about it. We considered our options and weighed the pros and cons. The potential pros were pretty clear—try to avoid additional surgeries.

Andrea's "Miracle of Montreal" brain surgery was super-natural. But it could only beat back—not stop—the NF tumors from continually growing at a slow and steady rate. Every four to five years or so, they attained a certain critical mass that required surgical intervention. Andrea went back under the knife for her eleventh brain surgery in 2006 and another in 2010.

Andrea's last surgery had been a technical success and a pragmatic disaster. That one left her in a coma for five days with so much swelling inside her head that her doctors were hours away from a craniotomy to open up her skull to relieve the pressure. What seemed to me was a Frankensteinian version of a cable box reset. My belief is that only divine intervention brought her back to consciousness.

Although surgeons removed significant tumors in each operation, they could not extract all of them. The inoperable "old" tumors matured, becoming more deeply embedded in her brain and spinal cord and more integrated with blood vessels and brain matter. More new tumors filled in around the older ones, creating a maniacal maze of lumps, channels, contours, and obstacles. Toward the end, this dense jungle seemed to become almost one undistinguishable mass, with scores of tumors hugging one another and vying for remaining space in her skull.

There was never any guarantee in any NF surgery that the surgeons would prune the right tumors and improve her situation, and there was always the chance she would emerge from surgery in worse shape than when she went in. Each surgery seemed more unpredictable, and each subsequent recovery was more difficult than the one before. She entered rehabilitation hospitals in increasingly diminished states. The stays in rehab were longer, and the recovery exercises were more grueling and draining. When she did get home, it took her more time to get back to "normal," and "normal" meant being able to do less after each surgery. On top of that, she wasn't getting any younger. So any chance to avoid or delay more surgery certainly seemed like a good thing.

Finally, trumping all that, after decades of surgery, Andrea was reaching the end of her emotional rope. She decided that she didn't want any more surgeries, and once she made up her mind, it was unlikely she'd budge off her position. While Dr. Plotkin and I had a certain amount of influence on her thinking regarding surgery, we were less inclined to exert that influence as she got older, as the surgeries became more perilous, and as the recovery process stretched longer and was less robust.

The final mitigating pro, and maybe the tipping point, was that Andrea sincerely desired to help others. She wanted to be a part of the team that found a way to beat this disease, which had caused unfathomable pain and horror to us, our family, and our friends. Maybe some incremental, if not monumental, good could come out of this trial that might move the needle toward a cure or, at the very least, improve the quality of life for other NF2 patients; or maybe, and perhaps more likely, it would turn into another good idea gone bad like her radiation folly years earlier.

This decision would become Andrea's ultimate act of courage, sacrifice, and altruism because the very significant cons were also crystal clear. AZD2014 was not approved by the US Food and Drug Administration for this purpose, so it hadn't gone through the rigorous process needed to validate its benefit and safety and release it to the public. Andrea would be the first human with NF to use this drug to battle NF2 tumors, and just because it showed success in rats didn't mean it would work in humans. Our understanding was that Andrea should expect some level of side effects, but there was no way to know if they would be mild, moderate, or severe. The drug had been used in trials on cancer patients, and the side effects were all over the map.

Then there were the business aspects of the deal. Remember, Andrea always shied away from the yucky business aspects of most things in her life. She wanted no part of them when it came to owning rental property, our investments, my job, or her own mosaic business, and certainly not when it came to the medical industry. As we would come to learn later in the process, for drug companies (and hospitals), clinical studies were big business. While these companies were in the game to develop and utilize drugs that could help sick people, they were also in business to make money.

My understanding of the drug company's business model seemed pretty straightforward. Develop or identify a drug that could help a segment of sick people. Determine the profile of the marketplace. Proceed to test this drug—first on laboratory animals and then on humans. Create a controlled environment to measure the impact of the drug, starting with a baseline, followed by consistent monitoring and good documentation. Evaluate the results, and if the drug seems effective and safe enough, package the data and submit it for review to the FDA to get approval to sell it in the United States. Once the FDA approves the drug, price it to the market, manufacture it, and market the hell out of it.

The cold fact was that it was a business model. To get the drug to market, it had to (1) work; (2) be deemed safe; (3) be FDA approved; (4) identify a market to justify the research and development, production, and marketing costs; and (5) be priced right for profitability.

It seemed to me that this model put doctors in a difficult position. Clearly, in our minds, Dr. Plotkin was doing all the right things for all the right reasons. But in reality, he had to walk a very thin line—selling hope to his patients to get them into the clinical trial while not understating the influence of the drug company or, of more immediate importance to the patient, the side effects. While he carefully explained the process, the pitfalls, and the potential upside and downside, we focused, at least initially, on the hope that we could be part of something that would help Andrea and maybe others also afflicted with NF. It's not that Dr. Plotkin overhyped the hope; it was more a case of human nature choosing hope over misery. Couple that human desire for survival with a fairly empty basket of alternatives, and it makes it easier to gravitate toward the new, unknown, but potentially game-changing option.

In hindsight, after we had a much clearer view of the bigger picture after having gone through the process, it felt like the old adage, "You just want to enjoy the hot dog. You don't want to see how it's made." We were hoping to enjoy the fruits of the clinical trial with as little hardship as possible. But that's not how this process played out.

This would be a clinical trial to test a drug was being used in an experimental setting, so the drug company officials had strict requirements and protocols for monitoring both the health of the subject and the success of the drug. Andrea would be subject to their rules—if they didn't like what was happening, they could drop her at any time.

The patient had to be stable going in, remain in overall good health (including maintaining their weight within certain parameters), and be able to tolerate the side effects. A baseline determination of Andrea's tumors had to be established. A full medical exam had to be performed every three months, including an MRI, to check the patient's health and to monitor the chemo drug's impact on the tumors.

Additionally, she had many other preexisting doctor's appointments and tests. Between all of these requirements, for the next couple of years, we wore out a track going up and down Route 3 on the two hour each way trip from Cape Cod into Boston.

The MRI segment of Andrea's requirement was of considerable concern because of the complexity of her MRI process. It was crazy off the charts, even by our insane standards. Andrea, among her many wonderful traits, had severe claustrophobia. MRIs sent her into full panic mode. She simply could not have an MRI without being fully anesthetized. Over the years, we tried everything—open MRIs, sedatives, acupuncture, counseling, and even hypnosis, but nothing worked. When Andrea's mind was locked, it stayed locked. This stubbornness no doubt helped her through some very tough times, but in other situations, it dramatically reduced her flexibility and willingness to adapt.

For most of us, getting an MRI is an inconvenience, something we can squeeze into our lunch hour. For Andrea, it was a four-day ordeal, involving fasting and premedication, hospital recovery, and a reentry process at home that included headaches, diarrhea, and nausea. She was allergic to the contrast dye and had to take medication thirteen, eight, and one hour before going under. This meant that no matter when the MRI was scheduled, she always had to wake up in the middle of the night for one of the doses. This was bad for her and created another level of stress for me, leading to a couple of slipups where I let NF get under my skin and led me to break some of my cardinal caretaker rules around maintaining good relationships and keeping my emotions under control.

For whatever reason, the last pill required right before her MRI was a Benadryl capsule—the over-the-counter allergy medication. One particular time, when we arrived at this point, I realized I hadn't given her the Benadryl and that, in fact, I'd forgotten it at home. Not a problem, right? We were in a world-class hospital with its own pharmacy and brigades of nurses, doctors, and nurse practitioners teeming with prescription pads. Ah, but this was Andrea's wonderful world of NF where everything was, or could become, a problem. When I told the anesthesiologist we didn't have the Benadryl, he furrowed his brow and told us sternly, "That's going to be a problem."

I said to him in my most endearing tone, "Right, like we can't get a Benadryl capsule at MGH." Well, the joke was on me—we couldn't get a sugar pill at MGH without going through the proper channels—and it was too late in the day anyway. They were going to have to cancel the MRI! No longer endearing, but certainly aggravated, I said to the doctor, "Then I'll go to the pharmacy and get the med." He said fine, but he was running behind schedule and told me I had fifteen minutes.

Like O. J. Simpson in the old AVIS commercial, I threw on my coat and sprinted through the hospital, out the lobby, and across the street to the pharmacy (which was fortunately directly across from the hospital). I grabbed the Benadryl, threw a twenty-dollar bill on the counter, and raced back—I had no idea what the clerk was yelling at me—flashbacks of our trip through Virginia when I kicked in the ladies' room door and hightailed it out of the state flickered in my mind. Back in the MRI room, we gave Andrea her dose, and in she went. In an act of frustration and immature defiance, I gave the remaining Benadryl doses to the doctor and haughtily remarked, "Why don't you keep these in your locker for the next disorganized jamoke?" and triumphantly (at least in my mind) exited stage right. Not my finest moment, but I would prove capable of even more boorish behavior when it came to this topic.

The combination of stress, familiarity, and sleep deprivation can make human beings act out in strange ways. Andrea also had a problem with her veins. I'm not sure if it was a result of the radiation she endured or just another bad card in her hand. In either event, the term they used was *rolling veins*, and it was very challenging to get blood out of her, and MGH seemed to have an insatiable appetite for her blood. In fact, she had so much blood work done that we were on a first-name basis with the phlebotomists in the brain tumor clinic and in the blood lab. These women were fantastic—competent, caring, and able to pierce her veins with a small butterfly needle with one "stick" every time. The blood draws came with a huge smile, an update on their kids and families, and a big hug at the end of the process. Nothing but goodness and sweetness.

However, when Andrea needed an IV for an MRI, it was a much different story. The MRI attendants weren't professional phlebotomists, just men and women who worked in the MRI department and, as part of the imaging process, had to insert an IV. We'd warn them about Andrea's veins, but with a cowboy/girl attitude, they'd barrel ahead and do what they had to do—always taking two "sticks" and sometimes three. It was clearly a painful process, but they felt they were capable (even when there was clear evidence to the contrary), and damn it, they were going to prove they could get the needle in. And they always did—often, however, leaving one or both of Andrea's arms red, raw, sore, and swollen for days.

It all came to a head one day when a young, overly confident assistant pooh-poohed our warnings and missed her veins for a third time—each time leaving an uncomplaining but visibly upset and hurting Andrea bracing for the next miss. He mumbled something about the fourth time being the charm when I verbally stopped him, and then I did something I'd never done in all our hospital interactions: I grabbed his arm and demanded that he stop. Needless to say, this didn't make

Mr. "Don't You Know Who I Am" in a white coat very happy. He pulled rank and said, "No IV, no MRI." I agreed and began to push Andrea onto her gurney toward the door. He asked me what I was doing, and I told him I was going to find Andrea someone in the brain tumor center who knew how to insert an IV with more than hit-or-miss skills.

What ensued was something like a WWF hospital-style wrestling match—I pushed Andrea, who was confused and upset, while he tried to pull us back as I jerked the bed forward into the hallway. We were tugging at the gurney from either end, much to the delight and horror of the gathered crowd who, themselves, were waiting for an MRI. Eventually, cooler heads prevailed, and I was allowed to call our phlebotomist friend to come up and, to my great satisfaction, put the IV in with one stick. It seemed like every aspect of our MRI experience was a zany adventure. Afterward, I felt badly. There were clearly better ways this stressful encounter could have been handled, and both the assistant and I knew it. We issued mutual apologies after the MRI and chalked it up to the full moon that night.

The day of the MRI was an all-day, outpatient process that included pre-op, being put under full anesthesia, the MRI itself, and post-op recovery. This was followed by a two-day respite and recovery process that kept her on her back while she reoriented and gathered her bearings. It was brutal, challenging, and even dangerous in many different ways. It was certainly a big check in the con column.

Of course, aways lurking in the shadows were the potential/likely chemo side effects. Many of us have witnessed family and friends who have gone through a chemo regimen. It's never pretty. It causes different side effects for different people in different situations, but they often include nausea, diarrhea, fatigue, dizziness, headaches, muscle aches, and a general feeling of having the shit kicked out of you. Andrea, as it turned out, would be *blessed* with all of these.

One other oddity (at least to us) was that, unlike most chemo treatments, Andrea would have to take a dose every day. This was not a "typical" chemo process used on many cancer patients that is cyclical and ends after an intense but foreseeable time period. Instead, this was an ongoing process that, if successful, would ensure that she would be willfully absorbing poison into her body every morning and living with the multitude of side effects for the rest of her life. A crazy definition of success, huh?

As one of the lab techs explained it to Andrea (thinking perhaps that she was new to the world of tumors, radiation, chemo, and the like), "Don't worry, honey. It's poison, but I'm sure it's going to help you."

Putting an experimental drug into a human for the first time introduces a whole different element into the risk-reward equation. A simple thing like what's the right dose was a relative unknown. The thinking was that too small a dose wouldn't have the desired impact on the tumor, and too large a dose might make the side effects intolerable. The impact on the tumors was a giant TBD, and the level of side effects a wild card. It would have to be a trial-and-error process—not the most soothing words you want to hear when you're about to enter the high-profile, life-altering world of experimental drugs.

Last but not least, was the cost. Because these drugs were experimental, they were not covered by insurance. The cost was astronomical – around $300 per daily pill. We were able to work with the drug company to mitigate a lot of these costs, but even when there was a small gap in the monthly delivery of the chemotherapy drugs and we had to purchase them directly from the compounding pharmacy, it was painful sticker shock.

While walking that very thin line, we were supremely confident that Dr. Plotkin ultimately had Andrea's best interests at heart. He knew Andrea and her history. He knew she was strong and strong-willed, and he knew the clock was ticking on the many tumors growing in her head. The only other option on the table at this point was surgery, and Andrea had poured cold water, at least for the moment, on that avenue.

There comes a time in any inflection point when you have to ante up and play, or fold and walk away. At some point in the analysis, I remembered a quote I liked from Winston Churchill: "Live dangerously, take things as they come. Fear naught, all will be well." Of course, this also had a religious connotation to us: Our faith had taught us to fear nothing because, ultimately, through God's intercession, all will truly be well. One more time, we piled into the car, and after a quick trip up to Saint Joseph's Oratory in Montreal and consultation with our spiritual advisor Saint André, we decided to move forward. Once again, we leaned back on our now time-tested belief of "in MGH and Saint André we trust."

So we blessed ourselves with the sign of the cross, strapped ourselves in, and braced for what turned out to be yet another roller-coaster ride. Andrea decided to enter the clinical trial. The upside was that, because of the drugs, Andrea would never require another brain surgery. The downside was that because of the drugs' side effects, she would struggle physically and emotionally almost every day for the remaining eight years of her life.

Once again, the serious and the absurd comingled together. Take the situation with Andrea's weight. Andrea had always been overly conscious of her weight, especially as her mobility waned, and in her mind, one positive side effect of the chemo was the potential for weight loss. And it happened—so fast and furiously that her doctors were concerned. (Andrea was concerned, too, that if she ever went off the chemo, she would put the weight back on!)

In addition to the weight loss, she was also experiencing almost all of the side effects we had feared. The worst was severe dry mouth, followed closely by bad diarrhea, nausea, an almost complete loss of appetite, and unrelenting fatigue. Daily life became increasingly more difficult.

But there was good news—really good news. The chemo actually appeared to be working! The tumors hadn't grown for two consecutive MRI cycles, and while the side effects were dreadful (Andrea's medical team worked feverishly with us to mitigate them as much as possible), the positive news, at least for the moment, outweighed the bad.

Later in the year, there was even more reason to celebrate: A couple of the tumors appeared to have shrunk. If this was true, it was the first time it had ever happened in an NF patient. This was a really big deal. Andrea was a rock star at the MGH NF clinic and rightfully so—she was literally sacrificing her body, and parts of her life, to advance this medical research.

But her problems persisted and, in fact, worsened. The weight loss situation was getting closer to a showstopper. The drug company had stipulated that trial patients who lost a certain percentage of their body weight within specified periods would be removed from this and future trials.

Despite the constant battering from side effects, Andrea amazingly maintained a pretty good attitude—at least for a while. We even tried our own remedies, figuring, "What the hell, why not?" As Bob Dylan sang in his classic song "Like a Rolling Stone," "When you got nothing, you got nothing to lose." So we went off-script and created our own little sub-trial clinic in our kitchen.

First, we addressed the weight loss issue—figuring if we could reign this symptom in, maybe some of the other areas, like fatigue and the general sense of feeling lousy, might follow. With little appetite for conventional food, Andrea happily went on a new diet—one of which the caloric maximums that would shame an ultramarathon runner in training. Her day started with two smoothies consisting of three bottles of the heavy dietary supplement Boost, two bananas, whole milk, and as much chocolate ice cream as I could jam into the blender. Lunch consisted of mounds of chocolate pudding and whipped cream, and supper was more ice cream, cookies, and amaretto.

At the same time we were pumping her full of unhealthy calories, we'd meet regularly with her nutritionist, whose job was to extol the virtues of healthy eating. Andrea wouldn't lie, but I would certainly spin the truth--walking my own thin line between her suggestions and our reality.

Despite our best efforts, she was barely breaking even, and she still felt shitty. She was actually beginning to tire of chocolate ice cream and pudding as an everyday culinary necessity. For a woman who had a sign over the door coming into the house that read, "Seven days without chocolate makes one weak," told me she was really sick! We used as many diversions as possible to keep her mind off the side effects: road trips, visits with the kids, and many Lifetime TV movies, but nothing worked for very long.

With her weight loss now at a critical point, it was time to get creative for our quarterly checkups. I had an idea that I thought was clever. While Andrea had a slightly different view (she thought it was stupid), she reluctantly agreed to go along with it.

She began going to her weigh-ins wearing increasingly heavier clothing. She dressed in layers, attempted to get on the scale holding her purse, and wore more ornate jewelry than a rapper. I must admit we got some strange looks when she came into the clinic in July with long pants and Uggs. While I don't think these actions had a real bearing, they provided a little comic relief and some peace of mind as we went through the process.

No matter the games and work-arounds we employed, as time went on, the pain began to outweigh the gain. We still attempted to live as much as we could on the normal side of our world, pushing the limits—going to Florida for the winter, even taking a trip abroad, and spending time with our growing flock of grandchildren—but the day-to-day turmoil was getting to be too much for even Andrea to bear. Although we tried to create as many diversions as we could, the incessant bone-numbing fatigue, unpredictable but increasingly constant nausea and diarrhea, and the inability to stop the severe dry mouth for more than a few minutes at a time were a losing and unsustainable proposition. As the old saying goes, "we could run, but we couldn't hide." We bobbed and weaved, but NF2 was never far behind.

The old motto "No pain, no gain" had been replaced with a new reality, "More pain, not enough gain." The time to reassess our plan and Andrea's tolerance was rapidly approaching, and as usual, NF would dictate the terms of our next chapter.

CHAPTER 21

What Doesn't Kill You Makes You Stronger, Right?

Finally, praise God, we moved onto a new, hopefully improved chemo drug in 2017, Brigatinib. Same goals as the AZD2014, but a different type of chemotherapy that targeted a variant signaling pathway. This version had different but somewhat lesser side effects. Andrea felt a little better, but even with this improved chemo, her body was taking a beating every day, and serious danger lay in wait.

One hot day in the summer of 2018, Andrea went to sit in the sun for ten minutes while I went out to run some errands. One dominant side effect, consistent across all of the trial drugs she used, was that they made her feel cold even in the middle of a heat wave. Unfortunately, an additional side effect of Brigatinib was extreme sensitivity to the sun that could result in sunstroke. Andrea knew this, but she figured she'd be out for only a few minutes to shake the chill.

Shortly after she sat down, she felt woozy. The sun was baking her compromised system. As she tried to get up to go inside, she lost her balance and fell. When I arrived home fifteen minutes later—thankfully I didn't run that one more errand I had thought about doing—she was in an unresponsive heap on the deck. I called 911. The EMTs arrived, treated her, and transported her to the hospital. The doctor at the hospital told me she probably had another five minutes before we lost her.

Her five-day hospital stay was a comedy of errors as these very caring but clearly overmatched doctors and nurses at the community hospital tried to connect the dots of Andrea's complex condition. We finally transported her to MGH, but even after her release, it took her several weeks at home to get back on her feet.

For me, this was a clear indication that the chemo had acquired the upper hand and had become too much. But as usual, Andrea fooled us all with her now almost legendary resiliency and determination. She bounced back, and as the summer drew to an end, she seemed to be tolerating her drugs a little better. It seemed to me she was able to will herself into another zone—she just didn't know how to give in or give up.

It proved to be short-lived. As fall rolled in, it became clear that we might be winning some of the battles, but she was losing the war. The tumors were stable or maybe shrinking (because of the mass, makeup, and numbers, it was difficult to get a definitive true measure), but the state of Andrea's health, diet, and lifestyle was unsustainable.

I decided the time had arrived to advocate for Andrea's well-being. We all wanted to keep fighting, including the drug company that wanted to complete a full trial to decide how to move forward with the production of the drug. But it had become too much for us. Andrea barely had the energy to get out of bed. Getting washed and dressed was an all-morning ordeal. She needed a long nap just to have enough energy to get washed and ready to go back to bed. Like NF had for many years, the chemo now owned her body and her mind.

Going into the last phase of the trial, we finally pulled the plug. Andrea simply stopped taking the drug and tried to reclaim and regain her health and a sustainable lifestyle. But it wasn't just as easy as stopping the chemo and feeling better. Her body, and to some extent, her psyche, was bruised and tattered. It was apparent that it would take some time before she, and it, recovered from this ordeal.

It's hard to imagine your body being so beat up and abused that even when you stop the abuse, it doesn't get better, but that was the case with this situation. Over the next two weeks leading up to Thanksgiving 2018, things took a dramatic turn for the worse.

Andrea wasn't feeling well, but she was more than ready to power her way through in order to spend the holidays with our kids and grandkids. The day before Thanksgiving, we were supposed to go to a basketball game with my sister, but Andrea was pretty lethargic, and we begged off. As the Boston Celtics' number one fan, she had to be pretty sick to pass on going to the game.

On Thanksgiving, Andrea was having problems standing up, but I managed to get her into the car for the two-hour trip to Connecticut for dinner. Natalie expressed concern over her mom's condition, and I promised her that if Andrea wasn't better the next day, I'd take her to the hospital. On the way home, we stopped at our son's house for dessert, and then I got Andrea into bed.

The next day, she wasn't better, so I brought her into a relatively empty MGH on the Friday after Thanksgiving for blood and urine tests. But most of the doctors were off for the weekend, and although the tests went quickly, we never heard back on the test results.

Andrea was really struggling over the weekend. Unable to get out of bed and, by Sunday night, talking in full-bore gibberish mode, I simply tried to keep her hydrated and comfortable. As I was going through my archives for this book, I found some of my notes I jotted down to relay to Dr. Plotkin. They reminded me of how sick she had become—she was "very confused", and "didn't understand simple phrases;" She stared down at the bowl of cereal with "no concept of how to use the spoon." She took a nap, but even after resting, "she was talking gibberish and I was unable to decipher what she was trying to convey."

By Monday morning, I knew I couldn't wait any longer for the test results and took her back to the NF clinic at MGH. She saw our usual nurse practitioner, Christina, who was alarmed by Andrea's condition and spent much of the day running her own tests, pumping Andrea full of fluids, and preparing her to be admitted for observation and scans. But as the old adage goes, "Man plans, God laughs"; because of a spike in severe flu cases over the weekend, not a single bed was available in the entire hospital. The NF clinic was closing at 6:00 p.m., so we were moved to the emergency room to wait until a room opened up for us.

We thought we knew a lot about the medical world, hospitals in general, and MGH in particular, but I had never experienced anything like the wringer we were about to be put through. The ER was windowless and dim, giving it the feeling of a medieval dungeon. It was crowded to the point of overflowing with people who were either there to be evaluated and treated, or being warehoused because there were no available rooms. Given the storm of coughing and sneezing and the requests for blankets from alternatingly freezing and sweating patients, I assumed there were more than a few people in close proximity with the highly contagious flu. Not good for anyone, but especially for people like Andrea with potentially compromised immune systems.

When I say crowded, I mean as jam-packed as a city subway at rush hour on Friday evening. All of the bays were full. There was absolutely no privacy; we all knew each other's issues whether we wanted to or not. We found out that in MGH-speak this is referred to as a "capacity disaster". New arrivals like

Andrea were simply rolled in their hospital beds into corridors and crannies while the doctors and nurses attempted to keep up with the overwhelming numbers. Each new siren heralded an ambulance that brought in another sick or maimed person on a gurney, and that continued every few minutes—all night. I had no place to sleep, so eventually, I sat on the floor and dozed on and off, not daring to fall fully asleep (as if I could with all the shouting, beeping monitors, and coughing) for fear of missing a call for a room that had somehow opened up.

During our almost twenty-four-hour stay, I observed many seriously sick people waiting for a bed (I later learned the term for this situation was *boarding*), and flu sufferers comingled with accident, stabbing, and at least one gunshot victim.

The room was saturated with the smell of the day's old gauze, unbathed masses, and trays of hospital food aging slowly and mostly untouched on tables, beds, and the floor. The entire area was filled with the constant moaning and cries of the weary and pained. And there was plenty of drama. A woman brought in by police was chained to a gurney and screamed obscenities for hours on end. A young man yelled back at the screaming woman, alternating between telling her to shut up and threatening to kill the doctors and nurses. Many people looked comatose, neither moving nor speaking for hours at a time, while others paced the hallways like zombies, expressionless and ashen. Some patients got out of their beds in hospital gowns and simply walked away. I don't know where they went, and in some cases, they never returned.

No one paid much attention to Andrea—not because of incompetence or indifference, but because of the overwhelming nonstop chaos. A truly heroic group of nurses, doctors, EMTs, police officers, and administrators did an amazing job of maintaining a semblance of control in what was a tense, heated, and often hostile environment.

As night turned to morning and morning to afternoon, our situation and the situation in the ER didn't improve. I'd been in constant contact with the clinic and admissions staff, to no avail. I tried to leverage all the positive lessons that I'd learned—go with the flow, trust in the process, pray, play the cards you're dealt, and the like—but as the day wore on and Andrea continued to get worse, I finally fell back on caregiver lesson number one: advocate, advocate, advocate. I knew if I didn't get Andrea a bed before 5:00 p.m., the day shift was going to head home, and that would mean another night in Crazyville.

Finally, I decided to take matters into my own hands. I left a message for the clinic to cancel the search for a room because we weren't going to wait any longer and I was taking Andrea home. I immediately got a call from an administrator who told me I couldn't do that because she was too sick to go home. I told them, in actuality, that she was too sick to stay where she was, and we were leaving. I wasn't even sure if I could get her out of there, but I'd seen other people walk out, and I figured I'd call their bluff. Ten minutes later, my phone rang. It was admissions. They'd found a room.

I don't know if the bluff worked, or it was a coincidence, but within the hour Andrea was in a private room, getting the kind of attention and medical care she needed. While she was getting better care, but she wasn't getting better. The doctors treated her for dehydration, exhaustion, and an infection, but she wasn't improving. They couldn't figure it out.

After the second day, I knew it must be bad when the attending physician asked me if I had any suggestions. I actually did. I suggested that they give her an MRI to see if any of her tumors had shifted or grown, and related our Florida trip story to them. I didn't really think that was the case, but even a long shot was worth a shot at this point. Little did I know it, but things were about to get worse—much worse.

On the afternoon of the third day, the doctors decided to take her in for an MRI. Although she had to go under anesthesia, Andrea was already pretty out of it, semiconscious at best. I went down with her, and I met the anesthesiologist. She was new to me, and that was unusual. Over the years, Andrea had had scores of MRIs, and I had met many of the anesthesiologists, but I'd never seen this doctor.

It all felt a little off, but I said to myself, "This is a big hospital, and you can't know everyone." Still, in the back of my mind, something didn't sit right. I had been through this drill so many times that I knew the routine and how the teams operated. This team seemed oddly disjointed. They were missing pieces of equipment, and they asked peculiar questions. I should have said something, but given Andrea's situation, I convinced myself I was just overtired and overanalyzing things.

I had learned a long time ago to question things in a hospital when I was uncomfortable, but in this case, my fatigue overrode my instincts and better judgment. They put Andrea under just fine. That was the easy part, but getting her to wake up proved to be a bit more difficult—she wouldn't open her eyes for another seven days.

It was one of the few times as an advocate when I hadn't trusted my gut. I was disappointed in myself for letting Andrea down. That marked the beginning of a torturous two months for both of us.

As Andrea lay in a coma at MGH in the neuro-intensive care unit for the next few days, I put the MRI situation behind me for a moment. Another lesson I'd learned from being in medical crises was that you have to be completely present in the moment, giving it your full, undivided attention. There would be plenty of time for reflection and analysis, but this wasn't it. Right now, all my energy had to be channeled toward resurrecting Andrea.

I knew from experience that doctors generally make their rounds twice a day, in the morning and in the late afternoon or evening, sometimes as late as midnight. A key rule for being an informed patient or patient advocate is to be present at rounds. At a teaching hospital like MGH, which is affiliated with Harvard Medical School, doctors make their rounds in packs, ranging from four to twelve people. Sometimes your own doctor is in the pack, but usually not. The pack is made up of a combination of veterans, newbies, and students, often wearing the same indistinguishable garb. Next important rule: identify the pecking order and home in on the leader of the pack, who ultimately makes the decisions.

The final rule in this area is to be prepared with the questions you want to have answered and speak up. If you're not prepared or ready to do these things, you run the risk of the pack moving on without getting any benefit from the only opportunity for interaction you may have for many hours.

Depending on the personality of the pack leader and the situation, the feedback you get can range from vague, quasi-reassuring non-answers to crisp, knowledgeable, declarative statements. My approach was to engage the lead doctor with context and questions. I felt this method helped the doctors fill in some of Andrea's back story, and gave me insights into their thinking and potential strategies. Even thought I barely knew these people, I thought of it as a team game with all of us having an important role.

In the first several days after the MRI, as Andrea lay virtually unresponsive, I used all the tactics I learned in the thirty-plus years of working with physicians in an attempt to somehow will her back to life. But this wasn't anything I could affect. Finally, during one of the updates, the lead doctor looked me in the eye and told me what I had been dreading. She said simply, "We have no idea why your wife isn't waking up." As bad as that was, at least I knew where we stood, and I appreciated and respected her for her candor.

Later that day, Dr. Plotkin came to see me. We'd all been through a lot together, and I always appreciated his generally optimistic attitude and his complete honesty. On that day, he was, as usual, honest but far from optimistic. He echoed what the lead pack doctor had told me earlier. He told me there was nothing more they could do for Andrea at MGH, and the best option was to move her to a special medical rehabilitation hospital. They simply didn't know what was wrong, why the MRI seemed to make it worse, or how long she'd remain in a coma, but hopefully, the rehab had the necessary medical resources and capabilities to bring her back around.

Uncharacteristically he lingered, and we had a long conversation about NF, life and death, life after death, his respect for Andrea, and her courage. It was simultaneously comforting and unsettling. As he walked out the door, I wondered if that might be the last time I interacted with him in the capacity of Andrea's physician.

I didn't have a lot of time to dwell on that aspect of our future relationship. I trusted Scott, and I felt for him. I knew from the pained look on his face that he was as unnerved as I was. Andrea was special to him, and next to our own family, her current plight ate at him more than anyone else. That didn't make the news to transfer her any easier to take. Andrea's road trip from our home to the clinic, then the ER, and finally to the neuro-ICU was about to take us to a new destination: a medical rehab hospital, whatever the hell that was! The only sliver of silver lining I could come up with at this point was that I knew that once again when Andrea finally did wake up, she wouldn't remember a thing. Thank God.

At the point when something has to happen in a hospital, anything from a test to an operation to a transfer, all the emotion goes out of the room, and process takes over. Of course, the process moves at its own pace, and that pace is usually slow—"hospital time" as we liked to call it. Andrea and I had plenty of experience with "hospital time" and ways to deal with it. Often, while killing time on "hospital time," we would use whatever props were in the room to amuse ourselves while we waited for the doctor; latex gloves, tongue depressors, and stethoscopes were some of our favorites. I would take the prop and put on a little variety show, while Andrea would alternate between belly laughs and horror.

One of our funniest memories occurred in one of the NF clinic exam rooms where there was a large plastic replica of a brain that opened up into four quadrants. In our own little weird world, we would demonstrate with a scalpel how brain surgery wasn't really "brain surgery," and even novices like us, using a YouTube video, could pull it off successfully. Piece of cake, we would proclaim. I wrapped up the presentation with the disclaimer that "I'm not really a doctor, but I did stay in a Holiday Inn last night!" We filmed it, and when we posted it, we got a bunch of likes and funny comments. I was surprised we weren't decertified on the platform!

Now, however, was not the time for frivolity. We had definitely moved into the vortex of "hospital time." What seemed like it should have taken an hour or two ended up taking eleven hours. But that was a drop in the bucket compared to what lay ahead. Our destination, Spaulding Rehab Hospital in Cambridge, Massachusetts, would become our new home for the next fifty-four days. Hospital time indeed!

As I watched them package up my unconscious wife for transport, it seemed to me that the chemo concoction meant to help her was more like hemlock. Recently, I looked up the documentation of the AZD2014 trials. A total of eighteen people, ages eighteen to sixty-one, participated. Nearly all exhibited noteworthy side effects. Twelve did not complete the trial because of a lack of efficacy, adverse events, physician's decision, or they just withdrew. The drug was not deemed sufficiently safe and effective enough to proceed, and the trial was discontinued in 2019.

Brigatinib is approved for the treatment of ALK-mutant lung cancer in the United States. While NF2 tumor cells do not have ALK, the MGH Synodos group studied the issue and figured out that Brigatinib also blocks the NAK receptor pathway. This is the active pathway for NF2 tumors. I suspect that Brigatinib will continue to have desirable antitumor properties for NF2 tumors. Progress? For sure, but progress at a big cost— in terms of time, money, and pain. I pray for those who submit to future trials. I pray for the doctors, nurses, and clinicians who have dedicated their lives to finding a cure. Finally, I pray for those who live and die with this despicable disease.

In the final analysis, chemo was reflective of just one front in the war on NF2. It reminded me that momentum and small victories were important, and that they often came with a cost. Like the epic clashes of WWI, where progress over weeks and months was measured in yards, not miles, gained; it was a gritty, bloody, painful war, often marked by subtle shifts and small triumphs.

Andrea and I still, even at this point, underestimated the severity of the battle, coupled with NF2's seemingly never-ending ability to bring waves of heartache and despair. The old adage about making progress, "You have to break some eggs to make an omelet," rings true in my mind regarding Andrea's role in NF research. She was special, willing to submit to the broken eggs' part of the equation, knowing full well she'd never get to enjoy the omelet.

People often ask me the sixty-four-thousand-dollar question: "Was it worth it?" It's a hard question because life with NF2 has very few absolutes; everything ends up being some shade of gray, even after you swear the issue presented itself initially in terms of pitch-black or transfiguration white. Nope, always gray. In that reality, I think what Andrea endured for seven long years was worth it. When future generations of doctors write the story of the demise of NF2, Andrea's sacrifices and unselfishness will be a part of that script. Through her willingness to allow herself to be abused (and make no mistake, it was pure physical and mental abuse), she ultimately contributed, in some small way, to a future where NF2 no longer ravishes and controls the lives of children, parents, families, and those supporting them.

Bless you, Andrea. Heaven holds a special place for you for all eternity.

CHAPTER 22

A Long, Strange Trip for the Grateful Living

It took nine hours between the decision to move Andrea and the time we arrived at Spaulding Hospital across the Charles River in Cambridge at 10:00 p.m. It was dark, with the rain coming down hard. By my math, we covered the 2.6 miles, averaging about a quarter of a mile per hour—pure "hospital time."

One thing to keep in mind when dealing with any hospital is that the normal processing day begins to shut down around 5:00 p.m. Usually at about 7:00 p.m., the night shift comes on and settles in for work. The night shift is a different animal. Their job is to maintain the status quo until the next morning when patients need to be fed, bathed, seen by doctors, do their exercises, and the like. Ten o'clock in the evening is not the ideal time to enter any hospital, especially with a comatose, deaf woman in hand.

And then came more "hospital time"—the admitting process. It always involves a lot of questions, often the same ones phrased in different ways several times over. It's annoying for the patient, but it's a requirement for the health-care provider (not to mention the insurance companies). And Andrea's deafness always made it take longer. Sometimes when hospital staff realized Andrea was deaf, they would gladly deal with me. Sometimes they would try to avoid me and deal directly with Andrea, which was almost laughable as they tried to articulate complex medical terms and then become frustrated when she didn't understand them. Sometimes they tried to use HIPPA privacy rules in an attempt to demonstrate that they were in charge, even though I had Andrea's full medical proxy. My only goal in this tiresome intake process was to move things along while keeping Andrea in the loop on any nonroutine questions.

They would always ask her if she wanted a sign language interpreter. Andrea always preferred to use me. She wasn't trying to make any kind of statement; it was just easier, and she was more comfortable—although I signed ASL, I also incorporated many "family" signs that were unique to us and more familiar to Andrea.

One time, against Andrea's wishes, the admitting nurse called in an ASL interpreter. When she arrived on the scene, she was a little pushy and hung around and refused to leave, even after Andrea let her know several times she was all set. Who knows, maybe she needed the money? Finally, Andrea smiled her sweetest smile and signed silently to her, "I told them my husband is going to interpret for me. Now get the hell out of here!"

The interpreter signed, "Thank you," and hit the road.

When we arrived at Spaulding, they didn't seem to quite know what to do with a deaf patient with NF who was in a coma. They'd seen a lot of things, but I suspected not this particular combination of ailments in one person. More "hospital time" drama as they debated what existing round hole fit best for Andrea's square peg condition. It was obvious that there was no good answer, so in my mind, any option would do—but I didn't run the hospital, and the back-and-forth continued for almost an hour.

At last, after midnight, we were assigned a room with *two empty beds*—these were the three best words we could possibly hear (short of "She is awake," of course). Because of Andrea's deafness, I was her designated hospital roomie/in-house interpreter. As I mentioned, she never felt comfortable being alone, and I never felt comfortable leaving her. As a result, we spent hundreds of nights together in hospital rooms, and I was used to sleeping in chairs, cots, or even on the floor. On rare occasions, there was an open bed in a semiprivate room, and often, the nurses would look the other way while I camped out there. Getting a bed, even only for a night or two, was a big-time luxury for me. That night, as I had often done over the many years Andrea was sick, I dozed off next to her and tried to imagine how this would all play out. I couldn't. So I said my prayers, pondered our situation and what kind of cards God was dealing us this time, and attempted to get some sleep and be ready for whatever tomorrow would bring.

I awoke in the still dark first flush of the morning to this strange new world and to an unfamiliar building with unfamiliar faces. Outside, the rain continued unabated, adding to the gloomy feeling of uncertainty. When you're admitted to a hospital, it takes a while to get acclimated. While all hospitals have many similarities, they all have their unique features and distinct personalities and rhythms. Our new dwelling was a medical rehab hospital, consisting of sick people (most with serious illnesses, like cancer or Alzheimer's) rehabbing from an event (e.g., a fall, an accident, or an operation). Nothing we'd been exposed to before, but it appeared to be well organized and well-run.

While the doctors and nurses were assessing Andrea's condition, I was getting to know the players, the system, and the schedules. I wandered around, checking out the cafeteria, the meditation room, areas where I could walk and stretch, and the amazing chapel. I also read up on the history of the building. What today is Spaulding Rehabilitation Hospital was founded in 1895 as the Holy Ghost Hospital for Incurables. The Sisters of Charity of Montreal (yet another spiritual connection), known as the "Grey Nuns," fulfilled the order's foundress, St. Marguerite d'Youville by caring for anyone with a chronic illness and disability regardless of background.

Originally a twenty-four-bed "cottage," the hospital grew over time to become Youville Hospital and Rehab Center, a 305-bed care facility, serving elders and those in need of rehabilitation. In 2001, Youville Hospital entered into a joint venture with Spaulding Rehabilitation Hospital, a part of the MGH umbrella; Spaulding purchased the facility in 2009.

All I knew was that, with the beautiful gardens, peaceful meditation room, and incredible architecture, this was a special place. Maybe because of my connection with Saint André and the "Grey Nuns" Montreal origins, I had a good feeling that Andrea was going to get the best care possible—and that proved to be prophetic.

For several days, the doctors and nurses evaluated, poked, probed, and consulted in hushed tones without any success. They were making no more progress than the team at MGH. We cajoled Andrea, I prayed, they switched medications, and we all became increasingly despondent. The doctors and nurses were more frustrated than I was. I'd seen this movie before, and I had a pretty good feeling Andrea eventually would wake up, although I certainly wasn't overflowing with confidence.

On the tenth day that Andrea lay in her coma, Natalie decided to drive up from her home in Connecticut and stay for the weekend to support me and comfort her mom. It was now early December in New England, and we were hit with a pretty good snowstorm the night before. I suggested she postpone the trip until the following weekend. But she would have none of that, and boy, was I glad that she didn't listen to me!

When she arrived, I could see the angst on her face. She'd seen a lot over the years, but the woman she saw lying motionless in bed barely resembled her mother, a husk of the formerly vibrant, irrepressible mom who raised her. Andrea was unresponsive; her skin was grayish; she had lots of tubes, wires, and monitors connected to her; and she'd lost a great deal of weight. Fortunately, Natalie had a large dose of her mom's strength. She didn't shy away in the least, greeting her mom with a big hug and a cheery hello, just as if she had walked into our kitchen for breakfast.

I asked her to sit and talk to Andrea while I went down to the cafeteria to get us some coffee. Natalie sat down, held Andrea's hand, and talked to her in a tone that belied the poor kid's anxiety and conveyed the sense that everything was going to be fine.

When I came back about fifteen minutes later, there was a lot of commotion outside the room, and nurses crowded around Andrea's bed. As I often did in those kinds of situations, I immediately imagined the worst case. But when I got inside, I saw Andrea with her eyes open, smiling weakly, and looking lovingly at Natalie. She had even softly mouthed her name: The word *Natalie* formed ever so slowly on her parched lips.

For the first time in this entire ordeal, my eyes welled up. They were tears of joy for a mother and daughter who loved each other so much that not even a coma, one that even the best doctors in the world couldn't figure out, could keep them apart. Once again, our prayers had been answered, and love had trumped another medical mystery.

Finally, we were on the bumpy road to recovery. Over the next few days, Andrea, who still could barely speak, and the nurses had started to bond. People really connected with her quickly and personally at a different level—through her trademark smile, eye contact, and physical interaction. Touching and hugging played a big part in how Andrea created more intimate relationships with almost everyone she came in contact with, including the cleaning staff, the food servers, and the maintenance guys. Andrea's recovery was going to be rough, but it would have been a lot rougher if it weren't for the phenomenal staff at Spaulding Rehab. While she still wouldn't speak for some time, I could see the connection forming through the smiles on the attendant's faces when they came into her room.

We quickly became family, getting to know one another, sharing stories, dreams, and laughter while agonizing and crying together, hugging, and offering mutual support. The young nurses thought Andrea was a hoot, and they would send her photos and videos of themselves out at parties or out dancing. Andrea wanted to know everything about their personal lives—where they lived or went to school, whether they had a boyfriend, and so on, until some of the questions started to make them blush a little bit. Several of the staff stayed in touch with Andrea long after her discharge.

Andrea slowly improved, but it was far from a even process. Sometimes it was two steps forward, one step back; other days, two steps back one step forward. After every operation or situation that required a stay in a rehab hospital, Andrea had to relearn almost every aspect of functioning as a human being. Speech, reading, walking, fine and gross motor skills, and using new equipment she would require all had to be rebuilt from a very basic level. Her focus and determination were so great, that I think even her closest confidants underestimated the enormity of what she had to go through to come back. They primarily focused on her progress and the end result, which were for the most part positive. But the physical pain, mental anguish, and emotional frustration were big parts of the process that few people had any insight into.

Rehab hospitals are generally structured to have one large area that contains the equipment, tools, and devices where patients are brought to work with their therapists. There's always a lot going on, and there is a constant encouraging buzz as the patients go through their paces. While it would not be unusual to hear a loud response, positive or negative, there were several examples of Andrea's frustration boiling over that brought the activity in the room to an abrupt, silent standstill. At one point, trying to improve her motor skills by building a structure out of blocks and failing again for God knows how many days in a row, she used her forearm to send the entire table of blocks flying across the room. Another time, she kicked the large balance ball off the wall and almost beheaded a therapist (to which the ever-upbeat woman shouted back, "Great leg strength!"). She had occasional outbursts with other patients who invaded her space, and she would be ever ready to hurl her infamous "You're full of shit" line at anyone she thought was less than truthful with her.

Relearning to walk was a particularly laborious and demanding process—especially during this stint at Spaulding. While I tried to keep Andrea's spirits up, especially in this area, I was getting pretty discouraged and wondered whether she would ever walk without a walker again. Again, her resolve overcame her aggravation, and she pushed herself beyond what was expected or reasonable. At the end of every session, she begged the therapist to allow her to walk farther, try new exercises, and work out on different equipment. Many a time, the therapist would say to her, "Okay, I think that's enough," and Andrea would retort, "No it's not, I want to do more." Often after a day of grueling work, she would implore me to help her sneak back into the gym to work out more. While visitors wanted to chat, Andrea wanted to "walk" with them to build up her strength.

One night when I was out to dinner and at a low point, her brother and sister-in-law called me with some long-awaited news: "She walked on her own!" they screamed into the phone. I didn't believe them and left the restaurant immediately to come back and check it out. It was true, and I cried for the second time since we had left our house a long, long time ago.

Despite the frustration, it was clear she was moving in the right direction. She flirted with her physical therapist, helped her occupational therapist with her dating life, complained about the food to her nutritionist as usual, and provided a great deal of entrainment to everyone who came into the room.

For example, one day the nutritionist brought in a lunch that Andrea, a gourmet Italian cook, turned her nose up at—and the following exchange ensued:

ANDREA. I can't eat this. It's lousy.

NUTRITIONIST. Actually, it's pretty good.

ANDREA, *eyeing the Tupperware container containing the nutritionist's lunch*. If it's so good, then let's trade lunches.

NUTRITIONIST. I would, but it's against hospital policy.

ANDREA, *in a voice loud enough to be heard at the nurses' station way down the hallway*. Bulllllllllllllshit!

The nutritionist could not stop laughing. Once again, it was Andrea's earthiness, honesty, and sense of humor that made her an almost instant, impatient patient rock star.

But behind the positive facade, it was tough for her. She had a catheter and wasn't eating well, and her eyes were troubling her. We were all trying to help correct these issues, work on her physical rehabilitation, and at the same time, reprogram her brain. It was, at best, organized turmoil. The longer it took her to get better, the more we realized just how sick she had been.

Even with the best attitude, there were many struggles. Andrea loved the holidays and family. She didn't remember Thanksgiving, so we arranged a Christmas party for her at the hospital. But she was very weak, and it was far from festive. The kids and grandkids tried their best to bring out some holiday spirit, but I could see in their eyes how painful it was for them to see their mother and grandmother in this condition.

While this level of trauma and heartbreak never became routine or even bearable, our kids knew the drill and dutifully slogged forward. But it was obvious to me that this latest ordeal dredged up a lot of old, bad memories. Their spouses hadn't seen anything like this before; they were simultaneously supportive and horrified. We limited the grandkids' exposure to the hospital, but they wanted to see their Noni, so we brought them in and out in small doses. As usual, our families stepped up big time. From spelling me to sneaking chocolate into Andrea, making food, doing her hair, and decorating her room, they made a tough situation as good as it could possibly be for all of us.

Many others at Spaulding helped Andrea recover—not only physically but also mentally and emotionally. They, too, were angels who helped us grind through the eight weeks we were there. For them, their work was clearly a vocation more than a job. Abiding in another of Andrea's lessons, we did what we could to show them our gratitude. We found out their favorite restaurants and got gift certificates and gave them heartfelt gifts. On New Year's Eve, we threw a party with Chinese food and party hats for everyone on the entire hospital floor. At 9:00 p.m., we moved the clocks forward three hours and popped a bottle of sparkling wine that I had smuggled in. That made Andrea nervous, to which I responded, "What are they going to do, throw us out?" The brand was André Cold Duck, of course.

Finally, we went home. Sixty-four days earlier, Andrea had gone to her doctor because she wasn't feeling good. From there, she'd been to the ER, was admitted to the hospital, did time in the neuro-ICU, and was transferred to a rehabilitation hospital. She still may not have been feeling top-notch, but she and we were so thankful and happy to be in our own bed and with our family.

God and a lot of good people were on our side, and they ultimately helped us find our way back home. A long and crooked path for sure, but we accepted it as God's plan, and we couldn't possibly have had a better guide!

CHAPTER 23

Some ABCs on QLAs
(Quality-of-Life Adjustments)

We returned home from Spaulding Rehab Hospital to the usual chaos of outpatient physical/occupational/ speech therapists, follow-up medical visits, incessant insurance forms, friends and family visits, and a new and pronounced variation of a chronic disease phenomenon that I had observed over the years. There may be a medical term, but I dubbed it "quality-of-life adjustment," or QLA for short. I have no idea what the clinical expression is, but in my experience as a care-giver, QLAs are of the utmost importance, can be obvious or stealth-like, and are one of the trickiest aspects of managing the evolution of chronic disease.

My definition of a QLA is a milestone, marking a major shift in your lifestyle. While QLAs can, in general, be positive or negative, when you are battling a chronic disease, they are almost always trending downward. When you have to stop driv-ing, for example, or have to move from a cane to using a walker, or can't get off the toilet without assistance, these are the types of markers you begin to use to evaluate where you stand in the evolution of the disease. While there can be positive QLAs, like rehabilitating after surgery or once again being able to relearn some things you physically could do prior to an event, in the cruel world of a progressive chronic illness, a positive QLA is like an oasis in the desert, too often delusionary or illusionary, and generally short-lived.

QLAs represent both practical and emotional challenges. From a practical perspective, the patient and the caregiver are constantly trying to stay ahead of the game, always cognizant of safety and comfort as the key priorities. This can be as simple as installing grab bars in the shower, pulling up the area rugs, or getting a lifeline device that automatically contacts caretakers and medical personnel in case wearers fall or wander off and get lost. This example of a simple adjustment, although a little challenging for a deaf person like Andrea, saved her from grave danger a couple of times she needed to activate it. It kept Andrea safer and, as a caregiver, provided me a sense of comfort and independence, which were like chicken soup for my nerves.

Other changes can be more extensive. It may mean widening doorways to accommodate a bigger wheelchair, building ramps, taking away the car keys, or moving from a two-story to a single-story house. These larger changes require significant logistical coordination and are often expensive necessities.

When possible, we used technology in dealing with QLAs. For example, setting up a camera system in the house so I could monitor Andrea's situation at home when I wasn't there. Some of my friends on the golf course thought it was a little creepy at first, but it was a godsend for me. They couldn't appreciate how much stress is alleviated and how response time is improved when caregivers and their loved ones know they can keep in contact with each other.

In Andrea's case, the cameras also provided security—a lot of bad things can happen when a handicapped deaf person is home alone. Sadly, there are people out there who prey on elders or handicapped adults. At one point, we had an issue with Andrea losing money—at first twenty dollars, then a couple of fifty-dollar bills, and finally several hundred-dollar bills. Certainly, Andrea had memory issues, but she swore she didn't spend the money and didn't know where it went. The security cameras revealed that our cleaning lady was sneaking back into the house and had been lifting cash out of Andrea's wallet. We caught her on tape and put an end to this unconscionable scheme. But the money wasn't the worst of it. Poor Andrea had been making herself crazy, traumatized, thinking she was either irresponsible or that her memory was failing at an accelerated pace.

As I mentioned, the practical issues of QLAs can be logistically challenging and expensive (we spent tens of thousands of dollars to redo the master bed and bath). But they pale in comparison to the emotional aspects. The potential for deeper depression is always simmering somewhere below the surface in people dealing with a chronic disease, and QLAs turn up the heat. Caregivers must be hypervigilant and quick on their feet to choreograph QLAs effectively and manage the rising tides of gloom.

It took me a while to figure out this QLA thing. I initially viewed a QLA as a mechanical exercise: If Andrea needed to use a walker, wouldn't she be safer and more mobile? Shouldn't she be happy? If Andrea needed an adjustable bed because she could no longer easily get in and out of the old bed, wouldn't that make her life easier? It's a practical move, right? When driving the car became dangerous, would anyone want to take a chance on injuring a pedestrian? What took me perhaps longer than it should have was appreciating the distressing emotional impacts on Andrea; to grasp and comprehend that it's not the walker or the bed or the ramp or even the car; it's the devastating sense that you are irretrievably losing your abilities, your independence, your dignity, and are another step closer to the bottom, from which there's no coming back. In pure layperson's terms, it really sucks.

Andrea seemed to know intuitively when a QLA was imminent, and her natural instinct every time was to fight it and push back with every fiber of her being. She would go contrary, resist the change, argue, and battle against it before she usually and gradually warmed to and accepted it and eventually came to embrace the new requirement. Not being able to drive was a real blow. With every QLA, there is a risk-reward evaluation. In the case of driving, at what point was Andrea putting herself and others at risk versus the impact of the emotional trauma she would suffer by giving up the wheel? As her driving ability diminished, Andrea protected her psyche by going into full denial and rationalization mode ("I have a valid license"; "I haven't been in an accident in twenty years"; "I don't care what you/my mother/my friends say about my driving. I'm fine").

Andrea's driving skills were further impeded by the fact that she wanted to carry on a conversation with whoever was in the car, and the only way for her to do that was to turn her head to read the passenger's lips—clearly a recipe for disaster. Even after she barreled down the driveway and demolished the Jeep trailer, she insisted it was a fluke. I was finally able to appeal to her mother/teacher/grandmother instincts and break through her defenses by asking her the simple question— "What if that trailer was a second grader getting off the bus?" She never again got behind the wheel of a car.

That's the "funny" thing about QLAs—the person affected often doesn't respond to bullying, persistence, or logic. As with the car, Andrea had to process it through her own way of thinking, which unfortunately made it appear to be convoluted or contrary to those of us trying to help. For many years, the only way I could get extra help around the house was to convince Andrea that the help was only for me, not her (which certainly had some validity). When she could no longer cook or garden, I argued that her insights and direction in these areas were more important than the chopping, mixing, or weeding, and there was a lot of truth to that perspective as well. My point is that QLAs have to make sense to the person living through the trauma and drama, not just those who are trying to help and support them. Looking at the process that way can help smooth out some of the inevitable bumps and make an inherently difficult situation just a little bit easier. I learned to observe, absorb, pray, communicate, and observe some more before taking action on a QLA; I tried my best to put myself in Andrea's shoes before forcing the issue.

Upon our return from the Spaulding ordeal, we encountered a critical QLA that crossed a red line for Andrea: permanent home health aides. Intuitively, Andrea knew this time it was different—these caregivers were not going to come in for a part of her home rehab stint and then leave, as they had in past situations; this time, they were here to stay.

This was a seismic shift. Another woman would be coming into our home to help her (and, as I pointed out incessantly, me) do the cleaning, shopping, and cooking and serve as another set of hands. Andrea understood the need, but she despised this idea. She was in no position to stop it, but that didn't mean she couldn't fight it, and boy, did she ever.

She took her displeasure out on the first few aides assigned to our case. These innocent victims cycled through, usually for a couple of shifts, because, for Andrea, they weren't fast enough or smart enough, or they didn't work hard enough, and their cooking certainly was not up to snuff. Andrea must have seemed like a raving lunatic. She would say do A, and they did A—to which she'd reply, "I meant B," and they'd do B, and she'd say, "You're not listening, I said A!"

The reason Andrea lashed out at these home health aides had nothing to do with their competence, personality, or ability to help; it was because she knew they represented a momentous QLA. Her own home would never fully be hers, ever again. These poor health-care workers were unfortunate collateral damage. We were both struggling with this cycle of frustration and beginning to wallow. That's when God sent us yet another angel.

Mary was just another person sent by the agency in what was becoming a long line of home health aides who, in Andrea's mind, weren't meeting her standards. As so many of our angels did, Mary entered our lives randomly, only to become a part of our lives forever, first as a helper, then as a trusted companion, and later as a close friend.

Mary was clearly competent and wanted to do a good job. She initially seemed nervous and a little timid (maybe she'd been warned about Andrea's antics). What broke the ice was, Mary started to banter with Andrea. Mary retained her professionalism, but as much as Andrea dished it out, Mary gave it back. This give-and-take sparked a connection between the two. It personalized the relationship and transformed Mary from representing a negative QLA into a real person Andrea liked and came to depend on. Mary made Andrea happy, and I think at that point in her life, that's what Andrea was searching for—a reason to be happy.

As an aside, it was interesting for me to observe and parse not only some of the emotions Andrea was dealing with, but also the impact these emotions had on her daily being. I provided security that gave her a sense of comfort and companionship; God contributed a deeper feeling of hope and peace; her kids and grandkids brought her love and energy; but it was angels like Mary who gave her a reason to laugh and experience everyday joy. You could see it in her anticipation of them coming, the look on her face when they would walk through the door, and the ongoing chit-chat that invariably brought cascades of laughter. This collage of different elements, each bringing their own bit of meaning to the party, was the fabric of the village that helped lift Andrea above the drudgery and pain that clouded her life.

Of course, Andrea had to put her own imprint on the relationship with Mary. Shortly after Mary started working, Andrea had this conversation with her:

ANDREA. I like you, but I can't call you Mary anymore.

MARY, *confused*. Why not? That's my name.

ANDREA. I have a sister-in-law named Mary, and I can only have one Mary in my life.

MARY, *a bit taken aback*. Well, what do you want me to do? Change my name?

ANDREA. Well, maybe. What's your middle name?

MARY. My middle name is Gertrude, and I hate it!

ANDREA. Well then, if you really hate Gertrude, then you can be Trudy.

And so Mary became Trudy, and from that point forward, Trudy didn't work for us; she was part of us. Whenever she was around, she was an extension of our family. It wasn't long before she and her husband, Bob, were coming by for a glass of wine before dinner, or I was out playing golf with Bob while the girls hung out, or we were showing each other our favorite restaurants. Trudy retired after a couple of years of working for us as a home health aide, but she never stopped coming to visit. Her effervescent personality always brought a whole lot of sunshine, laughter, and goodness into our lives.

Trudy is a shining example of how a person, with the right degree of empathy, can singlehandedly transform a seemingly hopeless situation into a long-lasting positive one. Andrea not only accepted Trudy's assistance, but through her, she also made peace with the necessity to take help from all the future home health aides we would need to utilize for the remainder of her life.

Acceptance is the key to QLAs. But often it takes time, and QLAs don't always move in linear directions or at a rate you would like them to. A good caregiver has to develop a feel, and balance off the need for action with the risks and rewards, as well as gauging the patient's willingness to accept their new level of capability and the changes it entails.

Andrea accepted and then embraced the home health care QLA, and Trudy was an enormous help for us during the transition period coming home. With her and a host of dedicated therapists, as well as Andrea's own drive, after just one month or so removed from Spaulding, we were cleared to go to Florida for a month of relaxation. Down south, we got a home health aide whom Andrea loved. I had to laugh because now she was all in and couldn't imagine life without her home health aide. We set up physical therapy, and with the help of family and friends, we were able to make Andrea safe and comfortable. Although still dealing with side effects from her daily chemo (which, believe it or not, she had agreed to re-start), she was feeling almost as good as she had before the long travail of chemo and rehab. By the time we left Florida and returned home to Cape Cod, Andrea had been riding her trike bike, going out on our boat, and socializing with our friends. Andrea was feeling better than she had in years, her tumors were stable, and we dared to hope again.

As a caretaker, I also had to deal with my own QLAs. Some of them were, of course, mirror images of Andrea's, only from a different perspective—moving to a one-story house, updating the house to be handicapped accessible, the surgeries and aftermaths, or the loss of independence—but the biggest one for me was retiring from ADS. For thirty-five years, I had regularly put in sixty-hour weeks and extensive, exhausting business travel. My position and role had become both my anchor and my identity. In 2014, Bill Gallagher asked me if I wanted to take over and run the firm, and while a scaled-down model could have been lucrative, my reaction was "no frigging way."

Andrea's mom had passed away in 2013, and with the progression of the NF, forever chemo, and never-ending rehab, once again, God shed His grace on thy; for the next eight years, I had the freedom and the time to support Andrea as she required increasing levels of assistance and attention. It was time to ride off into the sunset, close the ADS chapter of my life, and be fully focused on my role as Andrea's caregiver. What a blessing and a gift that turned out to be. God was once again directing traffic.

One old lesson I relearned during this timeframe was to "be in the moment." I had made my living for over thirty-five years by hustling, compartmentalizing, and multitasking. I had no spare time or energy to stop to smell the roses. In fact, I flew by the flowers so fast I didn't even see the garden. For the next eight years, not only could I be present for Andrea, but I also relearned the old lesson of being in the moment.

To be a truly effective caregiver, you have to be physically, mentally, and emotionally present so you can pick up on cues, interpret signs, and absorb and assess what's happening—good or bad. In the early stages, it's frustrating beyond comprehension because you don't have any context or experience. And it only gets more difficult as you face the realization this is going to be a long-term role, and each successive QLA becomes more difficult, more draining, and more distressing.

And boy is there is a huge caregiver community in the United States grappling with these issues. AARP's "Valuing the Invaluable" 2021 report estimates caregivers provided thirty-six billion hours of unpaid care worth six hundred billion dollars; the average caregiver pays more than seven thousand two hundred dollars annually in out-of-pocket costs (e.g., transportation).

Still, some people just can't accept this type of situation, ignore it, or walk away from it. No judgment here—it can feel like a lifetime sentence that saps your energy, your independence, and your spirit. For me, actual acceptance came slowly, in increments and degrees. Initially, it came grudgingly—the "Why me?" stage when I wanted to blame everyone and anyone: fate, doctors, all the "idiots" in my life who didn't get it, and God. Especially God. The times I grew angry and resentful it was never directly at Andrea because I knew she wasn't responsible for her plight. It was sometimes at other people, often times at God, but mostly at NF2, that damned evil entity methodically banging away at Andrea's brain and ruining our lives.

The next stage for me was focus. I began to realize that this was serious— "true business," as my born-Deaf friends would sign to me (meaning something was true with full certainty). It was a never-ending, always-morphing challenge. Here, I started to understand that while I didn't have any control over NF, I did have control over myself and my relationship with NF. This realization was key for me; my mindset shifted from "Why is this awful thing doing this to us?" to "Let me figure out areas I can focus on, control, and improve." My years of solving business problems and managing complex technical projects were invaluable in allowing me to conquer this phase.

During this stage, I really analyzed the disease, dug into NF studies in medical journals, joined NF support groups, worked closely with Andrea's doctors to understand our situation and devise potential alternative ways to help her. I homed in on the Andrea Cahill Foundation for Neurofibromatosis Research.

The foundation and fundraising gave us the greatest element of control over this beast. NF couldn't stop us from raising money to support researchers as they made incremental but important progress against it. After years of getting our asses kicked by NF, we were finally helping to turn the tide and have an effect on the game. It felt even better than the Red Sox finally beating the Yankees and going on to win the World Series in 2004. (Sorry, Yankees fans, I just couldn't resist that jab!)

While every year we staged our fundraising bike ride, the training got tougher, the Green Mountains in Vermont seemed to get higher as I traversed them, the wind was always blowing harder into my face on the final leg from Lake Champlain to Montreal, and the final mile up Mount Royal to Saint Joseph's Oratory—that testament to hope and salvation for us—got steeper, it was that much more pleasurable knowing we were helping to hasten the demise of NF2.

We, of course, saw our plight through the lens of Saint André's life. If this humble man who stood barely five feet tall could create such a glorious cathedral and international pilgrimage site through prayer, devotion, and faith, why couldn't we be a part of another seemingly impossible goal like eradicating NF? Faith gave us a reason to try and keep going back to that well again and again.

In the midst of this long, strange trip of caregiving, the old Grateful Dead song lyric would occasionally come to mind: "Sometimes the lights all shining on me, other times I can barely see." There were times, as a caregiver, I was so focused that I felt as though I was on an island by myself. Other times, I'd get a lot of positive feedback from people observing the situation and appreciating what they thought I was going through. Their comments ranged from "Boy, you're doing a good job" to "I can't believe how committed you are" to "You're a rock star. I don't know anyone else who would do what you're doing."

It's flattering to have people appreciate what you're doing, but I had to be careful not to let it take on a life of its own. It wasn't all that difficult to get swayed off course and start listening to and believing my own complimentary press clippings. It can be enticing to worship false idols, especially when the devil disguises these idols in the image of goodness.

And that's when I crossed over into the "gracious stage"— fully comprehending it wasn't about me; it was, and always had been, about Andrea and the damned disease, and the only reason I was put in this role was to support Andrea and wrestle with NF. This understanding allowed me to deflect any adulation, realizing it had no value toward the cause and could only serve to skew my focus, dilute my attention, and put me out of position as I attempted to assist Andrea. No hero ball allowed;

caregiving really is a team game, and everyone needs to play their part. I felt content in the role God had given me.

The final stage, for me anyway, was gratefulness. I'm not sure when I crossed this line, but I'm sure glad I did. I don't know if it was one or a series of QLAs that moved me, or if it was simply a natural progression. I do know that, for me, prayer was a key component because, by this point in our lives, prayer was the basis for almost every move we made. I began to thank God for choosing me to fulfill this destiny, realizing how much joy, satisfaction, and comfort I'd been given through my relationship with Andrea.

This stage was not as utopian as it may sound, but it certainly brought me a deeper sense of serenity. It gave true meaning to what I/we were doing—in the day-to-day sense and in the bigger picture. Small things and individual moments became clearer, more poignant, and more important. I felt my faith was enhanced and rewarded. It was a shining example of a positive QLA.

It also improved my relationship with Andrea. She never fully accepted her NF, which is probably why she was able to fight so hard for so many decades. But I finally did, and that made for a good counterbalance.

Sometimes, Andrea's endless questions could be annoying, and her stubbornness and her cognitive issues could make her challenging to live with and turn the simplest issue into a maddening morass of confusion. But I was usually able to ascribe her curtness, crabbiness, or sometimes downright mean comments as a product of NF. I fed off the gratefulness, more likely than not to be looking at life's difficulties through the lens of "It's nothing personal. Move on to the next situation/adventure and hope things will be better."

Living more in the moment made everything a little clearer, more vivid, and easier to deal with; I really began to slow down and better appreciate the little things in life. I laughed a little more at our trials and tribulations (and much more at myself). I worried less about the future. I had an even greater appreciation for our angels. I smiled more frequently at my wife, we spent more time on the beach parking lot watching the sunset with a glass of wine, and I held her hand like I meant it.

In this final more enlightened part of our journey, I came to believe even more that we were all put on this earth for a reason, as part of a plan. We can't just be random bits of matter with uninhibited free will floating around the universe and bouncing off one another haphazardly. I ultimately believed that what happens to, and between, us is fate. It's defined, orchestrated, and ultimately judged by a higher power. I call that higher power Jesus Christ, but to me, it doesn't matter who or what you call it, or if you call it anything at all. All I can tell you is that Andrea's and my little world, riddled with mysteries and contradictions and scarred by NF, was tempered and lit by faith and love that emanated from a higher power.

People would say to us, "Your life is so difficult. You've lost so much. It must be such a struggle." My reply was, "Some of that is true, but from that, we figured out how to create a happy, loving, and caring relationship by looking past NF and focusing on the goodness in life." I'm not sure folks believed my answer, but it doesn't matter. I'm at peace with how things played out.

Focusing on the moment, Andrea and I spent pretty much every minute of every day together in the last three years of her life on Cape Cod in the summers and in Southwest Florida in the winters. Sure there was sadness, trauma, and burdens to bear; pain and the ever-present danger of a fall or an accident; and the certainty of a not-so-happy ending. But there was also the joy of making each other's lives better, bringing smiles to our faces, easing our mutual burdens (even if it was only for the moment), and having shared experiences that only we could appreciate and could never have had on our own. These things happened by being in the moment, being fully committed, and by outsourcing our earthly burdens to God.

For me, for example, taking Andrea on a boat ride exemplified how, as a caretaker, you can both give and receive great satisfaction from this role. When I looked back and saw Andrea gleefully spotting an eagle, yelping with joy when she saw dolphins swimming along with the boat, flashing an enormous smile as she closed her eyes and relished the winds on her face, or giving me a big hug when we docked, any caretaker malaise I had would disappear and float away in the breeze. We were both fully in the moment, and in those moments, the world was our oyster, negative QLA's be damned!

CHAPTER 24

Day Is Done, Fades the Light, God Is Nigh

I will never forget the time when Andrea and I went to see a bullfight in Mexico City and barely escaped the arena in one piece. We went in with innocent excitement, anticipating the matador would conquer the evil bull and woo us and the crowd with his skills and bravery. But the scene went unexpectedly topsy-turvy for us.

It was a brilliant summer day, with the festive crowd smiling and chanting, teeming with the anticipation you feel when you attend a big sporting event. And for this crowd, this was sport—a cultural ritual that brought joy to the assembled masses. Long before the matador appeared, the bull charged into the ring—full of life, feisty and free, healthy and headstrong. But then, for us, the spectacle turned into three drawn-out acts of increasingly painful cruelty. First came the picadors, men riding horses protected with mattress-like padding who wielded sharp lances that they repeatedly jabbed into the bull to cut the muscles in its neck. The second act involved the bande-rillas, men who stabbed the bull's shoulders with colorfully dec-orated sticks tipped with sharp spikes to tear muscles, nerves, and blood vessels.

Finally, in the third act, the matador arrived, taunting the bleeding, weakened, confused bull with his cape before thrust-ing a sword into the bull repeatedly to try to pierce the heart, cut a major blood vessel, or sever the spinal cord.

This was not what we expected and didn't seem like much of a fair fight. Eventually, the matador wore down and killed the bull—much to the delight of almost everyone in the stadium, except Andrea and me. We were firmly in the bull's corner and loudly rooting for beast to best man. Our previously polite seat-mates subjected us to a lot of jeering before we hastily escaped the stadium. In a most bizarre twist, we went out for a drink and something to eat at a local restaurant—only to see a bull's head mounted over the entrance. We quickly found another place to dine.

It wasn't much of a stretch for us to relate to the bull's quandary. It had entered the ring vibrant and spirited, but sud-denly, it found itself in unnatural circumstances—overwhelm-ingly and, to us, unfairly beset by powerful, inexplicable forces. The bull drew on its determined instinct to fight back, even as it got more disoriented and diminished and progressed toward an inexorable fate.

So it was with Andrea and NF2. She had grown up happy, optimistic, kind, inquisitive, and determined—blissfully unaware of the harsh realities to come. NF2 upended all of that. Without warning, she was beleaguered by unpredictable and unrelenting danger. To survive, Andrea had to adapt to whatever was coming next and depend on her unwavering will.

NF2 reconfigured both her body and her mind. It created what I dubbed "dead spots" in her brain that sometimes made her cognitive processing go sideways. Sometimes she would tell me, "I know what I'm trying to say, but I'm talking ragtime." In Andrea's brain, illogical sometimes became logical, and vice versa. And when that phenomenon combined with her natural inquisitive, outspoken, and headstrong nature, her kind and caring personality, as well as social norms, could go out the window, and she became contrary, stubborn, cutting, and even nasty. When she herself was confused, she became confusing to others around her.

It's no wonder she developed dual personality traits. Andrea was a paradox in so many ways. At any given time, she could be happy but sad, healthy but sick, bubbly but troubled, nice but nasty, clear but confusing, simple but complex, smart but ditzy, aware but forgetful, straight-talking but vague, soft but hard, strong but vulnerable.

Her ability to juggle juxtaposing traits is one of the things that made Andrea so interesting and endearing to me. She could appear disjointed and confusing to all of the people some of the time, and some of the people all of the time. But I felt like God had provided me with a secret decoder ring that allowed me to decipher and appreciate the yin and yang of these opposite but interconnected feelings within her.

Her paradoxical personality was overlaid by yet another level of complication: having to toggle between her public and private lives. I've touched on this, and we all do it to some extent, but those fighting a chronic illness have a more dramatic schism between these two worlds. Some choose to fight it full bore (Andrea for sure), some (I suspect most) pick their spots, while others turn inward and become reclusive.

The fight in Andrea allowed her to maintain a public persona that was often not much different than before she became ill. Always smart and sharp, she learned how to make sport of herself when she had mental lapses, and her ability to read the room allowed her to channel many of her altered capabilities into being ditzy and charming. On stage, she was always caring, attentive, happy, and accommodating. That was how she wanted to feel and how she wanted the outside world to see her. It took a lot of effort, and certainly, it wasn't phony, but it also wasn't sustainable.

NF2 also reshaped her psyche. When she was triggered or had too much time to think, another side of her personality was on display. She could be withdrawn, insensitive, and angry. When she retreated into this dark part of her world, her favorite retort was, "I don't care," and she didn't. She didn't care about what she said, how she said it, or who it hurt. She didn't care about things that helped keep her going and were necessary for her health and well-being. She didn't care about me or about herself.

Oddly, this dungeon was also a necessary sanctuary for her to maintain her sanity. She needed a place to feel lousy about the world and herself, where she could lash out and not give a crap about anyone or anything. If you don't care, you can't be hurt by anyone or anything, including NF2. I came to appreciate that she not only *needed* to escape to this place, but she also *deserved* to go there. It was her way of taking back some control and refocusing. Then from this dim, gloomy yin side of her personality, the bright yang side of her being would reemerge.

NF2 was never able to quench her desire to be with people. They energized her and buoyed her spirits. Her love of people kept her slips from turning into slippery slopes of depression and despair. Over the last chapter of her life, as Andrea's discomfort and loss of function and dignity mounted, her kids and grandkids often acted as the guardrail that kept her from falling off the cliff.

Our daughter and her family lived about three hours away, outside of Hartford Connecticut. When she decided to settle there and raise a family, Natalie made a commitment to us that they would be an important part of our lives, and she stuck to that promise through thick and thin. She drove to the Cape at least once a month. Her house was always open, and we always felt welcome, and we were happy to drive to see their family at least once a month and sometimes more. In my head, I never wanted to go more than two weeks without seeing them face-to-face. As a school teacher, Natalie had summers off, so she and our grandsons, George, Harry, and Trey, spent large chunks of time throughout the summer at our house on the Cape. Friends would ask us if it was too much to have company all the time, but Andrea and I loved every minute of it. There were regular trips to Martha's Vineyard, birthday celebrations, Cape Cod League baseball games, playing soccer in the yard, trips to the beach, and many board games—all filled with the laughter and beauty of three young boys loving their time by the ocean and with their grandparents, Papa and Noni (from *Nonna*, or *grandmother*, in Italian).

As the boys got older, they began to learn sign language, and by the time they were seven, the older two were proficient enough to be able to engage in conversations with their deaf grandmother. Ever the teacher, Andrea would create elaborate games to increase the boys' sign language vocabulary. Most of the time, they were having so much fun with her that, like her first-grade student's decades earlier, they didn't even realize they were learning.

They climbed up on her lap, even in the wheelchair, and became very protective of her. It was special to watch, and I know they'll grow up to be better human beings as a result of the time they spent with their Noni.

As for our son, Peter, while Andrea loved his and Ali's company, and cherished the many adventures we had with them on the Cape and in Florida, she had worried that they weren't going to have any children. This bothered her greatly, and she would occasionally raise the issue with them. Given Andrea's outspokenness and her Italian family upbringing, it was useless to tell her that she was crossing a line that she shouldn't.

The day she found out that Ali was pregnant, I thought Andrea was going to lose her mind. For the remainder of the pregnancy, whenever we were with the kids, Andrea would pretty much ignore us and talk to the baby and rub Ali's belly.

When Peter called to tell us they were on their way to the hospital, we were in Florida. Andrea was determined to get on the next plane so she could mother the mother and the baby. It took a couple of days, but when we did get home, it was as if baby Lou was the first and only baby ever born. She gobbled him up.

When Andrea held her new grandson, they would often lock their eyes and enter a different zone. Andrea's smile beamed when she held baby Lou in her arms. She would sing and sign to him, "One, two, three, four, five, I caught a fish alive!" Maybe it was Andrea's voice or her hand movements, but whatever it was, Lou would be mesmerized until the end of the song: "Why did I let him go? Because he bit my finger so. Which one did he bite? The little one on the right!" And when she pretended to bite his finger, he would reward her with his own big beaming smile.

But as time progressed, even the joy of her children and grandchildren couldn't offset the steady erosion created by NF2. In the last years of Andrea's life, NF2 had worn her down like that bull in the ring. Her legs were giving out, and she was falling often. She couldn't always make it to the bathroom on time. More frequently, she was forgetful, and sometimes things didn't make sense to her. She didn't want sympathy or to be a role model or to be lauded; she wanted to be able to eat a roll without choking and wondering if she'd be able to breathe again, have a glass of wine without worrying if she would fall over when she tried to get up, or get through the day with being bone-tired, even with two naps.

Increasingly she'd say to me, more often than I would have liked, "I don't want to live like this anymore." And what could I say? "Don't worry. Things will get better. There's a good ending in sight"? No, she was right, and we both knew it. The problem was that neither one of us knew how to stop. We'd been battling this thing for so long that now, like that bull, it was our last primal instinct. We had melded into one entity, dedicated to shielding her from the horrors of the disease.

As the sand in the hourglass of her life steadily emptied, she pondered the ultimate paradox—while she cherished the people in her earthly life, she longed for the peace and serenity of a heavenly eternity. The greater her challenges, the more difficult it was to reconcile her battle here on earth.

In the final acts of her life, I feel like we both found a measure of peace. We created a simple but effective routine that dealt with the realities of NF2, but didn't allow the disease to take control of our daily process. Andrea got up, ate breakfast, and got washed/dressed—an everyday sequence that now took us about three hours. Often our helper and wonderful friend

Donna was there to assist Andrea and do the cooking and cleaning. Donna would be the last in a line of marvelous, giving, and caring women who became enmeshed with Andrea and helped to elevate her will to push forward.

Even in the monotonous rhythm of the morning routine, Andrea found nuggets of joy. For her last birthday, the kids got her an electronic picture frame that rotated hundreds of photos that they fed it. Every day, Andrea would delight in looking at the photos—new ones or old ones, it didn't matter to her. Our conversation over breakfast usually went something like this:

ANDREA. I love these pictures!

ME. Me too, but are you going to talk to me or just look at the pictures?

ANDREA, *not responding, continuing to look at the photos.* I love these pictures!

ME. I'm not going to sit here if all you're going to do is look at those pictures over and over.

ANDREA, *cue the eye roll.* I love these pictures!

Our wonderful daughter-in-law Ali also made sure to send Andrea a good morning text message every day with a new photo of baby Lou.

ANDREA, *squealing with delight.* What a cute picture of Lou Ali sent me this morning.

PETER. (*No response.*)

ANDREA. Did she send it to you?

PETER. No, she only sends it to you every day.

ANDREA, *cue the eye roll coupled with a mischievous smile.* Oh,
that's too bad.

By early afternoon, we would lumber out the door, and
I'd push her down the new ramp our neighbor and friend Clay
had built for her and help her into the car. While she hated the
need for that ramp, it made life so much easier for us. We'd tool
around for several hours, doing errands and making observations about what was happening around town. In a real-life version of "Driving Miss Andrea," she would order me to go here
or there, tell me my errands were boring, and have long debates
with herself about what she wanted for lunch.

Our daily excursion always included driving by the beach
at the end of our street on our way home, where years ago, we
had spread Andrea's mom's ashes into the ocean. Andrea would
say a prayer, ask her mom a question, or fill her in on some
goings-on (which frequently included complaining about me!).

Since we lived only a quarter-mile from the beach, we'd
sometimes go home and grab a bottle of wine and a snack, go
back to the beach, talk to each other and her mom, and watch
the sunset. If I hadn't prepared anything for dinner, we'd go
out to eat, usually at our favorite restaurant at the other end of
our street, the Quarterdeck, where the wait staff and bartend-
ers treated us like the locals we'd become, and Andrea like the
queen she aspired to be.

Getting ready for bed was the inverse ordeal of getting up in the morning. Two hours to get washed, get her pajamas on, and take care of her eye. I'd always complain about how late we went to bed, and she'd complain about how I read too much before falling asleep. When I finally turned the light off and rolled over to give her a goodnight kiss, every single night, she would sign off by saying, "This is the very best part of my day." And every single night, even after forty-three years of marriage, it still touched my heart, just a little bit.

In November 2021, we had our last discussion via Zoom with Dr. Plotkin. He told her, as gently as he could, that she had many tumors, including several that were large and now on the move. Even the chemotherapy was no longer stopping their relentless progress. The conversation was unusual for its bluntness and clarity:

DR. P. I'm afraid I have to recommend that you have surgery.

ANDREA. No!

DR. P. I know you don't want to hear this, but I think it's the right solution.

ANDREA. No!

DR. P. Will you think about it and consider it?

ANDREA. No!

DR. P. It could improve the quality of your life and keep you safer.

ANDREA. I don't care.

DR. P. You know I'll never badger or try to force you into anything you don't want to do, so if you change your mind,
let me know.

ANDREA. Thank you.

When the call ended, she asked me if I was going to side
with Dr. Plotkin and try to talk her into it as I'd done many
times before. But this time felt different, and I said, "No, not
at all." She'd earned the right to make her own choice without me chirping in her ear. We snuggled up on the couch as
the late afternoon dusk turned to night, lost in our individual
thoughts, but united by Andrea's steely resolve to go forward on
her own terms. At this point, more profoundly than ever, we
leaned heavily on our belief that we are spiritual beings, living
through a human experience—it gave us both great comfort.
Once again, her suffering brought us closer to God, now at the
point where life, suffering, the after-life and faith had metasta-
sized into the very foundation of our being.

In December, we were scheduled to go to MGH to meet
with Dr. Barker who was going to elaborate on why he felt surgery was the best option at this point. We'd then make a go/
no-go decision on the proposed operation. Andrea woke up
that morning and said, "I'm not going." This happened all the
time, and normally, I would have cajoled her into the car to
make the appointment. On this day, I said, "That's fine with
me," and canceled the meeting.

The lure of being in heaven with Jesus and her beloved mother was starting to seduce her. Like the Blessed Mother and her seven sorrows, Andrea's suffering was bringing her closer to God. She said she felt too worn out to go to our niece's wedding out of state. But the pull of people and socialization revived her once again. She somehow garnered an inner strength and decided we should go.

It took hours to get ready. We had to navigate a muddy parking lot in a deluge of rain, with three ushers carrying her in her wheelchair up several steep flights of stairs. But it was a wonderful time filled with family, joy, and love, and Andrea was an active participant. As I watched her rally, with all of her brilliant paradoxes on display, I marveled at how this incredible woman could once again rise above her trials and tribulations and laugh while she was sad, radiate happiness while she was troubled, and show strength while she was weak and vulnerable—demonstrating to all of us one more time what it meant to live life to the fullest.

For December, we rented a mobility scooter for her to get around in. Andrea had fought using this device for years, but like many QLAs, she now loved it, bopping around and apologizing for running into the walls and chipping the paint on the trim and the doorways. I could have cared less. Watching her have even a little more independence and mobility was worth a hundred dented walls.

The week before Christmas, we hosted our annual "Cahill Family Christmas Party." This was a forty-year tradition—the one time each year that most of our very large family got together in one place. With a crew of about fifty relatives laughing, singing, and yapping away, Andrea held court at the kitchen table. Always with someone's baby on her lap, she thoroughly enjoyed the day. Much later, one of my brothers and his family told me that, as they were leaving, Andrea called them back and gave them an extra, harder hug. On the way home, they talked about something feeling different; to them, it felt like Andrea was saying a bigger kind of goodbye.

On Christmas, we went out to brunch with the kids, and although Andrea seemed tired and disjointed, she was in her glory at the restaurant, bouncing baby Lou and showing him off to everyone and anyone who walked by our table. Back at the house, she was exhausted, but she wouldn't sleep and wanted to spend as much time as she could with the kids.

On the day before New Year's Eve, Andrea had one of her "episodes." She woke up, but she wasn't awake; she couldn't speak or get out of bed. I called Dr. Plotkin, and we came up with a plan to try to build her strength and see if she'd come around. She didn't, and the next day, with great difficulty and help from Donna, we got Andrea into the car and onto the hospital. Donna had a lot of experience with Andrea and illness (she cared for her own husband for years before he passed away), and I caught the worried look in her eye.

Andrea was severely dehydrated and had a bad urinary tract infection. We spent our last New Year's Eve together in the hospital. But as was her MO, within a couple of days, she was feeling better. Natalie drove up from Connecticut to help. She put on a good face, but I could see the same look in her eyes that Donna had two days earlier.

In retrospect, I think they, Andrea and God, were trying to alert me that the end was near, but I certainly wasn't in tune with the plan. We traveled to our condo in Florida for the season in an upbeat mood. Making the decision to stop having any more surgeries seemed to energize Andrea. We were in Florida for five beautiful days. We purchased a scooter for the condo, went out to our favorite restaurants, and took what turned out to be one last glorious boat ride on the backwaters of Bonita Bay that we'd come to love so much. Andrea was ecstatic at the number of dolphins jumping near the boat and putting on a show for us. The last picture I took of her, sitting on the boat with her trademark smile, summed up the momentary inner peace she was feeling.

The next night, she passed peacefully in her sleep—forever free at last. Waking up next to her that morning, waiting for the EMTs to arrive, giving her CPR for fifteen minutes, and holding her one last time before they pulled the sheet over her face were the hardest things I've ever gone through, but I thanked God for taking her without even one more day of suffering.

We had tickets to the Tampa Bay Buccaneers playoff football game the next day—a chance for her to see her favorite sports hero, Tom Brady, play maybe in his last game. When I lamented to the priest who came to comfort me that my biggest regret was Andrea never got to the game, he rewarded me with my first piece of post-Andrea perspective: "She has the best seat in the house, looking down from heaven," he reminded me gently.

Andrea wasn't afraid of death, and in many ways, she welcomed it. We both had come to grips with the idea that life on earth, compared to eternity, was like a grain of sand on a twenty-mile stretch of our favorite beach. We believed that we would be together again shortly—with Andrea going straight to heaven and hopefully having enough pull to drag me across the line—and that comforted both of us.

In her last months, she had finally found a modicum of peace with NF2. She believed that God never gives anything to those who can't handle it, that we all have our crosses to bear, and that it's all part of God's plan. The only thing that really nagged Andrea was an irrational level of guilt. She wondered what she did wrong to deserve this. Did she hurt someone and was being punished? Was God angry at her?

We discussed this topic ad nauseam, and she decided that these questions and doubts are too hard for mere humans to decipher, and unfortunately, she'd have to wait for an audience with her God to get the answers.

I, on the other hand, thought I had the answer. But Andrea didn't believe me, or by this point just didn't care. I believed Andrea was put on this earth to make the world a better place— by getting so many people to think beyond themselves and positively interact with others. In my theory, Andrea touched the lives of innumerable people. The breadth and depth of her influence were pretty impressive—family, friends, neighbors, acquaintances, countless medical people, students, and complete strangers. Boatloads of people who came away with an inclination to listen a little more attentively, care more deeply, and show a little more love. And when some of these people also touched a few other people, Andrea's impact and love spread exponentially.

Is it possible that Andrea suffered all those years so that more people could do more good? That's my theory, and I'm sticking to it. Andrea would tease me during her medical appointments that I always had a lot of follow-up questions. I'm also hoping to ask a few more if and when I get the chance to meet with upper management in the afterlife. I'm banking on Saint André's ability to guide me through the unknown and back to a smiling, radiant, healthy, and heavenly Andrea.

For me, I was drained, with the only regret that I hadn't done enough—enough to make Andrea comfortable, enough to ease her physical and especially emotional pain, and enough to keep her spirits up. One of my favorite Quincy Jones songs summed up my emotional state: "I did my best, but I guess my best wasn't good enough." NF had managed to keep a solution at arm's length, making us feel like, "I gave it my all, but Lord knows we're not getting anywhere. Seems like with all we've got going, we haven't got a prayer." But I momentarily snapped out of my distressed state to realize once again that we did have a prayer, and in fact, our prayers had been answered—Andrea was at peace, in heaven, without pain, and with her beloved mother and Saint André.

Well played, my dear. We did trick NF; it was both the journey and the destination that mattered, and your landing spot was the perfect reward for not only what you endured but also for the grace and faith through which you endured it. Amen.

Our life was hard, but it was good. Our frustration with NF was real, but we abided. Our faith was tested, but it was never broken. In the end, Andrea was finally able to shed all her paradoxes. She could be simply joyful; she could be vulnerable; she completely embraced God; and when she finally stopped fighting, she was at peace and blessed with perpetual happiness at long last.

CHAPTER 25

Stormy Headwinds, Spiritual Tailwinds, and the "Rainbow Connection"

Time seems to stop when you lose a loved one, but eventually, it continues ticking on, and life moves forward. The calendar dragged painfully from winter to spring and then rolled into summer—my time to start training again for our fundraising bike ride for the Andrea Cahill Foundation. The 2022 ride was going to be unique. Andrea would be with me only in spirit. The training and the fundraising were similar, but like many aspects of my life, the whole vibe was a little off-key.

As the ride approached, I had more time to reflect on what I was doing, why I was doing it, and what it meant to be in this game without Andrea. I questioned myself and my motives. Was I doing this for the right reasons? Should I have just wrapped it up with the 2020 ride rather than continue without Andrea? Would I be motivated without Andrea's presence driving me? What would it be like by myself, in solitude, for the entire trip?

I tried to give these questions their due, without allowing them to consume me. It was harder to sustain my incentive without a real sounding board and a perpetually quiet house. Finally, I once again put my trust in God and my faith that everything would work out however it was supposed to. Determined to control only what was under my control and leave the rest to fate, I pushed aside my doubts and carried on with a heightened sense of vigor and purpose. I pushed myself to train harder and fundraise with more enthusiasm, laser focused on the real goal of helping those living with NF2.

In some ways, it was easier. I certainly had additional flexibility and time. I didn't have to rush to get home for Andrea. I wasn't worried that I'd been gone for too long and was courting disaster in the form of a fall or a choking problem. For the first time, I had full freedom and unlimited time to go about my business to get physically ready for the ride.

But strangely, not having to worry about Andrea left my head eerily empty. I often resorted to playing association games with landmarks I passed on my bike that had some meaning to us: a restaurant, a park, or even an intersection where we'd laughed, conversed, or argued. To counter these dark flashbacks, I started to listen to music and tried to be more in tune with my surroundings—not only for self-preservation reasons, but to soak in the beauty of the road and quiet my chattering mind.

I came to realize that building up my endurance on the bike could also be a wonderful opportunity to become more immersed in the magnificent environment I was pedaling through. This not only gave me a sense of peace, but it also led me to a greater level of awareness of some of the interesting things taking place around me. I started sharing my observations with the four hundred or so people who had traditionally donated to the Andrea Cahill Foundation in the form of what became my "musings from the road."

To my surprise, these musings became popular with the readers and a lighthearted diversion for me. I had conversations with animals (turkeys were the most prevalent), noted the beauty surrounding me, pointed out historical landmarks, and made whimsical observations about biking, geography, and life.

I received a lot of positive feedback from people who either enjoyed the nonsense, learned something new, or just liked hearing about what I'd observed from my perch on the bike. It was a win-win deal; it helped me keep a positive focus during the training, and it made our supporters chuckle and look forward to the next iteration. Here's a sample of one of my musings (which could have just as easily been labeled, "The rants of a biking madman!"):

> *Happy Friday!*
> *Some of you let me know you enjoyed my musings last week—well, it doesn't take much encouragement, so here's round 2:*
> *I've reached an understanding with the turkeys—they let me down the back roads*

unimpeded, and I promise not to bash them in my musings. You might say we got together and "talked turkey." Let's hope the truce holds.

This is how bike math works: 45 miles Tuesday + 40 miles Wednesday = feeling like you're 85 on Thursday.

There was a time in my life when I thought it might be a good idea to buy stock in Budweiser Beer—right now, Advil would be a far better choice.

As Albert Einstein told his son, "Life is like riding a bicycle. You can only keep your balance if you're moving forward."

To break things up, I did a training ride on Martha's Vineyard last week—can I count the miles on the boat to get to the island and back toward my daily goal?

Riding around Cape Cod, I see some beautiful street names—Seashell Lane, Oyster Pond Road, Ocean View Ave.—but I also see some odd ones: Would you want to be a pig living on Bacon Farm Road? How about a caddy on Putter Drive (maybe just use a wedge?)? Or anyone living on Leather Leaf Drive? The town of Falmouth must have been running low on street names.

*One street name that makes perfect sense is
Presidential Road in Bourne; the summer house
of President Grover Cleveland still sits there
majestically overlooking Buzzards Bay.*

*My six-year-old grandson thinks I should
ride from Montreal to Cape Cod because it's all
downhill on the map—do they start teaching
geography in the second grade?*

*It's been a great week of training—the rain
gave me a day off yesterday, but I'm back at it
today. October 2 is coming fast!*

God bless!

In many other ways, the training period was disconcerting.
As much as Andrea shunned the spotlight in the fundraising
effort, she was still the star of the show and my active, behind-
the-scene partner. I was used to telling Andrea about my training ride when I came home, but now I was met only by stark
silence. I'd tell her anyway, even though I knew her answers by
heart. The emptiness was deafening. and the best I could do was
put on some music and linger for longer than necessary in a hot
shower. The music sounded artificial and tinny, like fake crowd
noise pumped in at a sporting event, and the shower, which
should have been therapeutic, was in fact draining and left me
with shriveled fingers and an even darker mood.

At night, as I worked on fundraising, a similar scene played
out. I missed the days when Andrea would yell to me from the

other room, "Peter, shut that damn computer off, and come in here and spend some time with me!" When I'd ignore her and tell her to stop yelling at me, her prophetic response still haunts me: "You're going to miss my voice when I'm gone!" As was the case so many times, she was right on the money.

Finally, D-Day arrived: October 2. I was feeling melancholy, and the awful weather matched my mood. Natalie and her family lifted my spirits with their genuine love and unbridled enthusiasm. They saw me off and would meet me en masse in Montreal five days later. Peter and Ali put together a huge fundraising effort the previous weekend that netted one thousand dollars and, along with baby Lou, stayed in constant communication with me throughout the ride. My sister Mary surprised me with balloons and a gift bag at the inn on my first night. All my family and many friends texted me their warm wishes and heartfelt support. My frame of mind began to transform to one of thankfulness—for being able to do this, for being able to honor Andrea, and for the support the monies would provide for NF2 patients and research.

Unfortunately, I was jolted from this emerging feeling of goodwill by the reality of the weather. I was pedaling into the remnants of Hurricane Ian, which had devastated the west coast of Florida, worked its way up the East Coast, and was meandering through New England. While significantly diminished from its earlier category 5 status, Ian still packed enough energy to have a significant effect on an old guy riding northerly into the face of a stiff north wind.

The first couple of days were challenging. With cold rains and winds averaging twenty miles per hour and gusting higher, the wind chill factors plunged into the lower forties. When the elements come at you hard on a long bike ride, there comes a time when you need to evaluate the severity of the weather and your endurance capacity and determine whether to push forward or pull back and wait it out.

I saw that the bad weather was going to stick around for a few days, but I felt I'd trained properly, so I decided to push myself through it. In some odd ways, the weather turned out to be a blessing in disguise. It forced me to pace myself and exercise more caution on the wet byways. I had less time for my mind to wander as I locked in on the rain-slicked roads, and I made more stops than normal to warm up and wring out my clothes. As a result, I got to converse with a lot more really nice people who were genuinely interested in the ride and the purpose behind it.

Some gave me blankets, some kept an eye on me to make sure my coffee was warmed up, and others shared stories of their own loved ones with chronic illnesses. One waitress sat with me for fifteen minutes to compose herself after hearing Andrea's story and relating her brother's struggles with MS, before contributing. A guy in a bike shop checked my bike over and replaced my speedometer/odometer at no charge. A postal worker in a tiny town in the middle of nowhere Vermont offered to drive me to the nearest coffee shop (I declined, even though it was twelve miles away in the rain and into the wind).

While Andrea was always on my mind, it was the weather that demanded my attention. I balanced my thoughts between what I was doing and why I was doing it with the very basic requirement of staying upright on the bike and getting to my nightly destination in one, albeit one very soggy piece.

Most of the roads I travel on are backcountry highways, usually one lane each way. In some of the hillier places, there are signs for an additional climbing lane for trucks, which, although it created a de facto bike lane, I never liked seeing, knowing the impending grade was going to be intense. The road shoulders usually have an informal "bike lane" that ranges in width from three feet to mere inches. Cars and many large trucks that travel between the small cities and towns connecting these roads often reach speeds between sixty and seventy miles per hour. In a tight lane, the draft from a big rig can be strong enough to push you off the road.

For the most part, I coexisted with the vehicles that blew by me. I was already soaked, so their spray didn't bother me. But there was one scary moment when a lumber truck passed me going fast. As I looked up, I was horrified to see planks of wood stacked side to side rather than end to end on the truck. These boards poked into my bike lane space and passed directly over my head. It shook me a bit when I realized I was less than two feet away from being decapitated!

The mountains around Ludlow, Vermont, are always a challenge, but even more so on this trip because of the weather. It takes many times longer to go up than it does to come down.

As a result, you feel like you're constantly going uphill, and it starts to wear on you mentally and physically, especially with age. That's why I say woe to the two twenty-something bikers who blew by me with mocking grins and disparaging gestures as I was going up the side of Okemo Mountain. Bad karma boys, you'll be old someday too.

Over the last days of the ride, especially as the weather cleared, I had plenty of time to contemplate life as I traversed the rolling hills in central Vermont surrounded by some of the most beautiful, colorful scenery in the world. Andrea's saga of courage and daily grit never stopped amazing me, as remembrances galore popped into my head like a string of firecrackers going off, one after another.

Some of the big stuff she endured was on display for the world to see, but I was an audience of one for the everyday small stuff she wrestled with that I found so impressive. In my mind's eye, her struggles were innumerable, her setbacks immense, and her triumphs often improbable. The minidramas I reflected on in the Netflix of her life, in my mind at various times, had me alternating between smiles and watery eyes, but they always made me proud to have a role in her epic performance. Consciously or subconsciously, I pushed and pulled harder on the pedals, and the miles disappeared behind me as wonderful snippets of her odyssey looped in my mind.

I had other inspirations as well. My father never gave up or stopped fighting even as his diabetes consumed him. Unlike Andrea, he had a prickly personality, and his impact was on a smaller circle of people, but I admired and tried to emulate his work ethic and perseverance.

I also thought of my eighty-two-year-old friend Noah, a brilliant architect and former athlete now plagued by leg and foot problems. But that doesn't stop him from slowly walking five or more miles each day with his dog, Lulu. While his determination is impressive, his attitude—making friends with almost everyone he passes—is the real tribute to his character. With my dad, Noah, God, and Andrea on my side and by my side, how could I lose?

I felt Andrea on my shoulder in spirit. There were lots of small signs from her along the way—if you are the type of person to be inclined to believe in such things—and I certainly have become that type of person. And even if I wasn't paying attention to the smaller or more subtle messages she was sending me, there was no way I could miss, or misinterpret, the giant butterfly.

As I was struggling down Route 5 toward Greenfield, Massachusetts, in the middle of one of those cold, wet days, looking for a place to get a hot coffee to warm my frigid fingers, I saw an enormous butterfly in the distance. It wasn't, as I initially feared, an illusion; It was a roadside sign for the Magic Wings Butterfly Conservatory and Gardens. To appreciate the significance, I have to share the backstory with you.

Two years before Andrea passed, she became obsessed with attracting butterflies and decided to plant a "butterfly bush." She loved the beauty, majesty, and freedom that the butterflies reflected. After much research, she found the type of planting she wanted. We ordered the bush, but Andrea didn't like it and sent it back; we ordered another one and finally got the right one, and I planted the scrawny thing. Of course, it was in the wrong spot and needed to be moved—twice! *But what the hell,* I thought. *It sure is going to be nice to see butterflies from our screened-in porch.*

For two seasons, we saw nothing—not a single butterfly. The bush seemed to be thriving, but much like Andrea's prior efforts to attract orioles and hummingbirds, we came up empty. Andrea researched solutions, pampered, and talked to the shrub, but to no avail.

But the summer after Andrea passed, I was sitting on the porch talking to Dr. Plotkin when a large butterfly appeared out of nowhere. I mentioned it to Scott, and we both laughed that Andrea didn't like us talking about her without her being included. The butterfly began bouncing off the screen and starting to distract me, so I walked in the front door of the house and damned if the thing didn't follow me. I walked to the back door on the opposite side of the house, and sure enough, there was the butterfly. I hung up with Scott and went back to the porch to enjoy the butterfly, but it was gone. From that point forward, the butterfly began to make frequent appearances—floating, spinning, diving, and lingering around the bush for my viewing pleasure.

Two weeks later, I was in Toronto with my son, his wife, and seventeen-month-old baby Lou, walking down a park path, when a butterfly began to follow us. I told the kids my story, and we laughed that Andrea wanted to come on vacation with us. The butterfly followed us for a long time, at times setting itself down on the sidewalk in front of us. I picked up the butterfly by its wing and brought it over to Lou, who squealed with delight. We let it go, and it continued to follow us for quite some time before waving good-bye and flying off.

A couple of weeks later, my sister and I were on our boat off the coast of Martha's Vineyard, reminiscing about Andrea, miles away from land when a butterfly came into the boat and landed on the windshield. As I filled in Ann on the story, the butterfly flew next to the boat for several minutes before flying off. There was no question in my sister's mind that Andrea wanted to enjoy the boat ride with us, as she had done so many times before.

So you might be able to appreciate my surprise at spotting the first and only butterfly conservatory I'd ever seen, at my lowest point in the ride. After resting, having a cup of coffee, and taking a lot of photos, I felt rejuvenated and eager to get back on the road and complete this leg of the ride. As I approached the road, the rain stopped, the sky brightened, and on cue, the sun snuck out. I rode the remainder of that day's ride like my bike had (butterfly) wings!

The butterfly conservatory was the turning point of my ride. The weather cleared and warmed, and from that point forward, it was smooth sailing all the way into Montreal. Coincidence? A sign from above? Andrea? A self-fulfilling prophecy? Or nothing at all. I'll leave that up to you to decide, but for me, it provided new energy, renewed determination, and a belief that Andrea was smiling down upon me and had my back.

As I finally raced through the city of Montreal toward my final destination at the oratory, I was filled with the emotions I'd worked so hard to tamp down—a compressed version of the story that had brought Andrea and me to Montreal in the first place and why it was so meaningful. As I turned the corner into the basilica, I almost fell off my bike. My brother, daughter, son-in-law, and three grandsons—George, Harry, and Trey— were at the entrance, cheering wildly, each of them waving a homemade sign, including the one that touched a real chord; it read, "Noni would be proud of you." My only thought was, *God, I hope so.*

The remainder of the weekend was a festive blur, a celebration of the successful ride, and a remembrance of all Andrea meant to us. We relaxed at the hotel, swam in the pool, and zip-lined in Old Montreal with my family. Per tradition, we had dinner at our favorite Montreal steakhouse, Le Keg. What was usually a pleasantly subdued, reflective dinner for Andrea and me this year became a raucous celebration with five adults and four kids. We toasted to everything we could think of, but most importantly, to Saint André and Andrea. The spirit of happiness, love, and determination hovered over our table.

Of course, we spent several hours the next day at the oratory, praying and giving thanks for another successful event. The boys were blown away by the grandeur and aura of the basilica, as well as the smaller crypt church, the prayer candles, the crutches on the wall, and the museum. Harry was especially intrigued by the display of Saint Brother André's heart.

I made sure to bring them into Saint Brother André's ten-by-fifteen-foot one-room Spartan dwelling with its bed, wash basin, hotplate, and a small table with the Bible on it. I told the boys that this was my favorite place on the complex, a testament to the man's character and dedication. I did my best to impress on them that a man can be bereft of money and possessions and yet still be the richest man on earth.

I also prayed to be able to accept the changes in my life, vowing to attempt to honor the past while enjoying the "new normal." From our secret garden at the oratory, I felt the presence and love of both Andrea and Saint Brother André. We spread some of Andrea's ashes on the grounds, in a quiet, secluded area. I smiled, really smiled, for the first time in a long time.

It was time to head home, put the finishing touches on the fundraising, and send out a boatload of grateful thank-you notes. We drove together from Montreal to Connecticut, stopping at our favorite winery, St. Jacque's, to say hi to the owner and his wife. Yvon gave us a personal tour of all aspects of the operation. I think Natalie was taken aback when Yvon teared up when he talked about Andrea. The depth of his love for her shining from his watery eyes.

Before I departed from Natalie's house to drive back to the Cape, Andrea had one more surprise for us. We were getting ready to say goodbye when Harry came running into the house, wild-eyed and screaming, "Papa! Papa! Come out front. You have to see this!"

I hustled through the door, and to my delight and amazement, there was a brilliant, double rainbow lighting up the sky. So vivid and clear it couldn't possibly be real—but it was.

And memories of Andrea flooded my mind and my heart—healthy and happy, teaching first grade. I would visit her classroom, and she would show off her guitar skills with the children, singing along to her rendition of the song "Rainbow Connection." Years later, now profoundly deaf, she would lovingly sing it to her children and grandchildren. It was so special to us; we had it printed on the prayer cards for her services. Trey sings it with his mother every night before he falls asleep.

So thank you Andrea, for putting a beautiful, colorful bow on this ride and letting me remember your voice one more time, through one of your favorite songs, selfless to the end, taking the time to remind me that life was going to be all right— here on earth and on the other side of the rainbow.

> Why are there so many
> Songs about rainbows?
> And what's on the other side?
> Rainbows are visions,
> But only illusions,
> And rainbows have nothing to hide.
> So we've been told and some choose to believe it.
> I know they're wrong wait and see.

Someday we'll find it, the rainbow connection,
The lovers, the dreamers, and me.

One thing is for sure, I'm looking forward to finding that rainbow connection, and someday being on the other side of it with you and God forever.

The rainbow connection!

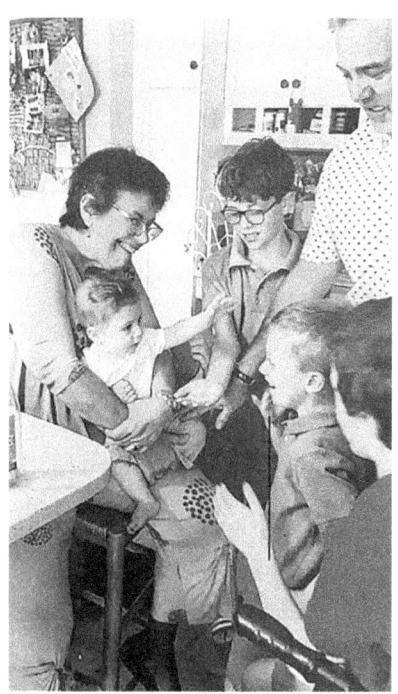

Andrea enjoyed every minute she
spent with her grandchildren.

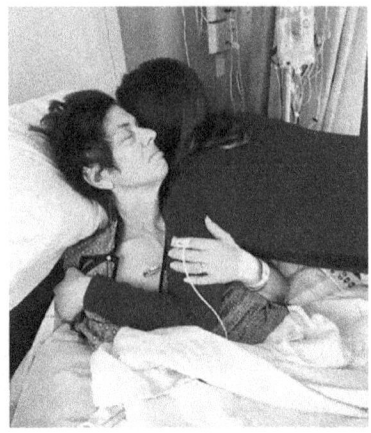

Andrea spent many rehab stints at Spaulding Hospital. Here, just opening her eyes after ten days in a coma, the bond between mother and daughter transcends even the harshest medical challenges.

Andrea on the boat the day before she passed; the smile on her face belies how sick she had become.

Three of our grandsons greeting me in Montreal at the conclusion of the first bike ride/fundraiser after Andrea's passing; the sign reads, "Noni is Proud of You!"; I hope that's true...

A check presentation to Dr. Scott Plotkin, Executive Director of the Brain Tumor Center at MGH, and Andrea's longtime neurologist— thank you to everyone who has been a part of our fundraising efforts over the past twenty years!

CHAPTER 26

Goodbye but Not Good Riddance

I'm now sitting in a hotel bar, in an old refurbished railroad station in Scranton, Pennsylvania, having a late lunch. I'm on the last leg of my car ride north from Florida to my daughter's house in Connecticut and eventually to our home on Cape Cod, with Andrea's urn keeping me company in the passenger seat.

I finished writing the original manuscript last night in Winchester, Virginia. The irony wasn't lost on me that the town in Virginia where I completed the manuscript has the same name as the town in Massachusetts where Andrea grew up.

I have to admit I'm worried. If you know me even a little, you know I'm not a worrier, and in fact, I view it as a wasted/ useless emotion. I learned long ago that worry is a yoke that wears you down, distorts reality, and lends itself to making poor decisions. But as I finish up my lunch in this beautiful setting, I suddenly seem to be worried about a lot.

I'm worried that, at some point in the future, I won't have this book to write anymore—I'll have to fill my time with other things, including, I guess, interacting with people. I've avoided a lot of that over the last many months. I've enjoyed spending my time with Andrea. I'm worried that "I have to get on with my life," and I don't even know what that means. I'm worried that, at some point soon when I go back into our home on Cape Cod, I have to attend to sorting through Andrea's clothing and personal items; I have to get used to sleeping in our bedroom, using our bathroom, sitting in the living room, and cooking a meal for one. Mostly, I worry because now I have to face life alone—without my constant companion by my side.

I purposely modified this trip home from my normal, direct one thousand five hundred mile highway-based sprint over two very long days, to a much more leisurely six-day sojourn covering over two thousand three hundred miles.

The ride, much like writing this book, has been cathartic. I drove through the heart of the middle south—through some of our favorite states, Georgia, Alabama, Tennessee, Kentucky, North Carolina, Virginia, West Virginia, and central Pennsylvania. I've been through several beautiful mountain ranges, spectacular rivers and gorges, and magnificent falls. It's truly God's country, in its beauty and in its people. I traveled through small towns in the back, back roads where there were more churches than any other buildings, where almost every house had a cross or a religious statue on the front lawn, and where the people were kind, friendly, and helpful to me. I enjoyed the ride, the views, the people, and most of all, the peace.

I also enjoyed the music. The new car I bought in Florida came with satellite radio so I could pick my genre, and the music held up even in the densest parts of the mountains. I listened to a lot of that '70s music because that was my era, and it was also the decade Andrea and I met and got married. The music, like everything else these days, seemed more profound and personal. Sometimes it made me smile, sometimes made me cringe, but always made me reflect. Songs like Paul Simon's "Slip Sliding Away" spoke to me: "God takes his time, God has a plan, the information isn't available to the mortal man." How true that is! Kansas sang "Dust in the Wind," reminding me that in the beginning and in the end, "all we are is dust in the wind." I heard Barbra Streisand sing "Evergreen," the song we danced to at our wedding; it brought me back to a happy time long ago while at the same time making it feel like it was only yesterday. We both loved James Taylor, and when JT sang our favorite song, "Sweet Baby James," it was all I could do to keep the car on the road.

The old hits just kept on coming. Each new song seemed more meaningful and poignant to me. I sang out loud, laughed, and stared blankly at the blue sky in front of me as if somehow I could see Andrea smiling. I got some odd stares from the cars passing by me, but I couldn't have cared less.

Mostly, I enjoyed the beauty, the peace, my solitude, and the time I had to reminisce—smile to myself, get a little emotional once in a while, and try to figure out what happened and what God wants from me next.

I didn't get a lot of answers from either Andrea or God. That's all right; I did get an inner peace that tells me things will be okay, both in the short and in the long run—the same feeling I had all those years ago when we made our initial pilgrimage to Montreal to confer with Brother Andre. Andrea used to say that when you ask God for something, you'll get one of three responses: "Yes," "Not now," or "I [God] have a better idea." That's pretty much where I am now, waiting on Andrea and God for that better idea. I'm good with that.

I talked to a lot of people on the ride, and they were very supportive—of course, my kids and grandkids, my family, and my friends. One thing that stuck out in my head was something my buddy Rich said to me. He told me, "You need to be happy and be happy about being happy. Why? Because you know that's what Andrea would have wanted." Of course, he's right; Andrea was the most giving person I've ever known. All she ever wanted was for everyone around her to be happy.

So, honey, I'll try, but I have to admit. I'm still just a little bit worried about this whole moving-on thing!

Writing this book was an act of love. It was not as the old cliché goes, "a labor of love." It wasn't labor at all. I never experienced writer's block. I could, and often did, write continually for hours at a time. If I didn't write for a day or two, I felt anxious and detached.

I wrote this book because I had to; I had to for myself—to give my jumbled brain a reason for being in the months after Andrea passed away. Without this exercise, I would have sunk much deeper into some of the dark holes I was in; so in that regard, writing this book was both a selfish act and almost a literal lifeline for me.

This book helped me organize and better understand Andrea as a person, our relationship, and our lives together. Of course, that sounds a little crazy, but like looking at one of Andrea's beautiful mosaics and having to move back to see how all these small pieces combined to make a piece of art, I had to step back and take a higher-level perspective with the benefit of hindsight to fully appreciate what I had experienced.

The second reason I wrote the book is for my children and their spouses, grandchildren, nieces, nephews, and future generations of Cahills, Keatings, and Piranis. Except for me, many in this group knew and appreciated Andrea better than anyone, but I'm certain they don't all know a lot of the stories and details I've included. The reality is that, with this group pushing ninety in numbers, there might have to be a sequel to memorialize many of the "Andrea tales" that I omitted, or that they have and may want to share with their extended family.

The final reason for writing this book was to pass on some of the lessons I learned from functioning as a caretaker for Andrea, as well as those I garnered from the health-care providers I worked so closely with, and from the many bright people who imparted their wisdom to me over the years. As noted, I'm not a psychologist, I'm certainly not a doctor, and I'm not even that smart. I've assuredly never attempted to write anything close to a book prior to this, and I don't like doling out advice unless I'm asked. But I do feel that Andrea and I went through something unique together that may have value to others who are trying to figure out how to be a half-decent caregiver or how to incorporate some of the things I've learned into their caregiver repertoire. If it helps one person do one thing better, gives them the smallest bit of emotional comfort, or eases someone's pain by even an iota, this whole exercise was worth my effort.

In the end, I spent a great deal of time writing a book that I don't know, and in a lot of ways don't care, if anyone will ever read. I have the luxury of not stressing out over trying to make money from a publication (all proceeds will go to the ACF), having publishers reject it, or it being reviewed and criticized. It wouldn't mean a thing to me if a critic read it, or whether they liked it or hated it; and I'm not anticipating it going to the top of the New York Times Best Seller list anytime soon.

It would, however, mean something to me if it made someone smile, if it gave someone a better appreciation for what Andrea accomplished in her life, if it moved someone to join our fight against NF, or if it helped a single caregiver or altered one life in a positive fashion.

It also means a great deal to me that I've had the honor of telling Andrea's story, cementing her legacy, and putting down in black and white for anyone who cares what an amazing, special, inspirational, heroic, intelligent, funny, ball busting, creative, and talented wife, mother, grandmother, daughter, sister, cousin, sister-in-law, aunt, niece, godmother, and friend she was.

So, as I get ready to pull into my daughter's driveway later today, I truly believe that while this might be the end of my drive, it's not the end of the road or my journey with Andrea. One thing I did learn on this trip is that our conversation will, and has to, continue—even though Andrea must be totally pissed off that I now get to do all the talking!

EPILOGUE

The outpouring of love in the weeks and months after Andrea died was overwhelming. Call after call, text after text, and card after card, all attesting to how Andrea touched hundreds of people, transformed scores of lives, and made almost everyone she met a better person. As I meandered through the unimaginable shock and grief of her unexpected demise, it dawned on me that I'd had a ringside seat for this command performance and hadn't appreciated it for the magnificent cinema that it was.

I felt like I'd watched a brilliant magician perform her mind-bending trick so many times that I'd become desensitized to it and failed to appreciate the fullness of its beauty. I realized then that I was in a unique position to glean a multitude of real-world lessons from this special, well-lived life and that maybe Andrea's legacy was one from which we could continue to learn.

Perhaps what she demonstrated every day and what I came to comprehend as her husband and her caregiver could be of real benefit to others struggling with similar issues. The combination of assuaging my own grief and hoping that our collective experiences could in some way help others navigate their own situations is what drove me to write this book and tell Andrea's story.

The book tracked our journey from a fairy-tale beginning, through our battles, losses, and triumphs with NF2, to a place where we ultimately found acceptance and peace.

The phrasing of the title is reflective; in both her head and her heart, Andrea's was as dogged and determined as anyone I have ever known—as I hope you came to appreciate, she used that attribute in a multitude of different ways, and it, not NF2, came to define her.

As part of our journey, I gained a lot of experience as a caregiver for Andrea. I have tried to engrain some of the lessons I learned as a result of my involvement in our situation into parts of the book. These lessons seem to me to be especially important in today's world, with middle-aged members of the "sandwich generation" simultaneously trying to take care of both their children and their parents; caregivers assisting a loved one with a chronic illness; and couples in my age group coming to realize that it's likely (more like inevitable) that one of them will have to deal with the illness, care, and ultimately, the passing of their partner. I've tried to impart practical suggestions that might be helpful in these difficult circumstances, provide greater awareness and perspective, and perhaps make challenging decisions a little clearer and easier.

However, we don't have to be caregivers to learn from Andrea's journey. We can all become better people by understanding the talents and purposefulness she brought to bear every day. I included many examples and humorous stories of Andrea's extraordinary human instincts, her wisdom, and the everyday lessons she demonstrated and lived. As you read her story—our story—I hope you were as amazed as I was at how special those talents really were.

In the book, in some cases, I altered the names of people and institutions if I felt that "naming names" would in any way be compromising, embarrassing, or otherwise potentially damaging. I struggled at times with when to use the label NF versus NF2. NF is the overarching name of the disease, of which there are two types—NF1 and NF2. I used the broader NF label when discussing or referring to the disease in a general sense. I used the type Andrea had, NF2, referring to her specific situation. There were a lot of fifty-fifty calls where I used my own, best, judgment. I also took much of my direction from Dr. Scott Plotkin, who so generously and graciously gave of his time to help me edit portions of this book. To make things even a little more confusing, the name of the disease has recently been changed to Schwannomatosis. As it was NF/NF2 when Andrea was alive, I choose to use those labels.

The opinions, recollections, and ideas in this book are strictly mine except where noted. These are my observations of what worked and what didn't for me. This book is not meant to preach at or to you or tell you what you should do in any situation. We're all different people on singular paths, and so we must apply any lessons we learn to our own deal. I hope what I learned with Andrea and our experience with NF may offer lessons that can be valuable on whatever your journey.

Finally, my deepest gratitude to my editor, Lonny Lippsett. Without his patience, skills, and willingness to work closely with me on this project, I fear this book would be more of a puddle of words as opposed to a finished product I can be proud of. My sincere appreciation to my cousin Tim Cahill; my children, Natalie and Peter, and their spouses, Marc and Ali; and everyone who gave their time and reviewed the text. You were invaluable to me in my quest to make Andrea's story come alive. Special thanks to Dr. Scott Plotkin, Marylyn Howe, and Leslie Boor for lending me their expertise on various, specific topics and helping to make me look smarter than I really am.

Peter Cahill
May 2024

ABOUT THE AUTHOR

Peter Cahill functioned as his wife's devoted partner for forty-five years, and as her caregiver for thirty of those years. Although always an avid reader and writer, his path took him in a different direction, and throughout his forty-year business career, he rose to become a senior executive in the information technology industry.

Peter is now retired from most things that don't include writing, managing the Andrea Cahill Foundation, golfing, boating, and bicycling. He splits his time between Cape Cod, Massachusetts, and Estero, Florida.

Donations can be made to the Andrea Cahill Foundation, https://because.massgeneral.org/acahill

www.ingramcontent.com/pod-product-compliance
Lightning Source LLC
Chambersburg PA
CBHW020346280925
33212CB00001B/1